D0014238

WITHDRAWN

WASATCH COUNTY LIBRARY
465 EAST 1200 SOUTH
HEBER CITY, UT 84032

S. Dilworth Young
General Authority, Scouter, Poet

S. Dilworth Young

General Authority, Scouter, Poet

Benson Y. Parkinson

WITHDRAWN

Covenant Communications, Inc.

WASATCH COUNTY LIBRARY
465 EAST 1200 SOUTH
HEBER CITY, UT 84032

Published by Covenant Communications, Inc.
American Fork, Utah

Copyright © 1994 by Benson Young Parkinson
All rights reserved

Printed in the United States of America
First Printing: January 1994

01 00 99 98 97 96 95 94   10 9 8 7 6 5 4 3 2 1

Library of Congress Cataloging-in-Publication Data

Parkinson, Benson Young, 1960-

       S. Dilworth Young: General Authority, Scouter, Poet: a biography, Benson Y. Parkinson.

       p.   cm.

Includes bibliographical references, photographs, and an idex.

ISBN 1-55503-660-0 : $14.95

1. Young, S. Dilworth (Seymour Dilworth), 1897-1981. 2. Mormons—Biography. 3. Mormon Church—Biography.
4. Church of Jesus Christ of Latter-day Saints—Biography. I. Title.

BX8695.Y84P37   1994

289.3' 092—dc20   94-5519
[B]   CIP

To Dil, Gladys, Young Dil, and Leonore.

Table of Contents

Foreword

This book is based largely on interviews of Dilworth's friends and family. As anyone knows who has gathered oral history, facts become skewed, sources contradict themselves and each other, things come out in the wrong order, people imagine, confuse, and forget. The same holds for personal histories and journals. I have picked these stories, knowing that any given detail might be wrong, because the gist is there: This is how people saw S. Dilworth Young; or This is his voice in telling his own story. Sometimes oral history puts forward less of history, but more of the man.

This book has been over ten years in the writing. In that time, the old Young home on 24th Street in Ogden, which Gladys called Rosemont, has burned and been rebuilt according to a new plan. I regret to say that in that time too, many of those to whom this book would have meant most have passed on.

I decided to write this book after reading my grandfather's unpublished Life Story. Those one hundred and thirty pages, with his military and mission diaries, could have formed the core of Dilworth's best book, but he never wrote it. My book would not have been possible without the cooperation of Dilworth's widow, Hulda Parker Young, who gave access to these and others of his papers and recordings, suggested people to interview, gave several important interviews herself, allowed me the use of personal materials, and criticized the manuscript. Leonore Young Parkinson, Dilworth's only surviving child and my mother, also made available primary sources, helped develop numerous contacts, gave repeated interviews, and criticized early drafts. Some of these memories were painful for Hulda and especially Leonore, which makes their contributions doubly valuable.

Carlie Louine Clawson Young, Dilworth's mother, left a personal history. Gladys Pratt Young, Dil's first wife and my grandmother, was a haphazard journal keeper, but her letters during their courtship survive in Dilworth's scrapbooks. She also left charming stories of her childhood, which with others of her writings came to me through Mary Pratt Parrish, her niece. Louine Young Cromar, Dilworth's sister, shared materials on Dilworth, including a transcript of some of Dil's stories, her own personal history, letters, excerpts from their late sister Emily Young Knepp's diary, and Emily's personal history. Much credit goes to Dilworth Blaine Parkinson, my brother, who interviewed Dilworth or taped him telling stories on five different occasions in 1977-78, and who also filled two 90 minute tapes with his own memories. Other family members who helped include Dilworth's brother Hiram, his sister-in-law Louise Young, son-in-law Blaine Parkinson, and grandchildren Charlotte Parkinson Fry, Robert Alan Fry, Annette Parkinson, and Wendy Parkinson Asay. Relatives on the Young side: Harlan Y. Hammond, Phyllis Wells, and Gene F. Deem; on the Pratt side: Boyd and Mary Pratt Parrish, Berta Pratt Whitney, Gerda Pratt Haynie, and Stanley and Juliette Cardon. From the Parkers: James and Giana Nielsen.

For memories of Dilworth's early life, I thank his lifelong friend Merlon L. Stevenson. R. Lamar Barlow filled in background on the 145th Artillery and battle in World War I. Missionary friends who contributed valuable information include Francis G. Wride, Dilworth's companion in the backwoods of Louisiana and in New Orleans, and Alexandre E. and Ethel Kane Archibald, Bessie E. Kelly, and Grace Valentine Price, fellow workers in the office in Independence, Missouri. Leland P. Draney, a previous mission secretary, provided documents and took the time to type out answers to my lengthy list of questions on that calling's duties. For memories of Rey L. Pratt I thank Hugh Barnes and Dell B. Stringham.

Ogden friends who gave me stories include Delora Hurst, Myrene Brewer, Mary Wilson, Maggie Gammell, George Frost, Heber S. Jacobs, Lloyd L. Peterson, Martha Johnson Barney, Betty Peterson Baker, Ben H. Davis, Helen Grix Plowgian, and Margaret Wilson Barlow. Ena Barnes, and Dorothy West, Gladys' pageant aides, were also very helpful. Among scouters I thank Eden W. Beutler, Percy W. Hadley, Paul S. Bieler, A. Russell

Croft; also the following scouts: Jack Davis, George H. Lowe, Thomas M. Feeny, James N. Oka, E. LaMar Buckner, Don Buswell, Max Wheelwright, Worth Wheelwright, and Wally Brown. The Ogden *Standard-Examiner*, in helping my grandfather publicize his program, in the process preserved his activities for posterity. Richard Sadler steered me toward Lyle J. Barnes' helpful master's thesis on corruption in Ogden. On this account too I must thank the *Standard*, also Cecil K. Parker, a juryman.

The following New England missionaries helped: Truman G. Madsen, Oscar W. McConkie Jr., Rex W. Williams, Blaine P. Parkinson, and D. L. Woodward. Boston students and friends include John Hale and Olga Gardner, Richard and Mary Lou Harline, Talmage and Dorothy Nielsen, J. D. and Barbara Williams, and Rosemary Fletcher. For his Salt Lake and Los Angeles years I relied mostly on published and family sources. However, for their varied contributions I wish to thank H. Smith Broadbent, Phyllis Peterson Warnick, Bruce R. McConkie, Levier and Cynthia M. Gardner, Eb L. Davis, and Reed and Thelma Brown.

Thanks and apologies to all those who helped whom I have neglected to mention. My thanks for secretarial assistance to my wife, Robin L. Parkinson, and to Charles Fry, also to my father, Blaine P. Parkinson, for financial support in this project. Finally, I would like to thank Covenant Communications and its managing editor, Giles H. Florence, Jr., for giving the family the chance to present this story to the world.

Benson Y. Parkinson
December 24, 1993

CHAPTER 1

A Salt Lake Childhood

Origins

Seymour Bicknell Young, Jr. was born January 11, 1868, in Salt Lake City, Utah Territory. As a young man he served a mission in England, returning early to attend the dedication of the Salt Lake Temple in 1893, then serving a second, shorter mission to New York. Seymour was a striking man, lean and broad-jawed, with a rich, baritone singing voice. He sold wagons and later automobiles for the Consolidated Wagon and Machine Company, and did well. Once he sold a hundred small white Buicks in a hundred days. As a publicity stunt, he and a mechanic drove one to the top of Ensign Peak before there was a road. He would race the engine and lurch forward, then the mechanic would rush to block the wheels, then he lurched again, and so on to the top. Seymour was the eldest son of Seymour Bicknell Young, Sr., who as an infant survived the Haun's Mill Massacre. He too served a mission in England, taking part in the eastbound missionary handcart company of 1857. Seymour Sr. studied in the east and became doctor to his uncle, Brigham Young. He served many years in the First Council of Seventy like his father, Joseph Young, one of the original presidents and Brigham's brother.

Carlie Louine Young Clawson, known as Lou, or Lulu, was born in Salt Lake on July 28, 1869. Family lore says that a middle-aged apostle once gave her a lift in his buggy and in the course of the ride asked her to be his plural wife, but that she turned him down. Lou was softly pretty—she and Seme made a striking couple—but was shy in company and retiring in the family. Lou was a daughter of Hiram B. Clawson, a pioneer entrepreneur with a dramatic bent, whose career included managing ZCMI and the Salt Lake Theater. Dilworth remembers the Clawsons always laughing. "They seemed immune to sorrow, they joked, they dramatized, they had physical fun." Lou's mother, Emily Augusta Young, was a daughter of Brigham Young by Emily Partridge, Bishop Edward Partridge's daughter and a plural wife of Joseph Smith. That made Lou Seymour's second cousin through John Young. In the days of polygamy, with its large families, this was not uncommon. Lou was old enough to have memories of Brigham, who called her his little beauty. Once when she was playing on the front steps of the Church Office building, he passed by and noticed her with a great mouthful of gum. "Lulu, I wish you wouldn't chew gum," he admonished her. "It is not a nice thing to do." She writes, "It made a great impression on me, for since then I never chew it or like to see anyone else indulge."

Seymour Dilworth Young, Seymour and Lou's second child and first son, was born September 7, 1897, at 5:00 a.m., in a house at 83 Canyon Road, Salt Lake City. The house sat on the west side of the street on a spot where 2nd Avenue now cuts through. "My father," he tells, "ran for the doctor. He had to go clear up on 4th East, to where our grandpa had his horses. And then he lost the key to the barn, and they had a dickens of a time, but they finally got a doctor there." "My mother," he writes on another occasion, "tells me that I cried constantly from the time I was born until I was about six months old, that I wore out her and half a dozen nurses. She also said that after that I would sit on her lap with my feet against her abdomen and constantly push, so that it was an effort at all times to keep me on her lap."

One of Lou's lullabies, a version of *"A Frog Went A-Courting,"* goes:

> *A frog he would a wooing go*
> *Hi-ho, says Rolly*
> *And whether his mother would let him or no*

With a rolly polly gammy spinach
Hi-ho, says Anthony Rolly
So off he set with his opera hat
Hi-ho, etc.
And on the road he met with a rat
etc.

The family lived for a time in a home on the west side of Liberty Park. Dilworth's early memories include watching Hiram, his younger brother, toddling across the street and into the park with their mother in pursuit. Dilworth, at two-and-a-half, worried she wouldn't be able to catch him. The family moved to 4th South, then again to 560 East 6th South. Dilworth remembers dolls and dress-up with his older sister Emily. Emily describes their mother putting a blanket over the dining room table for them to play house, Emily and Dilworth taking the roles of mama and papa, with Hiram for the baby. Dilworth also remembers playing under the table when his mother was preparing food for a party. Dilworth, pretending he was in a tent, would slip out and snitch a pickle when his mother left the room. He mentions a neighbor boy small enough to crawl into his family's chicken coop by the hens' door. He would hand out an egg, which the two of them traded for candy at the store. The Youngs had a sandpile "on the west side of our house in the morning shade and there I spent a lot of time. I remember thinking that sandpile playing was the greatest objective in life." He mentions being afraid of thunder and lightning, hiding himself in his bed and covering his ears with his pillow. "One day I sat on the porch against the door during such a storm and discovered that I did not need to be afraid."

Dilworth says his father was "a very good pianist, and he had a fine singing voice." He says, "In those days there was a lot of singing going on in our parlor. Father . . . gathered about him a lot of people who liked to sing. They had happy, good times, and I enjoyed listening to them." Seymour originally intended to become a musician and would have taught piano and voice. "Grandma talked him out of it, foolishly. Ought to have let him do it. He'd have been happy. That was his natural bent." Seymour was active and busy in the 2nd Ward, holding positions such as Sunday School Superintendent and Chairman of the Music Committee. Hiram says the Bishop told him at one time he might as well be bishop, as much time as he spent doing church work. One year Seymour put on a minstrel show for the ward. The normal pattern was to have a semi-circle on the stage, with two "end men" and the chorus, all in blackface. An actor without blackface, called the interrogator, sat in the middle and asked questions, while the two end men cracked jokes. Seymour's innovation was to make it a ladies' minstrel. Lou sang in the chorus, the only time Dilworth remembers her participating in any public performance or meeting of any kind. Hiram and another boy did a dance called "The Golddust Twins in Clogs." Golddust was a brand of powdered laundry soap with the twin girls on the label. Dilworth remembers the black underwear and greasepaint and yellow skirts and wigs and being so jealous he hardly knew what to do with himself. "I learned to do the clog. I said, 'Daddy, I can do this.' And he said, 'Well, let's see you. So, what are you going to sing?' I said, 'I'll sing, I'm a Yankee Doodle Dandy,'" and he sang and danced but his father still would not put him in the show. Dil remembers the Danish members in the 2nd Ward.

> In fast day meetings, testimonies were often unintelligible to me as the Saints struggled to testify in English, their new tongue. In Sunday School the room was divided into classrooms by green curtains hanging from wires overhead. If I was not interested in what my teacher was saying, I could choose from five other classes, all of which I could hear. It was always interesting to try to solve the problem of the identity of the boy who kept poking me in the back through the curtain at my rear.

The Young children went through mumps, measles, rubella, whooping cough, and perhaps scarlet fever. Likely they had rheumatic fever as well, for both Dilworth and brother Scott Richmond developed heart trouble later in life. "Grandpa Young was the doctor. I remember Mother putting some chairs together, putting a sheet over them, and we three children crouching under and breathing fumes of menthol tinged with turpentine and a drop of carbolic acid." The whooping cough developed into pneumonia in Dilworth's infant sister Florence, and she died. "I remember seeing Mother being led from the room by Father. She was weeping violently and Father was trying to comfort her. I remember going into the room and seeing my tiny baby sister lying like a wax doll on the lap of the nurse. It seems to me they had a funeral at the house—at least I remember a lot of people being there."

At Christmas time Dilworth tortured himself trying to figure how Santa Claus got through the six-inch stove pipe, around the kinks, into the stove, then opened the door from inside to get out into the dining room. (Christmas morning was held in the dining room, the parlor being reserved for formal occasions like Christmas dinner, Sabbaths, ward teaching visits, and "lickings.") One Christmas, probably when he was five, Dilworth pined for a wood jigsaw puzzle he had seen in a store window, showing an old-fashioned, horse-drawn fire engine. With the horses running and the dogs barking underneath and the smoke billowing out from the fire making the steam to pump the water, Dilworth couldn't imagine anything more exciting. His mother insisted they eat a bowl of mush in the dining room before they could open their presents, "to fortify us against the candy, I guess." Dilworth finished and went out to the dining room to his chair to empty his stocking, which besides the candy held an orange, a novelty in those days. Then on to the presents—a new clipper sled, which Dilworth says at that time beat flexible flyers "all hollow," and a smaller package. Dilworth recognized it immediately as his puzzle.

Their father let the children play with their toys for about an hour, then approached them and said, "Well, Boys and Girls, you remember that Danish family over on 7th South?" These were the Olsens, a immigrant couple with children more or less the same ages as the Youngs. Dilworth remembers not liking the boy his age. "His dress, smell, everything was different, strange and

Danish." He admits to having had a "little tiff" with him a few days before. Seymour went on, "Now, we're going to take them our Christmas dinner. Are you willing?" The children agreed, though without really understanding the implications. Then his father said, "I want each one of you children to decide to give your best toy, the one you like the best, to those children." So it was decided. They would leave at noon.

> I had an awful fight with myself. I sat there and looked at that clipper sled, and I wanted to give it to him, and I wanted to keep my fire engine puzzle, but Father said, "Give him the one you like the best," and I didn't want to disobey Father, so finally I decided I'd give that boy my fire engine puzzle.

The family made their way down the back alley, Father carrying the turkey, Mother the dressing and gravy, the children toting pots of potatoes, sweet potatoes, plum pudding and dip, and cranberry sauce. They knocked on the door of the Olsen's tiny two-room house. Dilworth remembers a table and two chairs, but no other furniture. Seymour said, "Brother Olsen, we brought you some Christmas Dinner." He didn't understand his English, but Seymour gestured and got the idea across. Brother Olsen had them in. Seymour demonstrated how to carve the turkey, and Lou showed how to serve up the dressing and what went with what. Dilworth remembers a single bucket of coal and a small fire in the stove, barely enough to take off the chill. Seymour said, "Alright, now, Children, it's your turn." Emily gave the girl her age her large, bisque doll. Dilworth walked up to the boy and said, "Here!" The boy grabbed the puzzle just as brusquely as it was offered, without saying a word. Hiram toddled over with his gift and said, "Here's sum'n."

> And all the way home, I was walking on air. I don't believe my feet hit the ground once. I don't know why, I just suddenly realized what giving was. And to give our best and to give all we had was the finest thing we could do . . . When we got home, I thought maybe my mother had a Christmas dinner tucked away somewhere, but she didn't. She opened up a can of beans and we had bread and butter and beans for Christmas.

School Days

Dilworth remembers his mother as sickly, and he asked her about it when she was old. She said it wasn't a matter of disease. "I had seven miscarriages. If I'd had all the children I had conceived, I'd have had thirteen children." As it was she had six, of whom five survived. The Youngs hired a woman to help with housework and tending, and she boarded with the family. Emily says, "She took pains with Dil and me to teach us to read before we ever started school. We could read the easy words in the newspaper when we entered the first grade." She tells of being asked to stay after school with Dil after only a few days (this would have been at the Sumner School, on 3rd East between 6th and 7th South) and standing fearfully before the teacher's desk and being asked to read from a second-grade reader. Both could do so easily, and on the basis of that, both were promoted to the second grade. Dilworth talks about reading in his history, but does not mention the incident. He writes he was a year behind Emily in the fourth grade, but then of the two of them graduating together. Given family circumstances, it seems likely one or both lost or gained a grade or two.

One thing is certain—Dilworth read well from early on, and he loved to read. Emily remembers him kneeling before a stuffed chair with a book on the seat for hours at a time. "Father would get out of patience when he wanted Dil to get a scuttle of coal from the shed for Mother to put in the range, for I can hear him say, 'Just a minute,' but he never could find the place he could leave his book, and Father would have to pull him up and see that he did it." His Uncle Lee (Levi Edgar Young) gave him a six-volume Horatio Alger set, the "Ragged Dick" series, and he read these and others. Once he gave him a year's subscription to *Cosmopolitan* (at the time a literary magazine). "I could not understand what I read, but I tried. It was my magazine, and I did my best to live up to it." Lee introduced him to *The Last of the Mohicans*. "Ever after that the Delawares were my Indians and the Iroquois were my enemies. I read the whole series by Cooper." He read classics and the Standard Works and every religious book he could find. Emily speaks of him spending hours in "Grandpa Young's huge library . . . Dil would go to see them early in the morning and they would never hear from him till late in the day. He was curled up in a big comfy chair in the library." Once his father promised to give him any book in his own library if he would read it. He chose one called *Character—Smiles.*

> I wanted to smile so I started. I didn't understand any of it except the "ands" and "its" and small words. Later—long later—I found it among my books and correctly read the label, *Character*—by Samuel Smiles, an essay for the middle aged, but Father kept his word and gave me the book.

Dilworth stayed out of school at times to help around the house. He remembers alternating with Emily to help take care of Richmond when Louine was born in December 1908. "We washed the clothes in a machine which we turned with a handle on a wheel . . . we changed beds and mopped floors, and we swept the Navajo rugs every Saturday which were in our linoleum-covered living room." On another occasion, he adds, "I learned to make bread. We had a [universal] mixer and Mother would tell us how to do it from the bed."

Dilworth liked school, but he was "bedeviled by a boy named Sigurd Simpson, a dirty fisted boy of about eight. I was so scared of him that my life was miserable. I invented excuses not to go to school. Sickness feigned, hiding my cap, or losing my book until it was past 9:00." His father finally complained to the principal, who told him, "Seymour, you baby your boy too much. He's got to learn to fight his way, and until he learns he won't be much good." This took him aback. That night he told him if any boy licked him he could expect a licking when he got home, "and that I was to learn to stand up to the other boys." He bought him a pair of boxing gloves and arranged for his Uncle Shirl Clawson (later a Hollywood cinematographer) to give him a few boxing lessons. Dilworth does not say whether they helped, only that the family moved soon after to a house on the southwest corner of 9th Avenue and "C" street, across from the LDS hospital. This would have been in early 1907, when Dilworth was in the fourth grade. "I suppose that ended it, for I had no trouble thereafter."

"I enjoyed the school—no boys bothered me and I had little trouble except with arithmetic. I was not a good analyzer. English, history, spelling, grammar, were no trouble." The class at Lowell Elementary, where he now attended, put on several dramatic productions, including the Iliad and the *Odyssey* and *Alice in Wonderland.* "I was the Cheshire Cat because I have such a broad grin. I was proud of the part; and when we presented it to the parents, I about split my mouth in two trying to grin as broad as that cat is supposed to have done." Dilworth and his friends were throwing rocks one day in the schoolyard. Dilworth aimed, but the rock went off at an angle, sailing up to the second floor and crashing through the window of his own fourth-grade class. Red-haired Mrs. Burmister came to the window. Dilworth, paralyzed with fear, suddenly found himself alone in the schoolyard. All the others ran. She said, "Dilworth, did you break this window?" Dilworth, with the directness that always characterized him, said, "Yes, Ma'am." She called him in and took him to the principal, William Bradford. When he asked, Dilworth answered, "Yes, Sir, I broke the window. I didn't mean to. This rock slipped out of my hand and got going the wrong way." He told him he would have to take it up with the school board. Dilworth passed an anxious weekend, then on Monday "I was called in and told that, because I had told the truth and had not run, I would be excused from paying for the window. That was my first experience in honesty being rewarded, and I have never forgotten it." Dilworth recalls Mrs. Burmister trying to honor him with a kiss.

After Hours

Childhood games Dilworth remembers include kick-the-can, pom-pom-pull-away, duck-on-the-walk, mumble-peg, marbles, hopscotch, jump-the-rope, and tippy-cat. For this last, "one whittled the cat from a broom handle. The bat was a flat paddle. One struck the edge of the cat, flipping it in the air, and while in the air, striking it with the bat, driving it as far as he could." The opponent would allow a certain number of bat lengths. The driver could take them or demand more, in which case they measured. "If the driver was right, he got that many more points." Seymour bought the children a donkey while they still lived on sixth south. Dilworth remembers mostly the older boys in the neighborhood stealing it from their yard and his mother going after them. Once it balked on a set of streetcar tracks. Lou pulled and Dilworth and Emily beat it with sticks, but they could not get it off. Finally, "the car came to a stop, the motorman and conductor and a passenger got off and pushed the donkey off the tracks and went on their way, much to the amusement of everyone on the car—and to Mother's embarrassment. I was embarrassed too."

Dilworth played with the Marron boys, Ben and Hen, back fence neighbors, "Irish kids, tough and mean, [who] liked to fight all the time." Once Hen and Lewis Larson ganged up on him. "I figured, well now, I've got to get Lewey out of this, because the Marron kid was quicker than he was, so I just kept hitting Lewey on the nose until he started to bleed, and that fixed him, he didn't need to go anymore, and Hen ran." The Marron boys and other neighborhood kids stole the Youngs peaches summer after summer, until Seymour got the idea of hiring the Marrons to watch them. "'You can have what you want to eat, Boys, but watch it so that the other boys don't take it.'" That did the trick "They, when on their honor to watch and protect, did not feel they should steal. It proved a good way to handle boys." When a streetcar line was laid down along 9th avenue, the LDS hospital put in a sidewalk to combat mud on visitors' shoes. Dilworth, Hiram and the Marrons waited until that evening when the cement workers went home and carved their initials in the cement—SDY, HCY, BM, HM and LCY for little sister Louine. There they remained over seventy years for him to read as an old man.

Dil and Hi also played with George Cannon Young, their cousin, who lived nearby. Once they got into some new houses on "C" street above 9th Avenue and played cops and robbers. "Our cap pistols echoed nicely." The owners arrived without notice. Hi and Cannon were caught, but Dil "went up over the hill like a frightened deer. That night Father told me I would probably have to go to the juvenile court. I went through the tortures of fear of going to court—whatever it was it had a fearsome sound." Seymour let his boys stew two or three days, then told them he had gotten them off with a promise never to do it again. "We were entirely unconscious that we were doing wrong, but we did climb to the attic through a hole in the ceiling of a closet—dirtying the plaster. I suppose Father paid for the damage."

Dilworth mentions smoking with Hi and Cannon. "There was lots of smoking done in those days by nearly everybody . . . We managed to find some old big corn cobs, and we thought it was kind of cute to make corncob pipes." For tobacco they used cedar bark from the back fence, which Hiram remembers made them sick. Dil says, "We sat there pondering the centuries and tried to decide where babies came from. Cannon held for the stork and I held for the doctor and we were both wrong." Their father found out and confronted them before the family, telling them if they were going to smoke, to do it in the open. That apparently put an end to it. Dilworth writes of himself, "My bump of honor and honesty must have been well developed. I didn't need to be told more than once that a thing was not right and I stopped doing it." Hiram tells of his father offering each one hundred dollars if they would refrain from smoking and drinking and keep themselves clean until they were twenty-one. When the time came he had no money and could only tell them he would make it up to them. Hiram said never mind, that they ought to pay him a hundred dollars. For all that, Seymour smoked—away from the family—and Dilworth remained aggravated and disturbed into old age after having found him at it one day.

Dilworth speaks of his father as kindly but nervous and strict. "I always thought Father was fair with us most the time. He punished quickly, he had a quick temper, and he spanked us, oh, yes, you bet . . . [But] he saw what we needed . . . Father understood us and he got us things to play with." He says, "when we wanted to play, he made us a little ball diamond outside and bought a ball and a bat, and showed us how." The diamond extended between their house and the east-west ditch (which they sometimes dammed for swimming) about seventy-five feet away. "We managed to make balls or find an old ball and knit a cover for it if the horsehide was irreparable." Seymour would not let them "play sides" on Sundays, but allowed them to play "rounders." "I remember one time I knocked a home run through our . . . dining room window, right almost in the lap of the bishop, who was calling on Father." Dil says the bishop used to walk around the block to avoid seeing them on Sundays and having to tell them to stop. After the streetcar line pushed through their field, the boys played on another patch of "not-too-flat land" below 10th Avenue and between "B" and "C" Streets. At one time they had a team and coach. "We persuaded our parents to buy us uniforms made of outing flannel. The uniforms were flimsy but gave us a real professional look. The cost was one dollar each. . . . Every Saturday in the fall and spring it was either football or baseball."

They sledded in winter, coming down the hill and over a footbridge crossing the ditch, the ground dropping away on the other side. "Sometimes we could leap three or four feet. Our bellies would be sore from the pounding when we hit." Riding in the Avenues, "we got as far as we wanted to go." Boys commonly "hooked" rides on the backs of grocery wagons. The wagons were reinforced with steel supports on the sides. The boys would pass a long rope through these and hold on while being pulled on their clippers. They steered by pulling on one end of the rope or the other. When they got tired they dropped off. Another type of sled was called a schooner, large enough to hold a dozen people or more. "They'd have a horse pull that thing up to the head of Federal Heights," (the Avenues were too dangerous for schooners), "and then they'd all get out and turn the thing around and . . . slide down around those curves on Federal Heights into South Temple. They'd go as far as fifth east before they stopped."

It may have been the schooners that inspired the four-man coaster wagon Dilworth's father built.

It was the only thing of its kind ever invented. Otto Oblad the blacksmith made it. It had real buggy wheels cut to about twenty-seven inch diameter. The steering was a bicycle rim run by a sprocket and chain beneath. It had a brake like a real wagon. We used to start at 10th Avenue and ride to Grandmother Young's on [48 South] 4th East. Then we would have to push it home.

Or they could leave it there until the next day, or the day after, as they often did. Hiram says, "Father was wise. He knew where we were. He knew we were coasting or else pushing, mainly pushing." Dilworth agrees. "No toy ever used up more boy energy than that coaster . . . We were never any trouble at home." Not that there wasn't trouble to be gotten into coasting. The wagon could have upset. The spokes of the wheels were uncovered and could have broken hands or feet. Once, he writes, "Hi and I and Cannon . . . conceived the idea we'd really like to have an adventure." The three of them pushed the wagon as high as the Veteran's Hospital. Dilworth steered, Cannon held onto the middle, and Hi worked the brake. Down they came, "lickety-split," over stones and sagebrush and molehills. "That thing bounced, cavorted—we hung on for all we were worth. It's a wonder we weren't killed." They turned onto the cement by the hospital "going about thirty-five miles per hour . . . When we ended up at Grandma's we were limp with excited exhaustion."

The boys finally discovered where they could ride with less effort. Starting on "A" Street and 1st Avenue, they could coast east to "D", then to South Temple, then back to "A" Street. Dilworth calls it "perpetual motion"—seven blocks coasting for one block pushing. Of course it was a steep push. Dilworth says the wagon took four or five kids to get up a hill when he first started, but that as he got older and heaver, he could finally push it from South Temple home alone. "That was my great thing."

Seymour paid forty dollars for a red Durham cow with the left front and back teats joined together, forming one large teat with two holes. The seller claimed she milked faster that way. "We children fell in love with her and proudly led her home." The double teat did give two streams, but proved hard to work, and before long the milk began to come out bloody. "Father went back to the man and told him that he had sold the cow under false representations and asked for our money back. The man just laughed and told Father that he should be less naive." With no money for another cow, they used the milk from the good side. Hi brought in the milk dirty two or three times, with some story about how it got that way. "Mother decided that we couldn't keep that up, so Hi was taken off the milking list. Years later he confessed to me that he had thrown a handful of dry barnyard manure into the milk each time to get out of milking." After about a year Seymour sold the cow to a butcher. "It about broke us up, for we had learned to love that old red cow. She surely was gentle and kind."

The Youngs attended the 18th Ward on "A" Street above 2nd Avenue. Dilworth writes of walking with Cannon and Hiram each Monday night to priesthood meetings as a deacon, also Sunday mornings to "pass" in Sunday school and again in the evening for sacrament meeting. "I used to envy the teachers who could carry the silver pitchers for refilling the silver goblets. These were passed from mouth to mouth." Hiram speaks of collecting fast offerings in kind and delivering them to widows in the ward. John D. Giles, the deacon's teacher, gave the boys pencils and books and had them write down points for attendance and participation. Dilworth won a prize when he was deacon's president, "a boy's history of 'Abraham Lincoln' by a man named Morgan. I read it altogether about ten times in the next few years." Dilworth thought highly of John Giles, "who made the business of being a deacon seem very real." Brother Giles writes of a presentation Dilworth made on behalf of the deacons before meetings were adjourned for the summer. "Dilworth arose and said in a rather commanding tone, 'Brother Giles, we would like you to stand right here.' I followed instructions. Then I listened to one of the most carefully prepared and appropriately presented talks I have ever heard from a boy." Dilworth then presented him with a book of poems by Tennyson.

Dilworth says, "I can remember that I wanted to learn and was very much annoyed by boys who wanted to disturb. I can't remember wanting to do wrong during that period. I heard of other boys and their mischievous acts and used to wonder why they wanted to be that way. But for myself, I didn't want to, nor did Cannon Young or Hi."

Most of the land north and west of the Young home was wild, still, and the boys liked to play in the hills. "Cannon Young and I would get the fever to build underground houses. And so every summer we would go over the rim of the canyon fifty feet or so and start to excavate." They heard of successful underground forts belonging to rough boys by the sand pits above "K" Street, but they never managed to get theirs covered. "We did not have the money to buy old lumber to roof them over and we would not steal any, so the holes were dug and the energy spent—with loss of interest when we could not complete them." Once in March Cannon and Dilworth went on an overnight camp in City Creek. They packed two quilts and enough canned food for a week, rolling everything in a wagon cover to be used as a tent. Each boy took an end and they started out for the new road cutting into City Creek from 11th Avenue. "The farther we staggered with our food, the more scared I got—and homesick. So I began to fake a stomach ache. By the time we got to the place where the road bends to go toward the State Capitol I insisted on going home." By now the sky was black and low with an approaching storm. "We staggered home with our load, much to Cannon's disgust with my babyness, and got there just at dark and just in time for supper. Father was just organizing a searching party for us." It snowed eight inches that night.

Cattle from the city roamed in the hills, which were covered in sego lilies. "We learned to recognize them and dug the bulbs for spring salads. As I look back, they seemed inexhaustible, but they are all gone now." Seymour bought Dilworth and Hiram a repeating .22 Winchester rifle one Christmas. "Every Saturday for about six months Father took us up on the hills in back of our house . . . and taught us how to carry the gun so we couldn't kill each other,

how to shoot it, how to never shoot at wrong things, target practice only on tin cans, never shoot at animals or birds . . . before he
let us take it out alone." Dil admits, "I think I lorded it over Hi
by carrying it more and telling him when he could shoot, but he
didn't seem to be very resentful." They never really hunted with
it, though once they took a pot shot at a bobcat.

When Dil was ten, a boy named Clarence Olsen was showing
him and Hiram and Cannon his mail-order Sears .22 pistol at the
edge of City Creek Canyon. The gun's spring was broken, so he
had stretched a large rubber band around the trigger guard and
hammer. Clarence was demonstrating how Buffalo Bill shot,
pointing the gun in the air, then aiming into the canyon, pulling
the hammer back and letting go. The boys were standing in a half-
circle facing the canyon, Dilworth opposite Clarence.

> All of a sudden my hand went numb. I looked down and saw
> an ever-larger spot of red on my white shirt. I yelled, "I'm shot,"
> and headed for home as fast as I could go. Over the back fence
> "belly buster" place, which Father had fixed to give us faster
> egress and ingress to our lot, Hi went. He had for once been
> faster than I. Into the house, "Dil's shot, Dil's shot!" Mother
> came out. The doctor came and soon discovered the bullet had
> gone through the arm and out, missing the bone and arteries,
> but ticking a nerve—which numbed my hand. The angle from
> which it was fired was such that it passed in front of my breast
> and into my arm. One-sixteenth of an inch to the left and I
> would have been shot through the heart. For three days I was a
> hero—then I was just commonplace—just another accident. I
> have often thought that the Lord must have had some purpose
> in my not getting the full load in the chest.

Clarence "ran like a rabbit up the canyon," finally coming
home that night. Seymour took away his gun.

Mountain Dell

Seymour B. Young, Sr., in the early days, invested in four hundred acres at Mountain Dell, near Little Mountain, where the
reservoir now stands. For a time he "grub staked" it—outfitting

miners to prospect for a month at a time in exchange for half of
what they found. He eventually built a cabin on the land. Other
families lived nearby, some who farmed, some poor Danish immigrants who worked replacing ties on the railroad. Towards the
turn of the century the community of Mountain Dell was large
enough to support a ward, dissolved in 1898 when the city
bought many of the homes to protect the watershed. Seymour Sr.
kept the cabin as a summer home. Dilworth's father, uncles, and
aunts brought their families here to camp each summer, "usually
about the 4th of July. We stayed until late August usually. We had
a tent frame on the bottom land next to the creek and did our
cooking in a two hole tin stove in the tent." The tents were suspended on wooden frameworks, over raised wooden floors. They
slept on cots. The men commuted fifteen miles to jobs in the valley, an hour-and-a-quarter by buggy, or stayed in the valley two or
three days at a time. Seymour often had company cars. One
Overland that he sometimes took to the canyon would quit without warning.

> Father would get out, unhook the gasoline line and blow. The
> dirt would go back into the tank and we would go until the dirt
> settled and was again in the line. Our lights were carbide gas,
> and our horn was a rubber bulb. One pressed it and forced the
> air through a reed. We had plenty of horses and wagons to look
> out for and of course always worried that we might get hit by
> the Park City train as it wound its way up or down the canyon.
> There were eight crossings and we were glad when number
> eight had been safely passed.

One of Dilworth's early memories in Mountain Dell was of
sassing his mother. After a few unsuccessful warnings, Lou threat-
ened to dunk him in the creek. He didn't believe her and sassed
her yet again. "She picked me up by one arm and one leg and took
me over to the creek and dunked my head under it. I thought she
was going to drown me. Scared me to death. That cured me of
talking to Mother like I shouldn't."

Louine says her grandfather kept horses at Mountain Dell and that the boys rode them a good deal. She says they had trout from the stream for dinner nearly every day. One summer Dilworth's Aunt Elma read Les Misérables to the older children. Dilworth remembers listening without really understanding. He tells of horseback riding, berrying ("wild currents, chokecherries and serviceberries"), and grouse hunting, though he says he and Hiram never hunted with the uncles, at least not much. "The camp was the most fun when our aunts were being courted, and our uncles were courting." Then, especially, there was singing around the fire, "campfire fun and storytelling." Grandfather Young would tell of his adventures crossing the plains and on his mission. Seymour Jr. and Levi and Clifford (who both later became general authorities) told of their missions as well. Phyllis Wells remembers how entertaining they were, singing and joking and dancing and carrying on. Levi was known for his Indian stories. "Seme" and "Lee," she remembers, were both good mimics. Levi danced the Charleston with cousin Florence Bennion, who was much taller than he. The brothers teased each other about their "Chinese" names: Lee Young, Seme Young. They told Pat and Mike jokes. According to one, Pat and Mike were parked on the fifteenth floor of a fifteen story hotel in New York City when a fire engine went by below, then another. "Pat, come quick, come quick, they're moving Hell and two loads have gone by already."

One night Lou found a nest of field mice in the cupboard where she kept Richmond's diapers. She called Clifford over. He, thinking to catch the mother, left the babies exposed in a corner. Lou put out the lamp and went to bed, only to feel something crawling on her a few minutes later. Carefully, she reached up, lit a match, touched it to the lamp, and then flipped back the covers. "Right there, lying on her nightgown, were three little naked mice. That mother mouse had brought those mice in under the covers and deposited them on Mother's lap." Lou called out for Clifford once more, who this time killed them.

On a Sunday afternoon once, when Dilworth was about seven, Grandma Young had invited everyone down to dinner in her cabin, when a cloudburst hit Little Mountain. Before long a wall of red, muddy water hit the cabin, picked it up, and floated it a hundred yards down the river, where it wedged against the brush and willows. Water flowed through the house two feet deep, so those around the table climbed up on it with the food. Dilworth ran up the stairs toward the attic and watched from above. "No one was hurt, nobody drowned, and the water soon subsided again, and then of course we had to be lifted out onto the higher bank, [with] mud everywhere. And finally around about 8:00 o'clock that night, they sent some carriages up from Salt Lake and took us home [to the valley]. All the bridges were washed out. They had a real time getting up and down." The tents were washed away. Dilworth says he learned never to camp in the river bottom, as storms even several miles distant could mean flash floods downstream. When they rebuilt the camp, they put it on higher ground. "If we'd have been in those tents . . . every one of us would have drowned."

Dilworth and Emily graduated from Lowell Elementary in the spring of 1911. Seymour had the money to send just Emily (perhaps because she was older) to the Latter-day Saint University, the Church-run, combination high school-junior college, located east of the Hotel Utah. Dilworth presumably would go to Salt Lake (later West) High. "I felt terrible. I had just turned fourteen and to be left out seemed to me awful. So I cried a lot, and Father somehow raised the extra money needed to pay my tuition." He remembers wearing knickerbockers to school. He says he did well enough in English and history but that "Latin and algebra were beyond me." That year Seymour's health turned bad. "He wasn't right down, but he was miserable for some reason. . . . He thought he had kidney trouble, and he probably did because that's what he died of." Seymour resigned his job and that April, before Dilworth could finish his school year, took the family to Mountain Dell while he recovered. "We couldn't afford to live anywhere else. We had no money." School was not really an option—certainly there was none in Mountain Dell. "Grandma Young helped us to get food, I guess, . . . We ate food, I don't know where it came from." They slept in tents through that summer and the next, spending the winter of 1912-13 in Uncle Mel Well's cabin, "which was better than the others, although it was unlined for winter use." That meant just a board between them and the weather. Dil says, "We learned what living in an unlined cabin was—it was awfully cold." Lou hung drapes—she writes in her history of an evening when a cup of water froze three feet from the stove.

Other families had been around during the summer, but with winter here, the Youngs had the camp to themselves. The children skated on a pond. The Youngs made a little money pasturing horses for some men from Garfield. "Twelve head or so wintered over the high ridges west of the camp and we could count them. In the spring we finally got to them and discovered that one had a colt. Herding them was fun, although we knew little about how to care for them." Louine remembers standing by the train tracks and picking up coal one of the engineers would throw off for them. She says her mother put their foodstuffs on the table at night, away from the mice, and wrapped them in blankets to keep them from freezing. Relatives visited occasionally. One day in February, Dil remembers, Uncle John Robbins came up on a sleigh.

> It was a warm day and the cabin had got warm through the roof and we didn't have a fire in the stove. Uncle John got out of his sleigh and he came in and he says, "My, I'm cold!" He went over to the stove and rubbed his hands on it and he got warm, and after he got warm Hi said, "Uncle John, open the stove door!" Uncle John opened the stove door, and there was no fire.

George Knepp, a strong, well-liked, good-natured fellow, not LDS, who ran the city farm farther up the Dell, visited more and more often. George, later chief sheriff's deputy in Salt Lake County, could play the mouth organ and call country dances. Dilworth did not realize it at the time, but George was courting Emily, and they married a year after the Youngs returned to Salt Lake. Once Dilworth took the "bobs" to town "and was too ashamed to drive them through the mud, so I took the wagon back." Once in the canyon snow he found the sleigh's tracks were narrower than the wagon's. He drove the horses four miles before they gave out with two miles still to go. George "came along, and with the tongue of his bobsleigh pushing against my tailgate, literally pushed me into camp. I learned there that false pride is a foolish thing. George never rebuked, just laughed and pushed me home."

The second August in Mountain Dell, George got Dilworth a job pitching timothy hay on the Hugh Evans farm in Marion, not far from Kamas. (George pitched at the Wotstenholm ranch nearby.)

> It was my job to . . . hitch up and haul hay for ten hours each day, milk five cows and feed them and the horses. The end of my first day found my muscles so sore that I could not hold my knife and fork if I had to put pressure on them. Mrs. Evans cut my meat. By the end of two weeks I was over my soreness and secretly felt my muscle each night and was pleased with its hardness. I consumed tons of food and must have eaten a pint of whipping cream each morning. I slept with Alva Evans upstairs and felt a little prickly at first. I did not realize it was bedbugs, but it was.

Dilworth remembers the Evans boys ran wild, especially on Saturday and Sunday nights, "but I never did indulge.

> They all had horses and buggies and took in the country dances for miles around. These were long lasting, followed by buggy rides home with the girls. Often they would race buggies down the turnpike road, which had quite a high center. It is a wonder they were not killed . . . At the end of the first summer Mr. Evans said, 'Dilworth, you cannot do a man's work, but you are so willing and tried so hard I'm going to give you a man's pay.' I got two dollars per day for thirty days work.

By that fall, Seymour had recovered enough to open a real estate office and move the family off the mountain to a home at 2002 South 13th East. Mountain Dell became once again just a summer retreat for the Youngs, until condemned for the new dam and flooded in 1917.

CHAPTER 2

Coming of Age

Granite Years

One day that winter Dilworth, now sixteen and six feet tall, went "uptown," presumably on foot, to LDSU to ask if he could finish the half-year he had missed. Osborne Widtsoe, the principal, told him he could. Dilworth asked, "'Well, could I do it on the money I paid on that year?' He said, 'No, you can't do that. You have to pay a half-year's tuition.'" Dilworth had no money, and neither did his father, so that was the end of that. He thought to try Salt Lake High School, but the school had a rough reputation, and in any case, Granite was closer to his Sugarhouse home. So he walked the thirty-five blocks out to Granite High and up to the third floor to the registrar's office. He told the man in the window of his project of finishing the half-year, adding that he had no money for entrance fees. Willard "Wid" Ashton, a math teacher who had been filling in for the registrar, enrolled him in the freshman class, explaining there were no fees. Dilworth signed up for English, algebra, agriculture, history, and physical education—Ashton taught this last. He asked Dilworth if he would like to sign up for seminary. "'What is that?' said I. 'It's a class you take in your spare time given by the Church for no credit unless you study the Bible,' he replied." So it was that Dilworth took seminary the second year it was ever offered.

"Those were happy days." Dilworth walked the three miles from home and back again each day. "I had no money to ride—

rain, snow or shine." Many of the students lived on farms and were a year or two behind, like Dilworth, from staying out to help at home. Adam S. Bennion, later an Apostle, served as principal. Dilworth remembers him and Wid Ashton as "high principled men [who] always insisted on high ideals in the students." He adds, "I enjoyed the school dances, and the girls were especially nice."

Dilworth made a lifelong friend in Merlon Stevenson, later head of engineering and math and head coach at Weber College and Dil's neighbor in Ogden. The two had much in common—both had been out of school, both walked long distances each morning and night (six miles for "Steve" at one point). Both liked sports, worked and studied hard, and had high standards. They resembled each other, too, at least enough to confuse their teachers. "Ike and Mike, they look alike," reads a caption in the 1915-16 yearbook. The picture of them together shows them with similar haircuts, in similar jeans and drooping, long sleeved shirts. They have similar pointed noses and similar jawlines. Steve says Dilworth was two inches taller and two pounds heavier. He remembers the two of them sitting in Wid Ashton's math class when Wid wanted to make a point about perspective. "He said, 'Well, a lot depends on the way you look at something,' and we kind of looked at him—'What?' So Wid came down and he had a book in his hand." Steve was sitting just in back of Dilworth. Wid showed the two of them the book and said, "'Now, what is that?' and we both spoke up at the same time . . . but one of us said it was a rabbit and the other said it was a duck. The bills for the duck were the ears to the rabbit, depending on which way you looked at it."

Steve thought Dil "as honest as the day is long, and that when he told you something you could depend on it." He thought him "just a good, solid American boy with high ideals, because everything that we talked about was on a high level. . . . I never in my life heard him ever use any foul language or ever tell anything that was even shady." They had fun and kidded each other, but perhaps having had to stay out of school made them more serious than they might otherwise have been. Steve remembers many of their conversations turning on lessons and helping each other along. Wid Ashton noticed their hard work and counseled them to keep at it, to prepare themselves well and then decide what they wanted to do and go at it. "Now I think both Dil and I listened very carefully. I know I did, and I'm pretty sure he did, too."

One year Dilworth talked Steve into taking a public speaking class with him. Steve, raised on a farm, recalls that speaking was not his forte, but he went along. Miss Wolfe, the teacher, apparently learned late of a division extemporaneous speech contest to be held at LDSU. Rather than have Granite unrepresented, she got Dilworth and Steve to go. Steve recalls it was Dilworth who persuaded him. "I still can't account for how I even agreed." Topics were to be assigned from a list three minutes before each speech was given. The other schools had all had the list for weeks. Granite's representatives were obliged to wing it. Steve recalls his topic was "The Mosquito." Dilworth's account does not mention his own. Steve says he "felt that Dil did a fairly good job," but calls his own performance a "fiasco." Dilworth writes, "I did poorly. Steve opened his mouth in his turn but no sound came forth." For their trouble the boys were awarded debate team letters. The winner of that year's contest: Wallace F. Bennett of LDSU, later a United States Senator from Utah.

Dilworth speaks of taking plane geometry from Wid Ashton, "to his despair, because I am not a mathematician." He says he played basketball under him his first year there. "I was like a fence rail in width . . . Whenever I would get in the practice, within ten minutes my legs would be so numb I could not feel them. The coach . . . would say: 'What's the matter, Young, you baking?' I would admit I was, a little ashamed of my weakness, and he would bench me for the next fifteen or twenty minutes. He knew what was wrong, but I didn't. I was growing so fast I had no reserve strength." That summer he returned to the Evans farm, stronger and better able to pull his weight and happy to pay back Mr. Evans for his confidence the previous summer. He and Lloyd Evans loaded one wagon against Alva and Dean Evans—"almost grown men. The first year we could not keep even, but the second year we made them sweat to keep up. This was a source of great satisfaction to me, and I came back home that fall able to keep up on the basketball and football teams without 'baking out.'"

Dilworth tried ranching the summer of 1915 when "a herd of cattle went past our place.

> Twenty-first South was a trail street from the stockyards on 8th West and 21st South to the mountains. These were wild Nevada cattle and dangerous. Get off your horse and you were liable to be charged by a cow or a bull. They belonged to Heber Bennion, and he was trailing them to Chalk Creek to the summer range. He had bought them from a rancher named McMillan. He, his son Heber Jr. (grown up), a McMillan boy and . . . a real Texas cowpoke . . . named "Big Jeff," were doing the trailing. I had a pony old and tough, and I asked for a job. Mr. Bennion hired me to help with the herd.

> I started out—no coat, a hat, the pony. We drove into Emigration Canyon for the night and bedded down at Little Mountain. It was an all night herd job. Next day we went over the Little Mountain trail up Killyon Canyon to Parleys Summit. We lost nearly 200 of our 500 in the oak brush in that canyon, and I lost most of my shirt and my pants in the same brush. I learned why cowboys wear chaps and, too, why they swear at the cattle. We didn't have enough punchers, enough food, enough anything. We bedded the second night on Silver Creek. By that time I was so tired that during the night I became obsessed with how to spell "cattle." I tried all night but had no peace until daylight when I stopped and wrote it in the dust where I could see it.

> Two days later we turned the cattle loose on Bennion's range on Chalk Creek—up near the Blue Lakes—and I ate one last breakfast of four eggs and bread and started home. I don't know how many of those lost cattle were ever recovered . . . I, who had never chased anything faster than a milk cow, really had my eyes opened to what a range cow can do. The McMillan kid had a good horse and a bullwhip. A bull was lying down and

McMillan popped him with the whip. Before McMillan could get his horse moving, that bull was on his feet, charged, and had gored the horse in the hip. That ended the horse—and the boy went home.

Big Jeff was in town a few days later and telephoned Dilworth to see if he wanted to go to a show. The Youngs had him over to dinner, after which Dilworth and he went into town. Big Jeff wanted to stop at his hotel to get something. Once there he tossed a manila envelope on the bed and, while he went into the bathroom, invited Dilworth to have a look. Inside were a dozen glossy prints of "naked women, in what they thought were striking poses. I saw what they were, quit looking at #4, and put them back in the envelope." They went to a movie, with apparently nothing more said. Afterwards Dilworth "bade him good night" and went home. That was the last he ever saw of him.

> I suppose he expected me to go with him to a bar, have a drink or two, and then seek out a house of ill repute . . . I realize now that I could have been in great danger, but somehow he sensed I was not the kind of boy who did bad things, and perhaps dinner at our house taught him a different culture than he was used to. He was a profane man but not meaning to be. It was all he knew, apparently, and I thought there was an innate courtesy in him that is in few men who work with their hands today.

When Dil had been an eighth grader at Lowell, an older boy had come to the playground and shown some of the boys a couple of pictures. "I saw only one of them. It was the worst sort of pornography that one could imagine. He strutted and bragged how he was indulging in the same stuff . . . It was terrible. I would like to forget it, but it lingers. It taught me that if I don't want to have it in my mind, I must not look." This became Dilworth's characteristic response. Louine remembers walking in Sugar House with Dil when they passed a group of teenagers having a lawn party. "They were playing kissing games—'wink' was the popular one at the time. Dil hurried me on, even though I wanted to linger and watch the excitement. 'No!' he said. 'Kids should not play games like that, playing with the emotions!"

Dilworth writes in his history of rummaging in a chest of drawers in the attic when he came across two large leather-bound "doctor books."

> One contained the anatomy of women, especially sex organs. It was well illustrated with drawings of the process of birth, from conception to entry into the world. It also described instrument delivery and even what must be done if the baby's head was too large to enter. The second book was about marital relations, and while not entirely accurate in some details, was interesting reading for a fifteen year old boy.

Dilworth notes, "We never asked [Father] anything about the facts of life and he never offered to tell. His only attempt was the night before I married Gladys, and then all he said to me was to remember that I was a gentleman. I nodded and agreed."

> It would have been a lot better if Father had instructed us in these things. It is odd to me that parents could assume adolescents would not be curious, but they were raised that way. It was hush-hush, but I suppose too that I personally was none the worse at the moment. Yes, I was too, for I often came back to those two books that year, and I am sure they indelibly impressed me like a phonograph record, constantly played, does. I am sure I thought too much about what I read—not analyzing, just caught up in the sex emotions it stirred up. Yet I did nothing physically—just imagined.

Dilworth writes that herding on Little Mountain "cured me of wanting to be a cowboy." Yet he gave it one more try in 1916. George Knepp, who managed Utah-Construction-Company-owned ranches, got Dilworth a job on the Big Creek ranch, near where Utah, Idaho, and Nevada meet. Dilworth traveled to Rogerson, Idaho, where he saddled up a company-owned riding horse and rode forty miles to the ranch. He doesn't tell of this stint in his history, but he mentioned it in speeches and around the dinner table. As a general authority he would explain the Lord's seemingly contradictory instructions to Adam and Eve in the garden by alluding to the mule teams on the ranch that, no matter how much you yelled and whipped and tugged on the reins, would not move until you swore at them. So too the Lord had to get the Man and the Woman moving by speaking a language they could understand. Dilworth learned the language, but found it easier to start swearing than to stop, and he never completely overcame it. "Vulgar talk is a great temptation," he said at a BYU devotional one time. "Little half-swear words, the damns and the hells, I guess, come easy. They've done to me. I punched cattle once and discovered that cattle didn't understand any other language. But I wish I'd tried the other language on the cattle. They might have learned something. And I would certainly have saved myself trouble." The cowboys sang to the cattle to keep them from spooking at night. "Yippie-Ki-Yi-Yo" was one of the songs. Dilworth's boy scouts would later sing its innocuous first few verses. Dilworth discovered the song had a hundred verses, ninety-five of which were filthy. He never mentioned going out of his way to learn any of them, and yet, as he told it, they continued to visit him throughout his life, in the least convenient of places, such as in meetings in the temple, and that all he could do was chase them out.

Emily remembers Dilworth calling her "his best girlfriend" and taking her to mutual dances. Louine, quite a bit younger, remembers the way he managed to get Rich and Hi to do his chores, sometimes trading books for the work. Louine he simply charmed into shining his shoes and helping him get ready when he went out. "I remember pressing his pants time and time again, and how I loved doing it." She remembers, when she was very small, him sending her after glasses of water while reading. "'That's only a sample! Please bring me another,' he would tease as I cheerfully trotted back and forth to wait on him." Dilworth was sociable at school and enjoyed walking with a large group of friends, male and female, including Wid Ashton's sister, and sometimes Wid. In his history he writes, "Those walks to and from were the best part of school." Most his group belonged to Forest Dale Ward, and Dilworth began to attend there, too. After a time he was called to teach a Junior Sunday School class. "I enjoyed that, although I can't remember making great preparations."

Dil's father, when he came down off the mountain, did not return to church. Perhaps he was afraid of callings because of his poor health. Perhaps he had gotten out of the habit at Mountain Dell and on subsequent long visits with Emily and George on the ranch. Perhaps he was embarrassed over not keeping the commandments—this is Louine's opinion. "Father and [one of her uncles] were close companions, and they broke the Word of Wisdom by enjoying their cigarettes. Father had his cup of coffee each morning, but he never let us see him smoke. He talked about having a taste of wine with Thanksgiving dinners, which he said was not breaking the Word of Wisdom. My mother was saddened by this, but she did miss church on Sunday, but did remain active in Relief Society, at least to be a Visiting Teacher." There may also have been an element of disappointment or bitterness on Seymour's part over being passed over. He was the oldest son. His father and grandfather had both been First President of the Council of Seventy. In 1909 his younger brother Levi was called to the Council. In 1941 another little brother, Clifford, was made Assistant to the Twelve, with authority higher than the Seventy. According to Dilworth's widow Hulda, this is the reason Dilworth gave for his father's staying home.

Louine remembers their father during these years as compassionate and given to service. "He was very thoughtful of neighbors, friends and relatives, visiting and cheering people. Often I helped him compose or correct letters of appreciation and encouragement to others." She remembers him as "solicitous of his own family, especially visiting and offering help for his invalid sisters (one deaf, one lame, and one completely incapacitated.)" She remembers family prayer and religious discussions around the dinner table. Her parents did not get around to arranging her baptism until she was eleven, but like the other children, she attended church and auxiliaries, and she feels her parents must have given her some encouragement. One summer when the family visited Emily on the ranch, Hiram held Sunday School for the children.

One day the bishop of the Forest Dale Ward told Dilworth he would have to release him from his call. He said the policy of the Church was that members could only hold callings in their own wards. He said he was unable to advance him in the priesthood, and told him he ought to go back to his own ward.

My ward, Richards Ward, was new and was at first meeting in a tent on the property of Willard Richards, 9th East and Hollywood. Later a chapel was built on Garfield between 8th and 9th East. But I was shy and strange and told the bishop that if I could not go to his ward I would not go at all. He said he was sorry, advised me to be obedient, released me from my class, and walked away. I was stubborn and scared and so I went home. I didn't enter a meeting house again until I was eighteen years old. I did no wrong things. I stayed home, read a great deal, visited my cousins up on the Avenues on Sunday afternoons, but attended no meetings . . . My father was not active and my staying home, keeping out of trouble, did not seem to bother him.

Hulda reports Dilworth spoke of having read the Scriptures, *A Comprehensive History of the Church,* and every other Church book he could get his hands on during his two or three years away. In his history, Dilworth reports, perhaps with some bitterness, that no one from his home ward tried to reclaim him.

Ward teachers came and went; they paid me no attention. The bishop, if he had ever heard of me, gave me no signs. . . . Knowing my disposition, I am sure if anyone had put forth the helping hand, been interested, invited me, I would have gone to Church, but I didn't have the courage to break the ice myself. . . . My father should have. My ward leaders didn't think it to be their responsibility. We were classed as an inactive family and to be left alone to stew in our own juice.

At age eighteen Dilworth made up his mind to return. He went to the ward and introduced himself to Bishop J. A. Rochwood, who assigned him to the priest quorum, though he did not hold that office. "If he had put me with the deacons, I would probably have quit again." Soon he was ordained a priest. He attended his meetings faithfully. "Hi and I were often the only two at sacrament meeting to administer the sacrament." He says he liked to talk to girls on the back row during the meeting. "I realize now I was a nuisance doing it. . . . I blithely went on having fun, not conscious of the offense I must have been to the people in the rows ahead of me. I suppose I got a bad name for it, but . . . no one called me in and corrected me. I would have quit in a moment had I realized. I was a noisy boy growing up." Dilworth later spoke of one Sunday simply deciding to listen. He concentrated on the speeches, meditated on them during the sacrament, felt the Spirit and left the meeting exuberant.

Dilworth dated Morris Knott, a Methodist girl. "During my senior year, I took [her] to the school dances three times, which was tantamount to saying you were pinned." He visited her at her home one Sunday, where they sat on the porch swing looking at the family photo album. At 5:00 she invited him to church, and he went along. "It was a nice service. No kids cried, the minister was young and a good speaker, the music soothing." Afterwards Mrs. Knott invited Dilworth and two other couples to her home, where she served ice cream and cake, then brought coffee to all but Dilworth. "She said, 'I know you do not drink coffee, but I have milk, root beer, pop. Please name it.' I took root beer. My large glass was the envy of the other boys against their demitasse cups." He left at 10:30, "as all young men did," and walked three miles home.

> The moon was out, the night romantic, and I liked that girl. But I thought as I walked along; and when I walked upon the porch at home, I made up my mind that I would never take out that girl again, and further, would not go with any girl unless she was eligible to go to the temple at the time I took her. I kept that resolve.

Dilworth dated Afton Love, one of the girls from Forest Dale, through graduation. Afton had a fused hip and walked with a pronounced limp. Merlon Stevenson remembers few people would pay any attention to her, and that Dilworth went out of his way to talk to her and make her feel good. Dilworth writes, "She reminded me of Aunt Elma Young and I mistook sympathy for love." He came to the realization he did not love her enough to marry her long before Afton did, and her feelings were apparently hurt. He found the situation painful and confided in Steve how terrible he felt. But as Steve puts it, "His whole purpose . . . was to help make her feel good and pay some attention [to her] . . . He had a heart of gold."

Sporting News

"While at Granite I tried all the sports," Dilworth writes. Track brought him the least success. He ran the half mile once without training, leading until the last 220. "My legs went numb and my eyes blacked out. I managed to finish but was badly beaten." Merlon Stevenson excelled at the high jump and pole vault. Dilworth says, "I liked the team games and played left field in baseball but was poor at batting." Steve, who proved a good athlete, remembers Dilworth as a consistent player and modestly refers to himself as the weak link. Dilworth's history describes an encounter at the mound with Stanley Johnson, whom the papers referred to as "The Terrible Swede."

> He was about twenty years old and pitched with man's speed. He threw a ball at me and I stepped back and it curved over the plate. He did it again. I resolved I would strike it the third try. It came on—didn't curve—struck me on the left cheekbone. I struck at it and was declared out. My face was swollen badly but apparently it did not break bones . . . I was just plain scared in that game, or I would have ducked the last minute.

He and Steve played football—without the padding of the modern game—both offense and defense with few substitutions. The team relied a good deal on these two big backs. Wid Ashton, coming off a championship year, scheduled a practice game with Utah Agricultural College. This was the first varsity game Dilworth played. "We were big kids," Dilworth remembers. "We

were as big as those college kids." Probably several were nearly as
old. Dilworth recalls his father as nervous and tending toward
over-protective during this period. "My father said to me, 'Now,
if you get hurt playing football, you have to quit.' He didn't want
me to play in the first place, and the only reason he let me play
was that I insisted." The game was held in Logan. Steve was fullback and leader, Dilworth halfback. Steve made a diving tackle at
a player's legs, hitting his head against the player's thigh pad,
twisting his neck and passing out. When he came to, he continued to play, but had little memory of it afterwards. The coach sent
in word for them to swap positions, but Steve couldn't keep it
straight and kept lining up at fullback. Dilworth says, "He could-
n't remember where he was. If you told him what to do he could
do it. So he'd say, 'What shall I do,' and I'd say, 'Go out there fifty
feet, and if anybody comes toward you, tackle him.' So he'd go out
there, and if the guy'd come toward him, he'd tackle him." Steve
remembers moments of clarity, during which he would wonder
what he was doing at halfback, but then he'd black out and go
ahead and play again. He remembers coming to, picking up a
loose ball, and making a good run, then once again he was out.

The team lost but felt good at holding them to 13-0. Dilworth
got his left cheek kicked hard enough that his teeth went numb.
"I thought it'd kill all my teeth." (His upper back left teeth eventually died and had to be pulled, but he didn't know whether to
blame this incident or Swede Johnson's pitch.)

> Anyhow, I was fine till the game was over with, and we went up
> in the hotel and bathed. And at supper I came down the stairs
> in that hotel in Logan, and halfway down the stairs I took my
> handkerchief out and blew my nose, and my face came up just
> like that, and my eye went shut just that quick, and puffed out
> till it was three times as big on that side. When Wid Ashton . . .
> saw me, he looked at me and said, "What in the world has hap-
> pened to you." I said, "I don't know, I just blew my nose." But
> I was worried because if I went home with a face like that,
> Dad'd sure fix me. So I sat up all night hot packing and cold
> packing that face, and by morning I had it down to where you
> wouldn't notice it much.

They played basketball together as well, Dilworth at guard, Steve at center. The guards mostly stayed back and fed the ball to the others, though Steve remembers Dilworth going in at times. The other teams thought it was Steve, who was right-handed, but Dilworth was left-handed. They would try to block his right hand, and he would put it in with his left. Steve scored on jump shots, leaving the ground at the free-throw line. If no one followed, he would shoot. If anyone came with him, he simply waited, and invariably they would fall away before he did, and he would still make his shot. Steve says, "I thought we were a pretty good ball club."

Dilworth records, "Wid Ashton would not let us play dirty. If we tried to retaliate on dirty play, he would jerk us from the game. We were long on ethics and often short on winning." He says, "I learned a great deal from him on how to be honorable. . . . Granite teams played clean." Steve agrees. "[Wid] was one who taught sportsmanship. He wanted us to play hard, but he wanted us to play it fair. . . . Very seldom did I ever hear. . . . any foul language, or any unsportsmanlike conduct on the part of any of our players." Of Dilworth he says, "I never saw him ever commit an intentional foul."

Not that they were short on winning. By 1915-16 Salt Lake High had been divided into East Side and West Side, with West the principle contender for the championship. Granite came from behind, though, beating West once and winning enough other big games that they looked like they might knock them out in their second meeting. West had developed what was called a "charging game," a fast, physically aggressive offense that overwhelmed the other team. Rumors that West was going to try to "take out" key players preceded the game. Steve's parents wanted him to sit that one out. Dilworth remembers, "As we dressed for the game, we could hear through the wall the coach instructing his boys. 'First, get Stevenson, then Smith, then Hausknecht.' Granite built up an early 10 to 5 lead, but then West began to overwhelm them. Steve reports that "very near the end of the first half, one of them came in and just smashed into me and tripped and tackled and took me

down, and another came and jumped on top of me and batted my
head into the floor. And it was some time before I even came to.
And when I did I was seeing double." Steve had bouts of uncon-
sciousness for three days after, and was out for the season. Granite
finished the half down 10 to 15. The rough play continued.
According to Dilworth, Hausknecht had both eyes blackened.
Smith broke his front tooth. Neither was in shape for subsequent
games, though Hausknecht played some.

West won this game 37 to 17. Dilworth reports, "at the game's
end, Adam Bennion walked over to the other principal and told
him about his bad sportsmanship and severed relations with West
High until they could clean up their athletics. East joined West,
and for several years LDS, Granite and Jordan played together,
and East and West played whom they could get to play."
According to the papers, this was accomplished through the five
Salt Lake schools withdrawing from the State basketball league
and playing as independents. The *Deseret News* reports the action
was "the direct result of the West Side-Granite game . . . which
Granite lost. There, it is claimed, is the heart of the whole difficulty—Granite lost. The coaches of this division claim that the
'charging game' which the West Side uses is dangerous and that it
was this style of game which put Stevenson and Hausknecht of
Granite out of the game." Adam S. Bennion is quoted as saying,
"When in interscholastic contests winning becomes so important
that the principles of true sportsmanship are only of secondary
importance it is time that our methods be changed. The action of
yesterday is designed to eliminate the 'win-at-any-price' spirit."
Other principals make similar statements—also without mentioning names. West's principal says he knows of no wrongdoing
on the part of his team, "but as dissatisfaction seems to exist, the
best way out of it . . . [is] for the schools to withdraw." In any case,
the move ended West's bid for the championship—there was no
league left to win.

Steve graduated that year, 1916, one year early. Dilworth took
over his position of center on the basketball team the following
year, where he began to stand out. His history records only one

event from that season. Dilworth wore a brace with metal hinges sticking out a half inch on both sides when he bent his knee. The LDSU captain examined it, made him bend it, then said, "If we were playing West, I'd make you take it off, but you're Granite so you can keep it on."

An Officer

Dilworth was elected Junior Class President for the 1915-16 school year. An article in the yearbook, possibly written by Dilworth or Secretary Morris Knott, lists the years' activities: The juniors beat the seniors in a tug of war, "awakening [them] to real life by means of a cold plunge in Mill Creek." Next they beat the seniors for the school basketball championship. "(Really we do not like to mention these things.)" One wonders which side got Steve, whom the Senior Class report calls "our Star." Then came the Prom, and an assembly, "a conundrum in pantomime, [which] amused the students after they had it explained to them." The juniors also treated the seniors to a matinee and luncheon in town and a dance in the evening.

Dilworth won the election for Student body President his senior year, which he was tempted to skip because, like Steve, he had enough credits to graduate early, or nearly so. "I wanted the experience." The student body council oversaw all extracurricular activities, including athletics, drama, debate, and of course picnics and dances. Dilworth says he has no particular memories of being president, beyond presiding at the meetings. "One time the student body wasn't very active and I bawled them out for not supporting the team better than they were supporting it, and that's what usually happens at student body activities." Dilworth could be gruff. Steve says Dilworth "showed leadership right from the beginning. . . . And he was one of the most kindly men, but I noticed . . . that he was just a little bit rough at times on people. And as I knew him, I've never been able to quite figure that out. . . . He really wasn't that way." He characterizes Dilworth's leadership as exceptional. "I never [knew of] anybody who took exception to [it] . . . They called it the Granite family. It was a very close-knit institution."

Dilworth decided he would like to be a naval officer. Noel Davis, an Annapolis "five striper" whose family had lived in the 2nd Ward and who visited the Young family each summer at Mountain Dell, gave Dilworth an introduction to Congressman Joseph L. Howell. Dilworth won the appointment. Adam S. Bennion told Dilworth he would graduate him on the strength of his Annapolis exams, assuming he passed. So Dilworth studied at home (the family had moved to 1882 South 10th East.) "Twelve to fifteen hours a day for [six] months I crammed information into my head—spelling, grammar, algebra, plane geometry, history and English." He came to school only for activities, games, and meetings. He obtained a book with the Annapolis test questions for the past fifteen years. "[I] solved every problem and answered every question in that book." In addition, he noticed the questions repeated every five years. "So I just figured that, five years back, I'd get that exam." Sure enough, that was the one he got. "I knew the answers. I knew it all by heart." And yet when he took the test, out of 4.0, he got 2.4, not quite passing. He received a letter telling him that, since he had come so close, if he could get another appointment, they would allow him to take the test again. Congressman Howell had been replaced by Milton H. Welling, who told Dilworth that with a first name like Seymour he must be a member of Dr. Seymour B. Young's family, and any member of that family could have the appointment. Dilworth dug into the books for three more months, then tried the test again. "I thought I was letter perfect. I knew every answer." And yet he only scored 2.6, barely passing.

"I was told to report June 15 to the Academy. Before borrowing the money to go East, I got an exam by the naval doctor in Salt Lake. He told me that I had a slight systolic heart murmur and that they probably would not take me."

> I didn't believe him so I went to several other doctors, and three of them couldn't hear it and one of them could. . . . They told me to do something like this, and I did it. "You leave this building,"

it was the twelfth floor of the Walker Bank building. "You walk home, four miles and a half, you cut wood all afternoon, (I had a woodpile and an axe), and then have your supper, and then after supper, wait awhile. Before you go to bed you will run a mile around the block, and take this dose of castor oil." So I took a big dose of castor oil and I ran around the block, a mile, that was [twice] around that block. "And the next morning you're to come up on a fast walk up to this building, and run the [twelve] flights . . . and come in our office." And they had three doctors there, and one was sure he could hear it and the other two didn't think they could.

But Grandpa Young said, "What's this?"

I said, "Grandpa, they say I have a systolic murmur."

"Let me hear it. Lie on this couch." So without any stethoscope or anything, he just stuck his ear against my chest, and he said, "Yes, you have it"—an old man 80 years old.

Dilworth never went to Annapolis. "I debated but somehow felt I shouldn't go. If I went and was turned down I'd have to pay the fare. . . . At the time I [thought] that it was the money which I didn't want to face repaying. But now I can recognize the Spirit." The United States had entered the First World War that spring. Annapolis would likely have meant a military career after the war, which would have prevented him getting his scouting job, would have kept him from a mission, and possibly gotten him away from Church activity. He wonders whether he would have been able to adjust to the school—"I was not of a temperament to handle Academy life"—and he speculates he might have failed to stay. "I believe the Lord influenced the decision. The heart never had bothered me until recently," he writes in 1972. "I know I was better than 2.4 or 2.6 in those exams. I knew the answers to every question they asked but something I did gave me the low grades."

Dilworth was one of the speakers at his graduation. "It must have been immature speaking." He worked that summer on a crew surveying a railroad spur in Idaho, Firth to Goshen—six miles. "All that summer I pounded stakes and learned how to figure 'cut and fill' on the project.

> We lived in a tent by the water tower at the Firth siding and ate
> our meals in a . . . freight car made into a dining car. We had a
> cook named Fred—an old-timer. It was an enjoyable summer
> and I learned a lot—about work and about men. These survey-
> ors were foulmouthed, bragged about their sex exploits, pro-
> faned—but they were honest generally. I found I could with-
> draw mentally and lose myself in a book.

Late in August the rodman quit. Dilworth had learned the job,
but the foreman hired someone else over him. The new man
proved incompetent—Dilworth found himself doing his job
while he got the pay.

> I went to the boss and said, "Do you think it's fair for me to do
> his rodding and him get the pay for it." And he said, "No, it
> isn't fair." I said, "Well, what you gonna do about it." He said,
> "Can't do anything." And I said, "Goodbye."

"And so the 1st of September 1917 found me at home, 1882
South 10th East, Salt Lake City, within seven days of twenty years
of age and the First World War six months old."

Artillery

At about age eighteen, Dilworth had a dream he did not understand. He saw a great field stretching as far as he could see, full of
countless men stripped to the waist, "doing some rhythmic
things—none alike—but in seeming unison, even so." During the
War at Camp Kearny, he stood on the edge of the parade ground,
two miles by one mile, and watched the 40th Division, forty
thousand men. "All were doing calisthenics—all doing a different
thing but all in rhythm. I saw my dream exactly."

Dilworth wanted to join the Army the fall of 1917. Seymour
opposed him. "As I was not of legal age, I had to have his permission. I would not lie about my age." Seymour agreed to have
Dilworth's grandfather, Seymour B. Young, Sr., settle it. Dilworth
went to his home on 4th East and found him in his library.

Dilworth explained his purpose and asked permission to go. He records the answer: "Your great-great-grandfather fought in the revolution. He thought the country was worth creating. Your grandfather fought in the Civil War. He thought the country was worth saving. I'm proud you'd want to make the world safe for democracy—by all means go." The 145th Regiment, originally envisioned as a machine-gun outfit but since reassigned as field artillery, was organizing at Fort Douglas with Utah volunteers, and Dilworth wrote Colonel Richard W. Young, a relative, about getting in. Colonel Young's response reads, "If an examination of your heart [showed] the murmur such as you describe, there would be absolutely no chance of your being accepted." Dilworth does not record the results of the exam, but he must have passed it, for he received one of the last posts in "E" Battery, made up of Salt Lake and Davis County men.

Seymour asked his son if he would like a father's blessing before he went. Dilworth said yes, he would. Seymour said, "We'll go to Grandfather; he's the patriarch of the family." They went to his home, where Seymour Sr. performed the blessing. "He promised me that if I would keep the commandments and behave, not one hair of my head would be harmed. He was prophetic for that is what happened."

R. Lamar Barlow, a fellow recruit, remembers mustering at the National Guard supply barracks on Pierpont. The sergeants would ask, "What size do you want," then plop down something on the counter, which might or might not bare any resemblance to the size requested. Dilworth was too late to uniform. "I wore a pair of my own 'khaki' pants, a borrowed army shirt, and a borrowed hat." The group marched from there to the train station, to the cheers and tears of spectators. "I was used to long steps and kept stepping on the heels of the man in front of me as we marched up Main Street, I for the first time."

Dilworth commenced a journal and kept it up throughout his training. He records that the towns they stopped in along the way applauded and sent out their school children and cheered. "This being heroized is quite the stuff," he writes. "I'll be getting so big-headed that I can't stand." In Los Angeles he and a friend swam, visited a "ten-cent dance hall," and toured a department store, bigger than anything they had seen. While the friend talked to the manager of the corset department, "I stood by and foolishly grinned, exchanging winks with the other clerks." Camp Kearny, a tent camp, was located on the upland desert northeast of San Diego. Dilworth, in his first journal entry after arriving, describes it as "bare and dreary on first glance, but one gets to like the place." Eight men shared one tent frame, each with a cot, mattress, and blanket. Dilworth's entry notes three of his tentmates are "fine fellows as far as morals are concerned (they don't smoke or tell dirty stories). They are all a pretty good bunch who seem to be all there."

The journal mentions drill, lots of it, from early on, and practice with three inch guns, but without live ammunition. In January the big guns, the 4.7s, arrived. Lamar Barlow remembers real shells in these, which they fired over orange groves into a bank of hills. Dilworth records a shell misfiring in February, driving the breech of the gun a foot into the ground. The "number 2" man, who loaded and unloaded, just happened to be off getting more ammunition. "When he came back a moment later and saw what had happened he was pretty weak in the knees." They fired from pits, which they dug with shovel and pick. "The solid rock baffles our efforts and turns the soft point of the pick into little balls, which will not even make it feel badly." Dilworth speaks also of gas mask drills, made painful for him by a case of boils. He mentions guard duty at the stables, "seven to eleven on, eleven to seven off." He sat on an oat sack trying to recite "Crossing the Bar" to himself when it got too dark to read. He tells of shots for paratyphoid, and KP with the sore arm. "They stick a needle about two inches long up under the skin into the muscle. Then they shoot about a pint of germs into our systems. It is great dope—I don't think."

Dilworth spent his liberty in the mess tent or the YWCA hostess house, reading books and writing letters. He swam in the ocean, walking six miles overland to La Jolla to do it. He records "galas" and "smokers" in the mess tent. In one he sang in a quartet ("I didn't smoke," he assures us). Refreshments at another included "dainty sandwiches," composed of "two slices of bread—an inch thick—and a tough slice of army ham." He made a trip to San Diego, visiting the bay and browsing all afternoon in a bookstore. Sundays he attended meetings. Billy Sunday, a famous revivalist preacher, visited the camp—Dilworth found him flamboyant but effective. He refers several times to sermons by B. H. Roberts, who accompanied the troops as chaplain, here and in France. November 3 was payday. Dilworth received $163, all but $13 of it in Liberty Bonds. Up until now he had been borrowing stamps (fifty per month, he writes in his journal, at 3 cents apiece). He sent home tithing and a little money for the folks, which left him "so close to flat that I can't tell the difference."

By November 17 the soldiers were ready for their first parade. "It was a huge success from the standpoint of the general. Over 20,000 marched by the stands. Among others our governor was there. . . . But in the ranks . . . the dust rose in such clouds that some of the time it was all that I could do to see the man in front of me. Dust behind, dust before, dust around. I breathed it until my lungs ached. My eyes were sore and my nose was clogged. [One] had to march at attention just the same." Governor Bamberger spoke, after which his daughter, "Miss Elsa," read personal messages to some of the men from the podium, a few of these "in the form of kisses." "Overhead twelve aeroplanes circled, wheeled and made evolutions in all shapes and forms." Dilworth fantasized about going to aviation school, though he suspected his heart would have kept him out.

Dust plagued the soldiers, sometimes whipped up by wind. The weather remained in the 80° range fall, winter and spring, but on November 20, Dilworth describes a blizzard, not of snow but of "fine particles of dust and sand from the surrounding country. We sometimes are able to see nearly 25 feet and the choking sensation is not much fun. . . . I have literally eaten dust for the last three days. It gets in our clothes, our hair. It sifts through the folds of the tents. It is everywhere. It gets in the tightest boxes imaginable." During this storm Dilworth drew the job of disposing of a load of ashes. "That was the ashiest, dustiest . . . dirt that I ever choked or smothered in." The occasional rains cleaned up the air, though if they continued any length of time they turned the camp into a "sea of mud." Sometimes this meant tent-bound liberty, "with letters . . . books and noisy fellows for companions." Sometimes they drilled or went to the gun pits anyway. "Just a little taste of what we might expect in France if we ever go."

Dilworth begins to lament "the straight and narrow trail between the canteen, the mess hall, and my bed." He keeps his chin up, does his part to keep the mood jovial. "The idea is to smile and make the other fellow grin." But he grows weary. "This sham of existence, this keeping up of appearances just to be talking makes me tired at times. To always brag about what a girl one has, to tell how many letters we get. . . . This being in love so bad that they can't live if a letter doesn't come every day is comical." Dilworth figures only one man in the tent ever loved a girl enough to marry her while in the army—no, he assures, he does not mean himself. "The little infatuations that wear off in about two weeks are the ones which make me laugh. Any fellow who will let anyone read the letters from a girl is not very much in love with her."

He waxes lyrical from time to time. He thinks longingly on the mountains of his childhood. "The rugged grandeur of their lofty summits is equaled by none on earth. Thank God I was born in them. Glad am I that I received a portion of their strength. Happy am I that the heritage of my fathers is vested in them." He worries over his parents. Of his mother, he wonders "how many nights she lies awake wondering what I am doing. Never mind, Mother, you need never feel afraid for the morals of me. I am wondering how many gray hairs my father is developing on my account. He says little but the drawn look on his face was enough to tell me that his love for me was too deep to be expressed or told." He feels "the bitterest regret" on being left out of the regimental football game at Thanksgiving, regret "that the greatest game in the world would never bark my shins or tingle my nose with dust. It would never again take all the hide off my face or leave me a lump on my elbow. . . . But if it had left me crippled I am still thankful that I can look back on a little of it in my experience and say would that it had been more." He adds as an afterthought. "I only hope that in the great game of war, I won't look back and wish I had had more."

There was some illness, but otherwise, death was as remote as battle in Camp Kearny. Dilworth's romantic allusions to it are mostly in quoted songs. "We march or we don't, we will or we won't/ Go to town on Saturday Eve./ We wonder if even we'll go up to heaven /If dead, or below on 'French Leave.'" He does his best to imagine battle in a passage composed between ten minute turns on a pick:

> In the trenches—the magic place. Overhead the shrapnel bursts and batters around like rain. Aeroplanes are searching the air and earth for artillery targets. The dull boom of the guns rumbles like thunder. The wind blows the dust of a thousand battles in our faces. It tells of the thousands . . . "out there" lying exposed to the elements and the blazing sun. The stench is terrible. We gasp as we endeavor to make the trench deeper so that we may find some small protection for our bodies. The bombs are finding us—one by one. We wonder who will be the next to go on the stretcher to the everlasting rest. There is a grave earnestness in the men's faces, a horrible endurance which must break sometime. It seems as tho we would go mad from the heat, the thirst, the smell, the driving—driving everlastingly— forward. Fighting inch by inch for some steel-torn piece of ground hardly large enough to die in.

He pauses to savor that last bit: "That is a beautiful thing to think of, hardly large enough to die in." He picks up again. Have we gone mad, how much can we endure, when, oh when will it end—and then it does, for Dilworth's turn on the pick has come again.

The journal contains several such sketches. He depicts a symphony concert in all its programmatic splendor. He describes the contrapuntal bustle of catching a train. He gives all the furnishings of the YWCA hospitality house, and all the garnishings of that year's Thanksgiving feast. He philosophizes: "They say that variety is the spice of life, and I guess that Seymour D. is getting some of the spice. It is mostly nutmeg with myself as the chief nut. Perhaps the thyme will help to make the pepper cool and the salt sweet."

He attempts poetry:

> *If you're on guard, or on KP*
> *What's the odds, to you—or me*
> *The work is there, so do it*
> *The time will come, you won't rue it*
> *A happy grin, will make lead time*
> *And takes the weight from off the mind*
>
> *Which isn't poetical. I do wish that I could write pretty things*
> *and make this a really interesting book.*

He longs to be like A. G. Empey, an Ogden native who joined the British army early in the war and published his memoirs, "or any other war hero. I might be someday, but at the present time— poor attempts."

Dilworth as a diarist aims for the "sentiment," yet in Camp Kearny as the months drifted by the dominant mood became languor.

> It is in times like this that one likes to sit and dream—aye, dream. There is no harm in thinking—nay, floating around in an ethereal way, nowhere in the land of no place, when time is forever and the road is lined with trees that are perpetually growing and giving leaves and blossoms to lovers . . . The whole world is one grand whirl.

"Forgive the dreamer," he concludes, after drifting a bit longer over home, holidays, Mountain Dell. "They will finally forget the giddy whirl and will gradually come to real things."

One other passage finds Dilworth with old friends:

> Books—the right kind—are the only reliable friends that a man has until he is married and then I suppose that a wife is the best. But books are the thing which make life worth living. The expression of feeling and thought in the works of the poets and

authors make up partially for the hardships, pains, mental suffering, loss of those whom we love—either through death or
circumstances. Then the books are a solace—and the only one
for me. So bring on the books and you may have the pleasures,
fickle friends, joys, hates, and other passions while I shall roam
in the world of books until the time shall come when I retire to
private life or another sphere in the after ages—Selah.

In March, "E" Battery was lined up and asked for three volunteers to leave immediately for France. The whole battery stepped
forward, so the captain had to resort to a lottery. "I never could
guess and so I was left behind," he laments. "I would like to be
going with them. That is what I enlisted for—active service."
About that time Dilworth was made a lance corporal. "This kind
gets the pay of a buck and does the work of a corporal." Dilworth
had complained in a January entry of the way the noncommis-
sioned officers rode the enlisted men. "They almost help us write
our letters." He complained about them jumping all over soldiers
without bothering to find out what really went wrong. Now that
he finds himself one, he muses over whether he will be able to
earn the boys' respect. He enjoys being able to stay in the tent and
read or do what he likes, "so long as the guard goes on alright."
Afton Love spent the last part of that month and the first part of
April in San Diego—whether with friends or family Dilworth
neglects to mention. "I was mighty glad to see her. We talked—it
seemed as tho there were so many home things to talk of." He
spent his liberty on trips with her to Coronado, Mission Cliffs,
Balboa Park. "It was three weeks of greatest pleasure. . . . Gee, I
certainly was sorry to see them go and I nearly bawled. There was
a lump in my throat for about five hours. I didn't think that it
would be so lonesome when they left, but it was."

"Wish it moved," Dilworth writes in late April. Wish something would come in a hurry. Sick of it—yet we haven't started."
He speculates they might be off by September. He reports a total
of $360 earned. "What a waste. It is certainly a shame that
humans can't live peaceably together." The next month he is

promoted to corporal, spending the first week sick. "We are soon going to be in one of two places—," he says, "over there or home." This time he is right. In late May sixty men from the battery received word they were shipping out as part of the June Automatic Replacement—filling slots in other regiments in Europe of those disabled or killed. Lamar Barlow remembers the enthusiasm. He says there lacked the moodiness of World War II—people had not had a taste of death yet. Noncoms, to Dilworth's disappointment, were to stay behind. "We are to whip the June draft into shape. . . . Another seven or eight months in camp and I'll be bugs." Dilworth records a several-day march before the Replacements left, up the coast to Santa Ana, including swimming in the ocean during rest stops, and dances and diners given by the towns they passed through. They returned to an empty camp and waited the new arrivals. "We are here for at least six weeks and probably until next spring." On the 28th of July he reports that "while I'm writing I am on the jump" because of rumors they would soon be leaving. Many of the other regiments had gone. "We are scheduled to be the last to leave Kearny and make up the rear guard." The next entry, August 5, is from the train.

Dilworth crossed the Atlantic on the Scotian, an English ship. "We were part of a large convoy of forty ships or so," he writes in his history. "Off on the horizon on both sides were cruisers, while occasionally a destroyer would weave in and out among the ships. At stated intervals the ships would change course, to confuse the submarines. This was the famous zig-zag course. Forty ships changing in unison was something to behold. His journal describes their quarters in the steerage as "a place of darkness and peculiar odors. With all of the ports closed and locked, our only air is through a temporary ventilator, so that it gets pretty sour here before morning." He is surprised at the variety of the sea, now a "heavy blue-green liquid slowly swelling," now "like frozen tar which slowly change[s] shape and color." He admires the moon, and the sunsets, "which rival those of old Saltair." He mentions lifeboat drills and the fear of U-Boats. He speaks

romantically of a ship on the horizon going the other way—
"Ships that pass in the night."

They rounded Ireland on the north and made land at
Liverpool, where they spent five days at a camp called Knotty Ash,
with inadequate supplies. The journal ends abruptly here until
after the war—soldiers were not allowed to keep diaries for fear
they would fall into enemy hands. He fills in a few details of
Liverpool after Armistice Day—throwing pennies at the children,
seeing all the sights, including an organ recital at the town hall,
"(but we Utah boys are spoiled for organ recitals)." He remembers
his disgust at finding prices at the YMCA as high as anywhere
else—a pattern that persisted in France. They crossed from
Southampton to Le Havre at night, then traveled by train (forty
men or eight horses to a boxcar) to Vouille, near Poitiers, and after
two more weeks to Bordeaux and Camp de Souge to continue
training on the 4.7 inch guns. "These were built like the 3 inch
guns but were much larger and more awkward to handle. We
never were good at shooting them, and they were less reliable.
These guns were likely the reason why we did not get to the front.
We never could shoot them straight."

Lamar Barlow, one of the Replacements, found himself in battle by mid-September. He and his group were given a one-hun-
dred-yard stretch of ground to take care of—beyond that they
weren't told a thing. Then on September 26, 1918, the Allies
coordinated an offensive—at zero hundred hours, every gun on
the front extending from Belgium to Switzerland went off at the
same time. From that moment on there were no more rotations—
he fought straight through, seven days a week. Beginning at 3:00
a.m. the captain would give the signal, and they would fire as fast
as they could on the enemy trenches with medium and heavy
artillery. When the enemy came up out of the trenches, the allies
followed, took up new positions, and dug in. Horses were brought
forward to haul the guns, then taken back again. The daytime was
business as usual—machine gun fire, shrapnel. Barlow says he was
hit three times. At night they dug trenches six feet long and deep
enough that their bodies were at least flush with the ground. He

remembers casualties by the hundreds, shell-shocked soldiers, sickness, filth, infection, unsanitary conditions. Dilworth and his battery were a long way from any of this.

Dilworth says the German submarines must have been effective in keeping supplies out, because their rations were poor. "We lived on carrots alone for three weeks one time." They got bread and cheese from markets, picked blackberries from hedges, and bought milk warm from farms. Dilworth, who savored these roadside meals, says they soon learned "what blackberries could do to a person unwashed." He tells of whittling the mold from one cheese until the cheese was mostly gone. Once Dilworth approached a chateau. A woman sat outside the kitchen doorway milking, the cow's head and forequarters inside the door. He pointed to the cow, the pail, his canteen, and said *"Du lait? Du lait?"* She didn't understand until he got down beside her and pantomimed. *"Oh, oui oui oui!"* she said and filled his canteen. He thanked her and tried to pay, but she wouldn't allow it. When he insisted she led him around the cow and inside, sat him on a chair, pulled a box from a bureau, and carefully unwrapped the portrait of a young man in uniform. Dilworth surmised this was her son, and that it was for him she wore her black arm band. She pulled a bottle of expensive wine from the shelf, poured a thimbleful in each of two glasses, toasted him, *"Vive l'Amérique!"* and drank. *"Vive la France!"* he said, and held the glass to his lips, but did not drink. She seemed disturbed. He tried to explain the Word of Wisdom, but couldn't make her understand his English. He gave her his glass, took hers, and gestured towards the pail. "Oh, oui," she finally said, and filled the glass with still-warm milk. *"Vive l'Amérique!"* she toasted him once more. *"Vive la France!"* he said and drank.

Dilworth's unit was ordered to the front on November 1, but before they could pack up and ship out, the Armistice was signed. "I took part in the celebration on Armistice night. Our band marched in a parade in the city and our job was to form a hollow square within which marched [the] band playing music. The guard was to keep the French girls from trying to kiss and hug the band members so they could not play." The parade finished at the *Esplanade des Quinconces*, packed with fifty or sixty thousand people, as he remembers, for the main celebration. The esplanade is dominated by the *Monument des Girondins*, a bronze statue of a woman, larger than life, in Grecian gowns, perched atop a white column several stories high. Dilworth says a drunken man climbed out on her upstretched hand, where he led the crowd in *La Marseillaise*. "He swayed—you'd think he was going to fall off, but he never did."

Then it was more waiting. Once one of Dilworth's friends suggested they go to "'Hill 13,' the army house of prostitution, just to look in. I refused. He went, but would not look me in the eye the next day." Another time, after a half-day's liberty in Bordeaux, Dilworth was waiting for the truck to take him back to camp.

> One of my battery mates came along and stood waiting under a dim street lamp. He did not see me and I kept quiet in the dark doorway. Soon a French girl came along and spoke to him in the universal language. He looked up and down the street, and seeing no one, went with her into the darkness. Later, when we arrived in Salt Lake City, I saw a woman, carrying a baby, rush up to him and thrust the baby into his arms. I stood watching and wondered what he was thinking—I'm still wondering.

He regretted later not having stepped out and prevented him, or at least made his presence known.

They waited out the great flu epidemic of 1918 in pup tents in the sand hills of Camp de Souge, cooking their rations on tin can stoves. Rumors flew—there may have been some question as to whether these green soldiers should be made part of the army of occupation. (Lamar Barlow felt bad that his group, who had seen battle, had to stay behind.) Dilworth played football for the regimental team at his old position of fullback. They line up a half-dozen games against other bases in Southern France, going undefeated and un-scored-against. The team was to travel to Paris to play for the championship of the American Expeditionary Forces

when the sailing orders came. They left Bordeaux on the Santa
Teresa, a United States "shipping board" boat, on December 24.
"Very few of us ate Christmas dinner." Dilworth felt queasy but
made it alright. Even with three-deep bunks he found the ship
more comfortable than the Scotian. "The crossing was pleasant
and warm for we were southerly most of the way, but the last
night out we nearly froze as the ship left the Gulf stream and wal-
lowed through the cold North Atlantic."

They arrived in New York Harbor on January 6. Hence to
Camp Merritt.

> [Here] we were deloused . . . Stripped naked we walked down
> a narrow corridor where at one point a cup of coal oil was
> poured on our heads. We then rubbed it in "good" and entered
> a cold shower with a piece of soap trying to get it out. Our
> clothes were given a steam bath and when they came out of the
> tightly packed barrack bags . . . they were permanently wrinkled
> as folded. We looked bad, but clean. I never had lice in France
> and did not need the cleaning but had to have it anyhow.

The 145th Field Artillery finished up its tour at the Agricultural
College in Logan, which had been more lightly touched by the
flu. Spectators at their parade wore cheesecloth masks. The boys
got fresh straw in clean ticks, boxes of candy, apples and cookies,
good light, unlimited bathing and a swimming pool. Dilworth's
discharge came around January 20, 1919. After nearly sixteen
months of waiting, there remained only the train ride home.

CHAPTER 3

Without Purse or Scrip

Interlude

In early 1919, Dilworth took his second railroad job. A member of a "maintenance of way party," his duties included "watching" the track between Salt Lake and Pocatello, which the party did from a three-wheeled track motor car. The car had seats for three crew members and a box in the middle for instruments and the engine. It lacked a windshield, which made travel difficult in summer, when the grasshoppers multiplied. The crew also planned new business spurs, including surveying the sights, drawing the blueprints, and overseeing the construction.

In his history, he describes himself at twenty-one as "girl hungry," eager for female talk and laughter, though "I had not dated." (It may have been around this time that Dilworth broke things off with Afton Love. Phyllis Wells, a cousin, remembers him at his home, still in uniform, and Afton hovering near him, sitting on the arm of his chair, putting her arm around him, and him not reciprocating. "He was not in love with Afton Love," she discerned. "We all knew that.") Dilworth describes himself as moral and idealistic at this time, but lacking a spiritual center. "No one could have had higher ideals than I did, nor was cleaner minded. . . . I had read all the books. I had been good and faithful to the principles, but I did not really know how to pray, and certainly I was conceited to a certain extent."

He drew the daily task of carrying blueprints from the Union Pacific Station to the office on South Temple and Main and bringing back others. Typically he carried books to work, which he read along the way. Each day as he passed two small houses set back off the street at about 150 West, he would hear a tapping on the windows and look up to see a girl in each, arm extended, gesturing to him to come and see. He hesitated no more than an instant, putting his nose back into the book and passing on. "One night during the summer I was sitting at home reading when my mind suddenly turned to those two houses. I felt that somehow I had to know what went on in [them]. My imagination was stirred almost beyond control. I had an overpowering feeling that I had to go to those houses. I arose (9:00 p.m.), walked four miles and stood on the sidewalk in front of [them]. The blinds were down, but light showed around the blinds. I stood there for about ten minutes."

Dilworth writes that he had not felt tempted in the army, but that this time the fire was hotter. "That summer, my constant passing by those houses plus some reading of sex material . . . lowered my resistance. That compulsion to go that night was powerful—and it was neither me nor my nature. That was the most powerful force I have ever felt." But he resisted. "Even while the urge was on I turned and walked back home. The further I walked, the less the desire pressed."

Not long afterward, the bishop arrived at Seymour's house to say he wanted to call his son on a mission. If Dilworth was "conceited," Heaven conspired in the manner of his call to teach him humility. Seymour was glad to hear the bishop wanted to send his son, and called for Dilworth. The bishop said, "'Dilworth? I don't want Dilworth, I want Hiram." Seymour answered, "Bishop, in my family my oldest boy goes first, so take Dilworth or nobody." The bishop took Dilworth.

Dilworth's mission journal doesn't mention the incident, but he must have fretted. He frets a little, fifty years later while writing his history. "What he had against me could only have been that I was noisy in meetings. I made the error of talking and kidding the girls on the back row in church. I guess I was a nuisance but all he would have had to do was to tell me about it and I would have quit."

He informed his mother that he would refuse a call to Missouri, Arkansas, or Louisiana. There, the missionaries had been persecuted—the Saints had been driven from Missouri—and he had simply made up his mind he would not go. The word in the foyer was that a group of new missionaries would be accompanying President Grant to the dedication of the Hawaiian temple and then finishing their missions in the Islands. News reached Dilworth, perhaps through one of his high-placed relatives, that he would be part of the group. He liked the sound of that. "There were grass skirts and ukuleles there—and I was romantic." His call, dated October 14, 1919, reads "Dear Brother: You have been recommended as worthy to fill a mission, and it gives us pleasure to call you to labor in the Central States Mission. . . ." The mission at that time covered the states of Missouri, Texas, Oklahoma, Kansas, Arkansas, and Louisiana. Dilworth told his mother he was going to have that fixed and walked downtown to do it. "I thought it would be easy. Uncle Rudger Clawson was President of the Twelve, and Grandpa Young was the senior President of the Seventy, with Uncle Lee as a member. I went up to the building, started to enter and get it done, but somehow felt it wasn't right. After standing on the steps and walking around the building two or three times, I walked back home and let the appointment stand."

Dilworth's grandfather did make his influence felt in one way. He asked Dilworth one day if he were a seventy. When Dilworth said no, he told him to have his bishop start action. "Just before I left [for the mission field], Grandfather said, 'Has the bishop done anything about ordaining you a seventy?' I said, 'No, Sir.' He said, 'Sit in this chair.' Then he called in Brother J. Golden Kimball from the next room, and they laid hands on me and ordained me a seventy. Then Grandpa said, 'Now go tell your bishop you are a seventy.' I did not tell the bishop."

Writing of the time prior to his mission, Dilworth says, "I think that I did not have the Spirit of the Holy Ghost. I had never experienced the warm glow." Yet in July came just the sort of prompting he would receive at many of the turning points in his life. "I learned that the ward choir was having a choir party up Lambs Canyon. I hinted around to one of our neighbor girls until she invited me to go with her." After breakfast at the lake at the head of the canyon, the group set out to climb the ridge in back of the camp. They overtook another party along the way, and joined them toward the summit. Dilworth's date, wearing "wool army britches, wrapleggings . . . and a pair of red three-inch high-heel dancing pumps," was soon near heat exhaustion in the morning sun and had soon lost her heels. Dilworth, coaxing her gently up the slope, had his eyes on another young woman, who bounded from place to place "like a gazelle," always seeming to have just lit on whatever boulder he happened to look on. This girl was sensibly dressed in men's blue jeans, hiking boots and a man's hat with a feather stuck in the brim. "I thought that if I had that girl as a partner, I would be able to really climb." Dilworth left his date to talk with the girl a few moments. Perhaps at her suggestion he climbed out to try to get her a little pine gum from a juniper, nearly falling in the process. He stumbled upon her again under the branch of a tree on the way down and slipped in beside for a moment, where they spoke of the columbines.

In camp his date went to sleep under a tree and he tried to take a nap himself. Suddenly, just off a little ways, there sat his "gazelle," among friends, gay, flushed, and brown. His journal reminisces, "I wondered what excuse I could find for going over and talking to you. Then you said that you wished that you had some willow for a whistle." He proposed a search, though he knew there were no willows at that altitude—and wondered whether she didn't know, too. His journal reads, "I remember of picking a large bunch of wild flowers for you. I remember my three French words and your reply in Spanish." (Dilworth's French consisted of "potatoes," "beefsteak," "cheese," "butter," "bread." Her fluent answer lasted five minutes.) "I did not ask her name," he remembers in his history. "She apparently knew mine." She embarrassed him by telling him they had already been introduced on a streetcar. That afternoon the party broke down into water fights "with my new friend trying to organize the rest of the girls to give me a dunking." When his own party began to gather around the truck for the ride down to the valley, Dilworth considered staying behind to ride down with her, but knew he couldn't really. So he accompanied his date to her house next door to his own, then walked the thirty paces home.

As I walked in the house, Mother came to the door. She said, "You are home early."

"Yes, Mother."

"Did you have a good time?"

"Yes," I said. Then I heard myself say, "I've seen the girl I'm going to marry."

"Oh, who is she?"

"I don't know . . . But I am!"

I hadn't thought those thoughts nor was I thinking them, and I was about as much surprised as Mother was when I heard myself say them. At the time I did not understand the way in which the Spirit prompts one to hear messages. I have since learned that this was one prompting that was true.

He wrote of watching for her on morning street cars, apparently boarding when he saw her—Lucille Wilcken introduced her as Gladys Pratt, formerly of Colonia Dublan, Mexico. She appeared in Dilworth's Sunday school (they may have dated once or twice between times) just as he was about to bless the sacrament bread. He got through the prayer all right but then handed the deacons the water. He went home with her after and looked through her album, longing for a certain photo. His journal mentions dates to the theater, a hike in Pharaohs Glen in Parleys Canyon, and skating at Liberty Park. She had not been before. "I had a lot of fun having her reach for my neck every time she would go to fall down—which was every time she tried to move." She told him on the way she was an F.F.V.—a First Family of Virginia. He replied that he was an F.F.V., too—a First Family of Vermont. His history adds a trip to Saltair and, that Fall, after a stint pitching hay on the Lost River Ranch with George Knepp, frequent train trips to Kaysville, where Gladys was living with her sister Amy. He says, "We just skirted the idea of engagement. I did not feel it fair to tie her up for twenty-six months (the length of a mission) and said so. She seemed willing to let it stand that if she was free when I returned, she would be interested. I did not try to kiss her—just held her hand. I suppose she thought I was a queer courter."

Dilworth's call instructed him to start for his mission November 12, 1919, but apparently there was some delay, as he and his group did not leave until January 13 or 14, 1920. He received his endowment in the Salt Lake Temple earlier that month. "No one went with me. Father was inactive and was too honest about it to try to obtain a recommend. Neither he nor Mother nor any of my relatives nor the ward leader said anything about it. I just decided to go one morning and went." He describes himself as "unemotional about it. . . . No one ever explained anything to new applicants and they went in with no idea of what to expect. . . . The temple ceremony at that time was not as refined as it is today. It was more blunt in its penalties, and it could and often did shock new recipients of the covenant until they would come out of the temple ready to give up." He sees another side: "I hadn't gotten humble. That is probably the reason that I was cold." His farewell, held Friday, January 9, featured a variety of musical numbers, both vocal and instrumental, according to the printed program. Speakers included J. M. Whitaker, "Dr. Seymour B. Young," the bishop, and Dilworth himself. There followed a time for "voluntary contributions." Dilworth refers to the affair in his journal as "that blooming farewell." He alludes to "the blunder I made there," something to do with Gladys, "and that speedy try to make it right afterwards in the dark." He spent an evening with her in Kaysville shortly before his departure, missing the train back to Salt Lake and having to sleep on a sofa in the living room of the house where she boarded. He arranged to wave at her when he passed through Kaysville, only to find his train went via Denver.

Shifting

President Samuel O. Bennion met with Dilworth's party of a dozen or so new missionaries at the mission office in Independence. A stout man in a white suit and a walrus mustache, he peered at the new arrivals one by one over wire-rimmed spectacles, assigning each to his area of labor. "Elder Jones, you go to St. Louis. Elder Peterson, you go to Canyon City." Dilworth describes himself at this period as having "a loud laugh, full and effervescent. . . . [I] liked to attract attention, and proceeded to do it. My laugh was like a horse laugh if you've ever heard one." As each comrade received his assignment, Dilworth let out with one of his horse laughs. "Ha Ha Ha!" Last of all, President Bennion came to Dilworth. "Elder Young," he said, "you go to Louisiana. You can laugh down there and they can't hear you."

Elder Alexander E. Archibald, mission secretary, and Elder Leland P. Draney, mission bookkeeper, then marched the recruits down to Bundschu's clothing store. The first order of business was to "introduce" each to the derby. "This consisted in placing the hat on our heads with the rim across the bridge of the nose and giving it a sharp rap. It made a dent in the nose and put a dent in the derby." The missionaries also bought "stick grips," small suitcases made of fiberboard with metal frames, suitable for sitting or kneeling on. These they packed with a shirt, a handkerchief, a single pair each of garments and socks, straight razor, soap, and brush, and a few other personal items. The rest of the grip they filled with books and tracts. One other purchase was an umbrella, carried inside the overcoat, dangling from the arm hole. "Then they took all of our money away and gave us back enough to get to our fields of labor, and two dollars extra." Dilworth and his companion, Boyd Rogers, were instructed to report to Elder Thomas C. Lyman, the Louisiana district president (responsible for missionary and member affairs for the state), stationed in Shreveport, but at last report in Delhi.

On the train the two used some of their money to buy buns and cheese. One of the first entries in his missionary journal, written during the train ride down, reads, "With faith and the inspiration of the Lord we shall find [Elder Lyman and his companion] when the time is right. We have no fear—only a fear that our knowledge of the gospel is not strong enough to serve us. You bet we'll study." They arrived in Shreveport at midnight, Sunday, January 15. They looked for President Lyman's apartment, but found they had the wrong address, so spent the night in the train station. Dilworth marveled at "all the classes of people" who passed, "dirty, clean . . . typical Southerners, Northerners." Telling the story half a century later, all he can see is the filth. "If anyone tells you Southerners can spit straight, don't believe it. That floor was covered with tobacco juice, and all over the spittoons. It was a miserable sight." In the morning the two took out their coupon books ("missionaries had . . . clergy books entitling them to one-half fair on railroad trains") and purchased tickets to Delhi, which put them back fifty cents each—half their remaining cash. For breakfast they ate bread and cheese left over from the day before.

The ride from Shreveport, in the northwest corner of the state, to Delhi, in the northeast, is about a hundred and thirty miles—a morning's journey. "All of the time the rain was falling, not heavily but steadily. I don't remember it stopping. . . . The clouds held low all of the time." Delhi, located on a tributary of the Mississippi, was a town built on stilts for just such occasions as this. "The water stood six feet deep among the trees. A boat was tied to each porch." Nowhere much to go, and no sign of the district president or his companion. They walked back to the station and asked the ticket clerk if a Mr. Lyman had purchased a ticket there. He looked in his ticket book and said "Yes, he bought a ticket to Shreveport." So they pulled out their cash and coupon books and paid the fare for the ride back. "We very likely will not find them, but that won't keep us from trying," he wrote while waiting for the train. "Or at least from doing what we can to spread the gospel." Without any apparent sarcasm, the passage continues, "This is a great town. . . . Well, pretty soon there will be no train back and it will be up to us to shift—by that I mean we will be out of cash. But we will work out of [Shreveport] into the country until we meet our president. It's discouraging but I suppose a part of the game."

So, without supper or breakfast, they spent Monday night, their second in a row, in the Shreveport station. "Somehow we got a map. On the map we saw that Mooringsport was a big oil producing town, like a mining town, with evil men." Mooringsport was north, so they headed south. "I had an overcoat. Elder Rogers did not, as I remember it. The drizzle dripped off our derby hats and down our backs. We got out of town and started to knock on doors. Every door we approached was opened by a black woman. We had a stock question for black people. We knew they should not have the priesthood, so we would say, 'Does John Peterson live here?' They would say 'No, Suh.' We would excuse ourselves and go on. One woman in response said, 'No, Suh, he don't and that ain't what y'all want. You got something fo' white folks that ain't fo' us niggers. That's what y'all got.' I admitted she was right and gave her a tract." In his journal he mentions knocking on a door "to see about getting something to eat." No luck.

A party pulled up in a motor car alongside the two elders and asked if they could give them a ride. Hungry and wet, they climbed into the warm car and asked to be taken to the nearest home with white people in it. Then they went to sleep. After awhile the driver woke them and said, "Here you are at white houses." They took their cases, thanked the driver and turned about to see the sign—Mooringsport Hotel. Dilworth writes, "Three times I had said that I would not do something on a mission and had done it: (1) I would not go to Missouri—I went. (2) I would not go to Louisiana—I went. (3) I would not go to Mooringsport—there we were. It took a lot of work on the part of those running my affairs in heaven to convince me that I'd better do what I was told and not drive any previous stakes as to what I would or would not do."

They tracted Mooringsport. "We decided to talk to each householder about the Articles of Faith. At one house I would do six and he would do seven. At the next house we would reverse. We went from house to house and got into quite a few. It did not take us long to explain our subjects. We were usually out of ideas in about twenty minutes." The people seem to have been indifferent. His journal records, "I never knew I knew so little about the Bible. . . . Fortunately we were not asked for any special proof of our belief." To his surprise, not one offered lodging or a meal. About dusk they decided to backtrack and ask those who had let them in for food and a place to dry off and sleep. Each turned them down.

Well after dark, Dilworth huddled up on the porch of a small schoolhouse and announced he wouldn't go a step further. Elder Rogers insisted on going to one more door. After talking to the man for a moment he waved him over and told him, "They'll give us some supper but can't keep us all night."

Two families occupied the tiny house, which had two rooms ten feet by twelve and a small lean-to kitchen. The two women prepared biscuits, fry ribbon, cane syrup, turnips and clabbered milk. Dilworth expected the milk would run, but found he had to let it slide out and then bite it off. Normally Dilworth disliked sour milk, but on a day like this, "that was the best of anything I had ever tasted." The elders made their presentation on the Articles of Faith. When their hosts began to seem tired, they got up to leave. One of the men said, "We can't let you out in a storm like that." They protested, but the man insisted. The elders and the two men slept in the back room, with the women and all the children in the front room. The men insisted the elders take the bed, then threw their own mattresses down against the door.

The men woke them before dawn, gave them breakfast, and showed them the door. They waited long enough to be sure the missionaries were gone before going off to their own jobs. The missionaries followed a set of railway tracks to Blanchard, halfway from Mooringsport to Shreveport. This was a log cabin town, "heavy with pine wood timber." Here a woman took them in, fed them a good meal, listened to their presentation, helped them dry off and clean up, but wouldn't agree to keep them that night. They tracted Blanchard's twenty-three cabins, teaching six families and placing some tracts, but failing to get a place to stay. Now it was dusk and still stormy, so they sat down in the waiting room of the railway station. About 10:00 p.m. the station master told them he was going home and needed to lock up and that they would have to leave. "We pled to stay but he said no. I said, "We'll protect it against the Negroes." He said, "Ain't any niggers going to bother this station." So they left.

> The agent locked up and turned out the lights, and [there] we were standing on the station platform. I could see the green light on the siding switch one-half mile in both directions. That is all. I was standing within three feet of the station and I could not see it . . . The lowering clouds seemingly at treetop height were impenetrable in the rain. I looked up and passed my hand in front of my face. I could not see it as it passed. Elder Rogers was there but until he spoke I did not know where he was standing.

> I said, "What do we do next?"

> He said, "Maybe we'd better pray!"

> Until now I had said regular prayers as at home, but we had not prayed together. It had never occurred to me that we should pray. So we knelt on our suitcases and I prayed we would find a place. Then Elder Rogers prayed. I think we prayed again, then I got up, stopped to pick up my case, and as I straightened up, off in the wood where we thought there was no house, a light flared up. First there was blackness—then this light.

They followed the light through the mud and trees. Dilworth tripped and fell into several feet of water in a borrow pit, losing his hat and floundering for it. The light proved to be a pine knot flaring up in the fireplace of a small cabin they had somehow missed, just visible through the open window. They knocked, and, responding to the faint voice within, called out that they were Mormon missionaries in need of food and a place to sleep. When there was no answer, they let themselves in, finding a young woman, alone, lying on a pallet, with a baby. "She was scared pink. She was so scared her teeth chattered. Mormons down there had a bad name. Her husband wasn't home. I finally sensed we were not in a good place. The Lord had answered our prayers alright, but whether we should stay or not. . . . She offered us two biscuits, and we each took [one]. I said [to Elder Rogers], 'we can't stay here,' for if her husband returned and found us alone with her, he could have us lynched. . . . We told her we would not harm her, we were there peaceably, [and] to prove it we'd leave and we'd go." Elder Rogers, years later, told Dilworth he felt they should have stayed. Dilworth thought Elder Rogers was probably right and yet couldn't see staying with a woman, alone, under those circumstances.

Still raining, still pitch dark. They thought of a barn they had noticed earlier in the day. "It was the only barn like it I ever saw in Louisiana. We started walking, hoping to find that barn. . . . We stumbled against trees, slid in the mud, and finally stopped, why I don't know. I put out my hand—it touched the latch of the gate leading into the corral of that barn." The barn sheltered mules, though with the darkness they did not know it until morning. "We crawled up into the hay and spent the rest of the night."

Next day they shaved and cleaned themselves in the brown water of a creek. When Elder Rogers bent over, his pants split wide open, leaving his seat exposed. They could think of nothing now but to go into Shreveport, so Dilworth gave his companion his raincoat and they started out. They must have done some tracting, for they got breakfast three miles down the road, then caught a ride the rest of the way. Now they telegraphed Independence: "Send President Thomas C. Lyman address and ten dollars." After several hours came the address but no ten dollars. They tracked down Elder Lyman in a poor white section of town. He asked them where they had been, shook his head when they told him, and said he was glad they were found.

Dilworth wrote of the episode in detail in his history and often told it. Looking back, he sees the Lord taking him and Elder Rogers by the hand and bringing them, a step at a time, where he wanted them. His journal gives no clue to the significance he would later attach to these happenings and leaves out all the important details—the light, the prayer, the woman in the cabin, the fear on her face. With his typical greenhorn enthusiasm he closes the section by saying he'll be going out next Monday "and see some of the country. I'm liable to have some experiences in that time—you bet."

Country Work

In the mission field one sometimes hears stories of elders working without purse or scrip. In these, people are impressed to provide the elders with a meal, a pair of shoes, or a night's lodging, so that, as they exercise faith, they rarely have to go without. The only thing that excites elders in quite the same way are rumors that missionaries will soon be pulled to open up new territory in remote parts of the world. The elders associate travel without purse or scrip with missionaries like Wilford Woodruff, and tend to think of it in the same terms as converting the United Brethren. (Anyone can do it, as long as he exercises Wilford Woodruff's faith.) One hears that travel without purse or scrip is against the law now, or that special permission from a general authority is required. In spite of these misgivings, most missionaries would probably jump at the chance to work that way.

In Dilworth's mission, elders worked with funds when stationed in cities and without when in the country. Generally they took apartments in the cities in the summer, when the danger of malaria grew high, but otherwise worked the countryside. Under President Samuel O. Bennion, "country work" was synonymous with travel without purse or scrip. They worked mostly on foot. Animals would have required money for their upkeep, and on Louisiana's thin dirt tracks there were few cars. Dilworth worked in rural Webster and Sabine Parishes, sometimes in what could only be described as backwoods. Francis G. (Frank) Wride, one of his Sabine Parish companions, says, "We nearly always had to have a rain coat. . . . Lotta mud. And it was red." Dilworth was surprised at how you might step from dust into mud, or visa versa, without any particular warning. Travel on these roads meant frequent crossings of "branches," as creeks were called, and sometimes rivers. He tells in his journal of one he couldn't get across. "After we had waded the [bottom]land up to our knees [we] decided we wouldn't try to swim." A man on horseback finally ferried them over the deepest part, one at a time. Besides mud and water, Dilworth remembers bugs. "There were sand flies, mosquitoes, red spiders . . . chiggers . . . etc. All bit and all itched."

"We tramped all over the parish, lost most of the time in the woods." These were turpentine pine woods, with long needles and trunks as wide as kitchen tables, harvested for turpentine much the way maples are for sugar. "The only way we could find a house was to sit down and wait for a rooster to crow or a dog to bark. Then we would follow the sound to a cabin." Dilworth records being lost with Elder Wride in the predawn hours of his first day in Sabine Parish, following trail after trail in the dark. Frank Wride tells of another day trying to make headway in a fog, only to run upon the same stream at the end that he left in the beginning. In early April Dilworth composed some lines of doggerel "After Trying Five Roads and Finding Out That They All Led to Robison's Ferry." Every time they asked, they'd be told:

> There's a ferry if you go this way about twenty miles
> And that way goes there too—oh quite contrary.
> And in a week we cannot seem to shake the happy smiles
> Of folks who show the way to Robison's ferry

Country work occasionally meant missed meals. One journal entry reads, "We started out in the sticks this morning with the idea of doing a little work. . . . We have done a little too I guess . . . and as yet we are waiting for a little luncheon to come along. It hasn't come so I guess we will call that one missed." A few days later he and his companion didn't get a place to stay until 8:00 p.m. They were offered no supper, and got no breakfast either. "That was our worst hardship," he writes of the trip. "It was not nearly as bad as I thought it would be." Country work sometimes meant missed sleep as well. In Cotton Valley, Webster Parish, they "asked various people where to stay, and when we asked that they generally said nowhere as far as they were concerned." Finally an aged man took them in, telling them he had hosted the elders twenty years before. Between Hatcher and Converse in Sabine Parish, he and his companion Elder Busby ran out of daylight without finding a place, and so camped in the woods. "This is my second time. We stayed near an old [shack], built a fire, lay down on a couple of planks, and dreamed away the hours. Elder Busby sang 'Oh Where is My Wandering Boy Tonight.' I retaliated with 'Who's on the Lord's Side, Who?'" Frank Wride says they tended the fires when they slept out to keep animals away. "I remember staying out some nights and the wolves would howl all night." He adds that "there wasn't many nights" that they weren't taken in.

Brother Wride speaks of using member or investigator homes as bases of operation while covering the surrounding countryside. L. P. Draney (who worked in Jackson and Clay counties, Missouri) says as much, though indicating that in his case members usually lived in small towns. "Country work ordinarily did not require constant duty in the 'sticks.' We left our heavy suitcases and excess supplies in safekeeping with friends when we were making our country calls." He adds that "it was our practice to work our way from town to town within our designated area, usually a county, so as to reach our pre-arranged mailing point to pick up our mail and supplies, and to get ourselves and our clothing cleaned up." At the mailing points they submitted reports to the mission office regarding amount of literature distributed (tracts cost 1/2 cent, the Book of Mormon 50 cents), the number and type of meetings held, money spent, and mailing address for the next week.

Missionaries cleaned themselves as well as they could in branches. The common way to do laundry seems to have been borrowing members' washboards. Dilworth describes using a flat iron warmed on the coals and wiped clean of soot—so used to electricity at home that this seemed to him a novelty. L. P. Draney says missionaries wore blue serge suits, white shirts with detachable collars "(celluloid for easy cleaning)," dark ties, "usually black bows," and derbies ("white Panamas during the summer"). He says they were expected to be clean-shaven (though Elder Bernice Parkinson, a missionary in New York State during the same period, was encouraged to wear a beard to make him look older). Brother Draney reports, "we often performed tonsorial 'arts' on each other" to avoid paying the barber. Shoe shining must have been an ongoing problem, since missionaries were told never to take them off while fording streams. According to Frank Wride, "they had what they call the stinging rattler down there and . . . the water moccasin . . . and they're deadly poison. . . . So we just had to roll up our pants and wade through, [then] take our shoes and socks off and squeeze the water out of them and go again."

Dilworth recorded his day-to-day impressions in his journal. He describes one old Civil War veteran as "tall, and as thin as a rail . . . emaciated . . . [with] a large Roman nose and piercing blue eyes which seem to see everything. His skin has . . . [a] clear, parchment-like texture. . . . He has a peculiar growth on his under lip that doesn't seem to interfere with his smoking an old brass pipe." He writes of a "most homelike" meal prepared by the Torraus family. "I suppose that we ought to have preached to them a little, but it was too hard—with a victrola for the first time in a month." He tells of sitting up all night with a "Mr. Watkins who is nearly dead with the dropsy. . . . He ought not to live very much longer. He is nothing but skin and bones now." In his history he recalls sleeping in "a twelve-by-sixteen cabin overnight with a family of backwoodsmen." Dilworth was impressed at how modesty was maintained in tight quarters. "At time to retire our host would say: 'Y'elders take that corner (throwing a straw mattress on the floor). Boys take this one; girls this one; we'll take the bed. ...Turn your back for five minutes and crawl in.' We all would."

He often speaks of sleeping with member families such as the Lees and Muses for days at a time. On one return visit to the Muses he found a box of candy waiting for him from home. Later "we made ice cream. I froze two freezers full." In the course of the week, branch members held a dance into the early morning, which Dilworth attended with his companion. "Elder Busby and I sat around and looked interested. It was no temptation, altho I would have liked to have shown 'em how." The Muse's home had burned, so part of the family was staying in a high-porched, unchinked log cabin, whose five-foot high fireplace caught Dilworth's fancy. With "the family cheerfully gathered around it reminds one of pioneer days, or Whittier's 'Snowbound,' or something equally romantic. . . . [It's] the kind I'm going to have when I move to Mexico."

The March/April Liahona places Elders Young and Busby in a "section of the country [that] has not been worked for 20 years." In spite of the pioneering nature of some of this post-war work, missionaries had more to rely on than the sympathy of the people. In the first place they came in the wake of generations of itinerant Protestant preachers. Rural and frontier folk had previously relied on traveling ministers for ordinances and preachment, and the tradition was not now so old that other ministers didn't sometimes work the same woods as the Mormons. In addition, LDS missionaries had themselves been working the countryside for generations. When missionaries entered an area, the office would provide them with a notebook listing members and friends of the Church they could call on. Frank Wride says that missionaries stayed with investigators relatively rarely. "It was nearly always members."

A portion of the missionaries efforts were in fact directed toward the members. Frank Wride says the missionaries were the main contact rural members had with the Church. "We would go to as many of those members in that area as we could and keep them on the straight and narrow as much as we could." Dilworth records heading up to "Carleyville to try to straighten out the Saints." At other times he mentions counseling, visiting, holding Sabbath meetings, and performing baptisms and other ordinances. Dilworth married three couples in Independence and mentions a marriage performed by an elder in Louisiana. The elder took his companion into the woods first and practiced with him and a pine tree. Travel without purse or scrip seems partly to have been a means of distributing the burden of the missionaries' support among local members. Dilworth states, "I thought the Lord would put angels on gateposts, so they'd ask us to stay." Many times he did, but often it was the angel of member hospitality.

But it would be a mistake to think country work put no demands on the faith of the elders. Some were tempted to stay too much with members, or to carry extra money, or to outright ask investigators for food. Dilworth says that's not how it was supposed to be lived. "When you go out in the country without purse or scrip, you don't go out and beg from house to house. That isn't the trick. You go out and preach from house to house. If you're humble enough and tell your message well enough, they'll invite you to stay." Ethel Kane Archibald, a former mission home housekeeper who married mission secretary Alec Archibald, gives as her opinion that country work was "to humble them. That's what Dilworth would tell you. . . . He'd say they'd get on their knees until they were sore." Alec agrees. "That was exactly it." Dilworth maintained that country work simply didn't work if it wasn't lived properly. "Boy, you get humble in a hurry, I'll tell you. . . . If you're humble enough, you don't miss any meals. But if you're not humble, you stay out and miss a lot of them."

Companions Near and Far

When Dilworth became a mission president in the late '40s, his first question in an interview was likely to be, "Does your companion get in your hair?" Dilworth's first permanent one, Melville Branch, got in his until he managed to learn a little patience. Elder Branch was about five-foot-four and walked with a limp, which irritated long-legged Dil. "Further, he had a . . . smile which never was absent. After a while that smile got on my nerves and I caught myself wishing I could rub it off." One more quirk that bothered Dilworth was Elder Branch's talent for getting the whole blanket when they had to share a straw tick. "No matter what I did to hold my share, Elder Branch in his sleep would get all of that quilt. I tried holding a corner, wrapping it around my arm and lying on it. I'd wake up coverless." Dilworth is much more judgmental in his journal. He doesn't mention the limp, the smile, or the quilt, but writes, "Elder Branch is a diminutive little fellow who can't say much and likes to do all the talking. He gives a line of vague nothings which no one could understand and then wonders why people don't get interested in the gospel. . . ." Dilworth in the course of time came to see things differently. "I learned to love and respect Elder Branch, to be patient with his physical infirmities and to accept and be built up by his cheerfulness. . . . He was a true saint."

Sometimes, as they walked down a set of railroad tracks, Dilworth would become lost in his thoughts. After a quarter of an hour or so, he would notice things had grown quiet and would look around to see Elder Branch a quarter of a mile behind. So he would sit down on his grip and wait for him to catch up. Then the process would begin again. "Finally I said to him, 'I'm very discourteous to you. From now on I'll walk behind and let you lead.' That slow pace was very trying at first, but I soon learned that compassion is better than fast walking."

Next came Elder Wride. "I'm going to like him," he wrote. "I'm sure of it. He is at least as tall as I am. That is something." Brother Wride recalls Dilworth spoke with ease, finding it natural to engage a family in an informal discussion of gospel principles. (Dilworth, the former student body president, records prior to a cottage meeting that he hopes the crowd will be large. "I can speak better to large crowds.") Brother Wride especially remembers how Dilworth spoke to children. "It seems like he could attract their attention when we'd go into homes, and he nearly always had a little ditty of some kind or little sayings or things that he read . . . and, well, those kids would just walk around him like anything." Brother Wride says he himself lacked education, having spent much of his childhood herding sheep and cattle in the mountains west of Benjamin, Utah. If Dilworth's former companion talked too much to suit him, this one spoke not enough, and he complains in his journal at having to do it for both of them. Also, if Elder Branch slowed the work with his limp, the case of boils Elder Wride developed kept his team from covering territory as quickly as Dilworth would have liked. These would become painful enough to keep him laid up at member homes for days. At one meeting, Dilworth conducted, spoke, blessed the sacrament and passed it, "as Elder Wride's boils wouldn't permit in his participating." Dilworth's impatience comes through in a passage written after the boils had kept the pair indoors for a week. "We hardly ever do anything as I'd like to. It seems as tho we don't have the courage or the ability to get out as we ought. But perhaps time will make us more bold and fearless."

Perhaps because he was made senior companion, perhaps because of increasing maturity, Dilworth is less judgmental of his other companions in the country. He writes in his journal of Elder Busby, who wore "a suit of clothes you can see a mile." His history elaborates. "Elder Busby was . . . freckled, five-feet-five-inches tall, redheaded with a large black Stetson ten gallon hat. He was the only elder I saw who did not wear a derby. He had a red-rust suit which did not fit. But he was cheerful and talkative. I would say: 'My watch says it is 4:00, time to find a place to sleep.' He would say: 'My watch says it isn't time.' I would say: 'My watch regulates the sun, moon, and stars.' He would say: 'Yes, but it doesn't regulate George M. Busby.' And it didn't." He tells a story of approaching a house with a dog and a high oak picket fence. Elder Busby pulled open the gate and watched the dog bolt out, then slipped inside and shut the gate before it could turn back. "I called, 'How are you going to get out?' He said, 'That's your problem; the dog is on your side now.'" After talking to the woman at the door, he opened the gate and walked out. "The dog walked past him stiff legged, ignoring him, hackles up, and entered the yard. The elder closed the gate and rejoined me, sitting out at the roadside. That was Elder Busby."

He led Elder Busby on an eighty mile tramp through a new section in the Red Land district in Sabine Parish. They were not unsuccessful in finding places to stay or people to hear them preach, yet they missed more meals than usual and slept out a night. Perhaps he remembered how dead tired he had been afterward when he counseled his own elders in a bulletin, years later, "Don't cover too much territory so that it becomes a race. One doesn't have to cover the whole country." Nevertheless the evidence is that he viewed country tracting as pioneering. The same bulletin states, "If there are Saints in the area, [you] are expected to visit them monthly and give the sacrament to them; staying over one night. The rest of the time is entirely with non-members."

Dilworth filled two mission scrapbooks with clippings of speeches and quips, plus letters, most of them from Gladys, his future "companion." These are occasionally humorous or topical, but more often Gladys' words are lyrical and high-minded. One letter describes a sunset. "When the great sun chariot dipped in the lake we saw the Sun God and his fiery steeds alight upon the water and be wafted away by the fairies back to their home by the way of the unknown sea." This particular day she has spent in the hills with her friend Sarah, but in the eye of their imagination, one other friend is present. "You were standing with your hat off and your arms folded [in] the breeze, putting the finishing touches to the tan of your face, and your eyes looking far away . . . and then you quoted something about the beautiful world." In other letters she speaks of school at the U. of U., Spanish club, a move to Salt Lake, a job at Keith O'Brien's, which she quits to become playground supervisor at the Kaysville Recreation Center. She tells of her loneliness for Old Mexico and a trip she plans to see her brother, Rey L. Pratt, President of the Mexican Mission, in El Paso. (Dilworth apparently wonders whether he might not conspire to be there at the same time, perhaps on mission business. She counsels against him going, but in any case the trip falls through.) She refers to books he's given her, sends a sprig of sage, and on another occasion, a snapshot of the house he was born in. She visits his family and reports them hospitable and friends of the beautiful and the worthy. (Dil's father writes of the visit, calling Gladys the "personification of refinement.") She preaches to him not infrequently, at one stage admonishing him, "Don't let me hear you speak of those people . . . as 'savages' again. . . . When you come home don't relate the incidents where you have had to put up with such conditions as you suggested—forget them—but remember the times when you have been befriended by some kind-hearted soul—clothed or fed or protected." More often she has occasion to build him up. "You mentioned . . . something of the dream of my desires. Have I met him? Have I met his steady gaze from eyes that look into your soul? I don't know—but something seems to say 'yes,' and then I think of a boy who is tall, straight, clean, virtuous, happy, gallant, and I think could even be tender—who loves me. Do you think he might be tender?"

Dilworth's journal describes a dream where he returns from the war to be greeted by his sister Emily. She turns for some reason and he loses her in a crowd. He tries to kiss her through the glass of a store window, but suddenly on the other side of the glass is a framed photograph of a girl he has never seen before. A few weeks later he dreams he is skating with Gladys, only the head and hair are Emily's. Then the ice changes to mud and then to a dance floor and he is dancing with Gladys, but with Emily's face. He describes daydreams, too. On one occasion he is trying his best to study, but "I can't seem to interest myself in it because every time I try to memorize a little scripture the picture always comes up of a glen in the high hills of the Wasatch. And [a] rock is rising out of it shaped like an immense hand. . . . There seems to be a girl climbing the rock, and dawgonit I can't drive her face from in front of my eyes." He continues for several pages now, addressing Gladys, telling each detail of the story of their meeting. Gladys writes with a dream of her own. Rey Pratt takes them to Chihuahua to the old mountain homestead. Gladys and Dilworth walk in the hills, drink from the spring, pause by a rose bush planted by her deceased sister, stop by the low oak branches Gladys had used for her "horses" as a little girl, and gather wild flowers, berries and cress.

He learned her birthday was March 24 (he didn't dare ask how old she was—he thought maybe 21 or 22). He managed to have Hiram send her violets, her favorite. At 25 and far from her family, she had been reconciled to not having a birthday that year. In his journal he records in code of writing to Gladys of his "affair," as he puts it, with Afton. "I don't know just what she will think or do. But then time will tell, so don't worry over it, Elder Young— but I do." Three weeks later comes her reply: "Forgiven!" and something on a past love of her own, which he in turn "forgives." He sends her a gold chain with the letter "G" for a pendant, which she wears. Several letters are exchanged—Dilworth wonders whether she likes it, whether he has been too forward in sending it. She reassures him, but coyly. "Many whom I meet are curious when they see me with it. One girl turned it over and looked at the name and with a little ejaculation exclaimed, 'Why, he was the nicest boy in Granite. How do you happen to have that?' I just laughed for I don't know why." Often she hints so broadly her affection cannot be mistaken, but never does she state it outright. Once she closes a letter, *"Recuerdo Ud. de mí siempre. Digame de tu amor, y vuelve Ud. a mí con corazón limpio, puro, y fiel."* The translation is "Remember me always, tell me of your love"—but in Spanish he could not read.

CHAPTER 4

City Work, Book Work

New Orleans

Dilworth's journal has him in the vicinity of Shreveport for the two weeks prior to the February district conference, working, comparing notes with other elders, and resting at member homes. He records attending The Wanderers, a play set in Ancient Israel, with a New York cast, and enjoying it thoroughly. Of the conference he writes, "President Bennion met with us at Shreveport with a result that we are going to be better missionaries." Dilworth was called on to lead the singing. "The only thing wrong was that I couldn't sing and beat time at the same time." In May he baptized Elman Miller, a child of record, in Carleyville, then took the train from Shreveport to Alexandria for his second district conference. Once again he mentions missionaries beginning to congregate a few days early, and having an enjoyable time with them. Dilworth took minutes at the conference and prepared a piece for the "newspaper"—he doesn't say whether the local one or a Church organ. He and three others were assigned to "reopen New Orleans," which had seen no missionaries since the war. "I was given charge of the work and am slightly worried as to the best means of carrying it forward. But I'm sure that the way will be opened for us if we strive to do our best."

The elders found quarters at 2333 Magazine Street. "Two large beds were in the front room, each covered by a mosquito net canopy. The other room was for dining and kitchen." They spent ten dollars for rent, and not much more for food, "so we would get by on very little over $25.00 per month." Money was a real concern. Dilworth's father wrote him that, "We don't have much business these days—but it takes all our time to get it." Dilworth remembers, "Meat was a dollar a pound, sugar about fifty cents. We no doubt overdid the navy beans and macaroni." His journal and scrapbook mention an overabundance of rice, as well as bananas. Once Elder Wride (who also spent that summer in New Orleans) and Elder Child came back from the docks with all the bananas they could carry—ninety-two they later counted, plus what they have eaten—for which they had paid the grand total of thirty-five cents. "Too bad everything isn't as cheap as that," Dilworth laments. Frank Wride says "we used to live on bananas almost," mentioning in particular the overripe ones discarded at the docks. "Those colored boys was good to us, they was. Sometimes they'd slip off some real good bananas."

L. P. Draney writes of summer work: "In Oklahoma City . . . we were expected to hold at least one cottage meeting each day and one street meeting each Saturday night. On those evenings when cottage meetings could not be arranged, we were on the street corners. . . . When doing country work, we always worked in pairs. . . . Usually, city tracting was done singly, except when recalls were made." Dilworth's journal for May 17, 1920, records one of his work days. "Went tracting for three hours. Out of 102 tries I managed to leave literature at 10 places. I loaned a B of M tho, and should therefore feel encouraged. In the afternoon I cooked dinner and went downtown with Elder Wride. Evening spent in study."

Street meetings required a permit, which Dilworth and Elder Wride sought the first Saturday they were in town. The mayor was out and the clerk, short, white-haired, Catholic and hostile, told them they would have none. Dilworth wanted to know what the city ordinance said and made to see the recorder and the city attorney. Now the clerk said they needed to talk to the mayor, who would be back on Tuesday. Tuesday they returned—the mayor was out, so they waited until Thursday. This time the clerk admitted the mayor was in and let them in to see him. "He was a pleasant-faced man of middle years. We stated our errand. The mayor said he would like to ask two questions: (1) 'Do you still practice polygamy?' 'No sir, we do not. We stopped in 1890.' (2) 'Whatever became of Reed Smoot?' 'He is chairman of the United States Senate Finance Committee.' He then called in that clerk and told him to give us a permit."

The angry clerk scratched deeply with his pen, spattering the ink. It read, "Permission is granted to preach on Rampart Street and the rear of the city." Handing it to Dilworth, the clerk said, "Don't get closer than six blocks to Canal Street." Dilworth wrote, "We can preach from Rampart north—or back. That is a pleasure which will not get us anywhere, for Rampart is so far back that we won't get a crowd in a year." The four elders walked the four miles Friday evening to Rampart and Canal, which immediately struck them as a good site. They showed a policeman the permit and asked how far from the corner they could preach. "Twenty feet." They paced off the distance, turned to face the passing crowd, swallowed their fear, sang "Now Let Us Rejoice," said a short prayer, and then all took a turn preaching. Dilworth went first, taking as his subject, "Faith and Works."

Frank Wride says they preached on that corner five days a week. He remembers "there was two other [groups] preaching on the . . . ritzy side, so they set the Mormons on the lower side of the street." He remembers scheming to get people to listen. Sometimes two elders would stand in the sidewalk looking up in the sky as if they had seen a meteor or an airplane. When people paused to see what the interest was, the other two missionaries commenced their preaching. He remembers a small black boy who used to sit on the corner and listen, who if they didn't watch closely would entertain himself by jumping on their "hard boiled" straw hats. Dilworth's journal mentions being treated to ice cream their very first day by a Mr. Smiley from Georgia who's parents were members. He indicates the preaching went well—"I wish that we could hold them as successfully as that each night." Dilworth on one occasion noticed he managed to draw bigger crowds than the others. Sometimes meetings went slowly. "Tonight we held another street meeting—result one strained voice and a good feeling." Other times the success was more gratifying. "Tonight I preached on a new angle of Authority. We sold 3 B of M—which is an exception and very wonderful for us. . . . The Lord was with us and we felt his all abiding power."

Forty-five years later, in 1965, Dilworth attended a stake conference in New Orleans.

> A brother bore testimony that he was one of the first baptized in New Orleans after World War One. He said he heard the elders preach on the streets and took a tract home. He followed with more until he joined. After the meeting I said to him: "What was the year you heard the elders?" "1920!" "Was it on the corner of Canal and Rampart Streets?" "Yes." "Were there four elders?" "Yes." "I was one of those four elders." After more than forty years, this was the first that I had heard of any fruit coming from that experience.

He writes in his journal, "Ah, if we only could all realize just what each evil impulse will lead to if only given a wedge in our character. A slight suggestion by one evilly inclined may be the changing point in the life of the honest youth. . . . Can you keep yourself unspotted from the world? So live up to the standards set by the pure and questioning eyes of a girl who says 'live clean[?]'"

He records two trips with Elder Child into the country, each time staying with members. On one of these, to Ponchatoula, they took down member genealogies, baptized a Brother Stevens, and held a cottage meeting on first principles attended by thirty people. In New Orleans they went to see a healer named Father Isaiah, who rubbed an old paralytic woman up and down "as far as he dared," as the journal puts it. He spoke, lifted her up and pronounced her cured, after which her family helped her off the stand, questioning her. "I-I- believe that I feel b-better." They tracted endlessly, trying unsuccessfully to avoid black neighborhoods, sweltering in the heat. "I am literally bathed in sweat all day when at work. I've ruined a couple of good shirts from my coat lining running into them." They swam in Audubon Park on 6 July (the 4th being a Sunday). A meeting fizzled because of a "car strike." People were nervous and not inclined to listen, "and of course the taxi men made it as miserable as possible." "So, Gentlemen, if you would get your greatest salvation—," concludes the elder. "Take a jitney all the way up Barowa Street," interrupts the driver. Dilworth comments on the weddings notices in the local papers, thinking perhaps of Gladys. Another time he attends mass, then holds a priesthood meeting with the elders, after which he means to study but gets wrapped up in the *Literary Digest.*

"And outside of dat, suh, why day ain't no news."

Secretary

Samuel O. Bennion, long-time president of the Central States Mission, came from a sheep ranching background. His brother Parley once said of him, "That Sam! There was a time when he could outrun a spring lamb; now he can't even stoop to tie his shoes. He's no good for anything except missionary work." (Gladys attended the Central States Mission reunion at April conference in 1921 in Whitney Hall, and wrote, "I walked up with Pres. Pratt, Bennion and Callis—I led the way so I took them up that steep 2nd Ave. hill just for fun . . . Of the three fat Presidents, I don't know which was puffing most.") L. P. Draney, mission bookkeeper, remembers President Bennion as, "to put it mildly, a character. Forceful, dynamic, demanding, often blunt in speech (as I found out on a number of occasions), but, at heart, a very kindly man. He was not what you would call an intellectual; as a speaker or a writer, he was not particularly impressive. But he got the job done."

Ethel Archibald, the mission home housekeeper, remembers S. O. Bennion talking about the elders at table. "S. Dilworth Young—that's a fine name. He's a good elder. Hasn't had any experience, but I think I'll call him in." On July 19, 1920 the telegram went out: "COME TO THE OFFICE AT ONCE. [S] O BENNION" Dilworth's journal records his goodbyes of the

21st and boarding the train. "[Elder] Wride had tears in his voice, and I felt kind of bad. I hate to leave Louisiana . . . and I'm sure that if I had my choice I['d] rather stay. I don't know yet whether it's a promotion or a calamity."

His history recalls a Pioneer Day party for members and missionaries at Swopes Park, baseball, and a boxing match with an elder who had been bragging just enough to get on everyone's nerves. "I did not want to do it. I don't enjoy either hitting hard or being hit, but the insistence was so strong that I finally put [on the gloves]. . . . I figured I was in for a black eye. I reached out and tapped him lightly on the nose. He rushed forward with a roundhouse swing which I ducked under, tapping him on the stomach as I went under. After four such swings and having his nose and stomach 'tapped' ever so lightly, I suggested to him that I had had enough if he had. He agreed he had. One of our slender elders who had been hazed by [him] and had been frightened by his bluster said later, 'If I had known he could not fight any better than that, I would have taken him on myself.'"

Apparently the party was the end of recreation for a season. Dilworth's first journal entry in Independence, a week after his arrival, fails to mention it: "I've hardly had time to move by myself. It is all work here." President Bennion called him to be mission bookkeeper. "I guess I'm to get a little of everything." Alec Archibald, mission secretary, says, "I think [he] hadn't had any training in bookkeeping and clerical work," but he remembers him jumping right in just the same. He and L. P. Draney trained Dilworth, though soon Draney would leave him alone with the books while he proselyted in Kansas City. Reports came due at the first of the month. Their principal other duty was mowing the long grass on the property, which they cut and raked by hand, hauling it off in a wheelbarrow to keep for the President's cows in winter. Dilworth's journal mentions the mowing, but dwells on the books. September kept him busy the better part of two weeks. On the sixth he writes, "It is all in the trial balance, you know. Sometimes, I think there is no such thing. . . . Elder Draney came to the rescue and here we are as tho just coming out of a pleasant bath. He is proving some of my statements and I'm awaiting the results with anxiety. I fear that the $15.25 we are out will be very hard to find—but it must be done. I have an idea that Pres. Bennion will kind of be mad about it—and poor Bishop Wells will be wild back in the P.B.O." He was up all that night and most of the next day, which was his twenty-third birthday, "the hardest birthday I've spent in a good long time. . . . [W]e finally hit it [three days later on the 10th]. Glory me."

On September 15, Dilworth was made mission secretary. President Bennion soon sent Elders Archibald and Draney together without purse or scrip to reopen the work in Jackson County. Dilworth lists as his first official duties writing checks and dictating a letter. He mentions having "registered" a missionary (Sister Dredge, number 1732), and "posting" it, his first of many. In his history he lists his duties as follows: keep the mission books . . . collect the rent on six houses, rent on pasturing from twenty to thirty cows on the temple lot, keep up the fence if they broke out, write checks weekly for 265 elders (133 checks), and in the absence of the President milk five of his cows and feed three hundred of his chickens. He was away about half the time." Adjacent to the mission office was the Church printing plant (Zion's Printing and Publishing Co.), where he sometimes also helped. "If the book wrapper got sick or behind in his work, I had to get in and fill orders and wrap packages of tracts and books each week. One hundred thirty packages had to be wrapped, weighed, stamped and taken to the post office in a little red tin wagon."

Alec Archibald describes further duties parallel to the role of Assistants to the President now. "The mission secretary's job was to oversee the mission in the absence of the mission president," including interviewing and assigning new missionaries to their fields of labor. If President Bennion were present, he conducted the interviews, but then "he'd tell us we need a couple here and a couple there," and the secretary would make the actual assignments. The secretary outfitted new elders at Bundschu's and put them on the train, and also helped returning missionaries get off. The office handled incoming mail for the elders and kept and balanced the missionaries' accounts, compiled reports and financial statements, and forwarded them to the missionary committee, all under the secretary's direction. Occasional duties Dilworth mentions include performing marriages and baptisms, administering to the sick, sitting up with ill members, and teaching a Sunday school class. One journal entry records a day putting in a floor for a sister in the branch, and anticipates another fixing her roof. Dilworth must have been relieved not to have to keep the elders' ledger anymore, but he still had to oversee it, together with balancing the petty cash and real estate books. His journal, month after month, lists his anxiety at being out of balance. (For the annual reports that January, Elders Draney and Archibald were temporarily called back in, then later sent out with fresh companions.)

Alec Archibald remembers Dilworth as hard-working and conscientious. "He was serious, and yet he kept everybody in a jovial mood, too." He remembers Dilworth's holding his audience when he spoke in public, starting off with a foolish joke. He remembers a certain amount of horseplay in the bedrooms over the offices at the end of the day, also that Dilworth read a great deal. Bessie E. Kelly, who held the position of stenographer, says he was blunt but "always cheerful and pleasant to be around, was always dressed neat and was a gentlemen and very friendly." She remembers him putting new words to songs for parties, also pranks: he got Sister Bennion to put cornflakes in the sister missionaries' bed sheets on April Fools' Day; he replaced a bottle of red pop with beet juice; he put little dabs of honey on each of her typewriter keys. When Alec Archibald returned home and began courting Ethel, Dilworth intercepted her outgoing letters and drew red hearts and angels on the envelope. Alec wrote back, "I received your decorated letter." Dilworth fessed up. Alec sent a necklace which Dilworth took for an engagement ring. Dilworth telephoned the mission home from the office (which was only across the driveway). "Sister Ethel, I have a package for you here. If you will meet me at the door, I'll be right over with it." He delivered the small box in a wheelbarrow. Ethel says, "He must have had a lot of joy in teasing me, because he teased me most of the time."

She remembers him hurting her feelings once or twice, "and I'd come back at him," but she couldn't stay angry long. She doesn't remember him teasing the sister missionaries much, mostly just her and another girl in the home.

The Archibalds speak of nightly baseball games after the office closed and fairly frequent outings, though on these last Dilworth sometimes didn't go. Dilworth's journal mentions an afternoon in Electric Park, and an excursion to Kansas City to see a forty-five foot fish being displayed there. "It is a fish alright. . . . I guess it could have swallowed Jonah, Mrs. Jonah, etc., ad infinitum." He mentions plays, (one, "The Return of Peter Grimm," he calls "splendid"), also Thanksgiving, Twenty-Fourth of July, and a steak-fry on his twenty-fourth birthday. He and Elder Rudger Price ran a fortune telling booth at a Halloween party in the basement of the church. "We made it very weird and scary." He played Christopher Columbus in an "entertainment given by the mutual," and later entered a mutual-sponsored speech contest. "I had the nerve to try in the readings—read 'America for Me[;]' and in the retold story, I gave one original, named it 'The Play.' Got beat, but it was good experience."

He writes of an outing to Far West, where his guide told him many of the homes in the area were built with stones from the temple, then to Adam-Ondi-Ahman, which "gave me quite a hallowed feeling." He visits Liberty, where he reflects on the suffering of the "prophet and the brethren. . . . It must have been something terrible. The jail is not there now. A house is standing on the old foundation." His grandfather, Seymour B. Young, Sr., surprised Dilworth with a visit only shortly after his call to the office, and took him to Haun's Mill. Seymour, a "baby in arms at the awful affair," was, according to Dilworth's journal, the only survivor of the massacre still living at the time. His journal describes a millstone in the Breckenridge town square that had formerly marked the well where eighteen victims of the massacre had been buried. The next day, according to his history, they located "a place which might have been the well site. The vegetation was high and thick there as against the rest of the field. Grandpa asked me to see to it that someday a monument be placed there." Of his grandfather he writes in his journal, "I love to be with him, he is so good and warm hearted." Seymour gave his grandson a piece of advice, and reiterated it in a letter some months later: "Smile but don't laugh."

Dilworth writes:

> Bedbugs were a pest and each Saturday we spent half the day pouring gasoline along the seams of mattresses and bed posts. By the following Saturday the bugs would be just as thick. Some beds were worse than others but actually all had them more or less.

> The seven year itch was also often contracted. The cure for that was a mixture of lard and sulphur, liberally kept smeared on the body for two weeks. The old style garments put on over this mixture were entirely miserable. We would get it from transferring elders who bathed in our tub. Elder Price and I finally concocted a solution of water and a weak solution of bichloride of mercury. We washed the tub with it, but got the itch anyhow. Then we washed our bodies with it. It took the skin off but it cured the itch in two days. It's a wonder it didn't kill us by mercuric poisoning.

The office elders proselyted some. Alec Archibald characterizes his time in the office as more manual work than preaching, though with occasional street meetings. Dilworth's history says, "We used to go over to Kansas City and preach on the streets. Most of the time we chose poor street corners and nobody would stop. No doubt people thought us queer to be preaching to blank walls. Probably we were, for we didn't seem to have enough sense to go to a better street or a better corner."

The Mailbag

Dilworth saved only two letters from his father, one from sister Louine and one from his mother. Mostly these are informal, affectionate, newsy, invariably with mentions of Gladys. "Modest and gentle in her nature," his father describes her, "yet with a strong personality back of it that stands out when you talk to her . . . so you see it makes no difference whether you like her or not. We have simply found a new friend." Another, typewritten, on his real estate company letterhead, begins with an account of the weather: "Dear Son Dilworth, Saturday afternoon; sky clearing; been raining all night after three days of real warm weather. Colder to night. Saw Gladess a minute ago; I said; where have you been and when are you coming to see us. I suppose I embarrassed her. She dont come to see us very often now. Hope you still write to her and she to you." He offers counsel:

> Now I want to give you a little advice along certain lines. IT IS UP TO YOU WHETHER YOU SUCCEED IN LIFE. It's your life; whatsoever you make it is yours. Now this applies to your health also. Dont say to yourself—nothing can happen to me for I am on the Lords business. I have heard missionaries say just such things. Dont you get in front of a fast running auto, for the Lords business is not to pull you out of the way.

Dilworth must have mentioned he was working hard. He does not say how he feels about his father's emphasis on health, whether he thought it was advice he needed, or whether he was disappointed his father had so little other counsel to give. (Seymour had traveled without purse or scrip on his own mission, though now he was inactive in the Church.) The letter continues in the same vein. "DONT WORK SO HARD AND LONG your president will like you better. If there is too much work let them call in more elders. . . . JUST SATISFY YOUR OWN CON-SCIENCE AND YOU WILL PLEASE HIGH HEAVEN. My dear boy; preach the gospel far and wide, late and early, and in so doing conserve your health so you can do it every day for a hundred years." Dilworth's journal records other words of his father: "I know you, Dil, that you are safe."

Gladys wrote regularly, and he wrote her. "Dil, all your letters are so wonderful," she writes. "They all seem to ring true as steel." She apparently didn't save them, nor did he keep copies. He kept enough of hers to fill two volumes of his scrapbook, and yet it seemed to him that "she hasn't written very often, but they are such dear, sweet, lovely, unaffected letters when they do come that they more than make up for any time in between them." She kept no journal, yet it is often her letters that give the clearest view. "Won't you please come down and talk to me," she daydreams, "—Oh! say until about 11:30. You know you could say all the clever things that were said, and I would sit in wonderment, trying to figure out how you remembered all those things. And then maybe . . . you would tell me about all the books I should have read and maybe you'd read to me a little, and then after that we would just talk together about things we like and don't like—and then all too soon you'd grab your coat and hat and run for the train." One letter in the fall of 1921 describes the pattern of her days as a new history and physical education teacher at Mound Fort Junior High in Ogden. At 7:15 she "arises whether she is asleep or awake," then eats, then "scrambles for hat, lunch, keys, books, gym suit, etc., . . . Catches car on the run," riding along Washington with eight or ten other female teachers. At 8:20 she "chases up and down stairs about 50 times, unlocks lockers that have been locked and the keys left home, winds the clocks." She takes roll and gives announcements, then dresses. At 9:00 "class kicking begins. They kick because it's cold. They kick because they have to change their clothes or because they have lost their shoes or something. But they kick mainly to keep warm." Then games, showers, the rush to beat the bell and so on through her day. Catfish or Old Maid at lunch. The streetcar back home. Night school (she says elsewhere her life so far has been "more schooling to get more money to get more schooling"). Then mutual or Parent Teacher meetings, or "the couch if there is no place to go." He apparently answered with a similar letter, which she refers to in another of her own. "I surely must admit, Dil, you certainly have a variety of jobs. It seems that keeping books is the least of your troubles. With weak-eyed elders and lame Saints, and sore nosed book wrappers, you nearly have the care of a family, don't you. Are you coaching the entertainments, too, or are you one of the principle entertainers, or just the doorkeeper." It is unclear whether she alludes to MIA activities, or just his role in the office. "I would like to know just your standing in these shows. And is there any after theater bouquets in compliment to that newly discovered sweetness of the bass voice?"

Gladys gives dancing lessons to children, makes candy, and hikes in the mountains. She is a passenger in a auto rollover, but comes out of it with only a few scratches. They exchange books—each uses the other's in his teaching. She alludes more than once to having called him on the phone. One winter evening she writes, "The wonderful mountains are glowing red in the rosy, golden hues of the departing sun. They tell me you have met a cold, hard world, but are melting it with the words of truth." She hints at her feelings for him. "The sun has been shining ever so brightly all the day, but the breeze has been nipping cold, portraying the gladness in my heart to know you are out in the world making good, but along with it the tinge of loneliness that comes from absence." She refers to Dilworth as "a man of the Hills with all their ruggedness, a man who is cultured, thoughtful and considerate, and above all a man who is willing to serve God. Can you blame me for being happy when I know that man remembers me." Once she seems on the verge of laying everything on the line, but she resists. "Dil, you are just what I thought you were, you've never proved yourself any different. You've lived up to my every ideal and that's the first time I have ever said that to anyone. Do you feel the least bit complimented[?] . . . Maybe in some future day, when mission and duties are done, maybe if 'God wills it,' and time 'brings no changes,' perhaps I can give a love like you have dreamed of, one of my whole being. I hope to give that kind of a love to the man I choose, Dil, for no other is my ideal. I am not going to write you very often in this strain, for I know your position and conditions too and can understand and sympathize."

For his second birthday in the field she sends him a pearl-on-onyx tiepin, "the oddest I ever saw. . . . She surprised me alright, and tickled me too. I certainly am in love with it. The rest goes without saying."

Dilworth seems to have developed a following as a writer while in the field. While still in Louisiana, according to L. P. Draney, he penned "'Dear Ma and Pa' letters, couched in Louisiana vernacular and relating to his missionary experiences." These apparently circulated around the mission and made their way to the office. "All of us in headquarters, from President Bennion on down, thoroughly enjoyed them. The result was that he was no stranger when he joined the staff." The Archibalds don't remember the "Dear Ma and Pa" letters, but do recall "Johnny Letters" in a similar vein. Dilworth mentions the Johnny Letters in his journal once, but he does not copy or quote from any. The back of the book though is full of jokes and anecdotes. He notes Elder Wride's prayer after sleeping on the floor of a member's home: "We thank Thee, our Father, for the night we have just endured." He draws up a list of "Missionary Definitions." A "Fine Experience" is "one good or otherwise . . . after they are over and no danger of them recurring." "Advice" is "something an older missionary thinks should be given to the new ones." He asks a postmaster if Louisiana is a healthy place. "'Well outside of getting malaria if you get in the swamps, smallpox if you go near the Negroes, yellow fever in most places, poison snakes every few steps, insects galore, pneumonia and tuberculosis in the very air, outside of these few things Louisiana is the most healthy state in the Union.'"

Dilworth from time to time notes feelings of unworthiness, and refers to the "evil in my nature." "Life is not very eventful in Independence," he writes. "And it would be the same old story of office routine and varying degrees of faith and spirit of goodness or wickedness in my soul. I have an idea that should I wish, I could be very good—but Satan wants me to be bad—very bad. With the help of the Lord I shall do what is right—and let evil pass me by." He frets over unintentional offenses he has given. "Dilworth, it is time you began to remember the things of your childhood and to not forget your ideals and your covenants with the Lord. Happiness comes only to those who serve him and keep his laws holy and intact. And if I can only have strength I shall do so." He writes less frequently in his journal as the months pass.

His doggerel gives way to more serious verse, including one published in the Liahona, an anthem to the Pioneers.

> *It is not hard to sing the praise*
>   *Of men who go to war*
> *It is not hard to do brave deeds*
>   *Amid the cannon's roar*
> *Brave deeds are sung the wide world o'er*
>   *With great applause and cheer*
> *But who has writ the epic*
>   *Of the Mormon Pioneers? . . .*

"At last something which I've written has been put in that paper," he notes with satisfaction. Sister Valentine recited it as part of the festivities that year on the 24th of July. But the piece that most nearly reflects the tone of his other writings is one entitled "Loneliness."

> *The lone peak, snow covered, like a saint*
> *Stands as a sentinel, lone and bare*
> *His head aloof from mortal taint*
> *Beneath his feet all that's of care*
>
> *He guards his spotless virtue well,*
> *Unknown to him that evil's sown,*
> *Nor cares he, e'en, when human ill*
> *Would try to claim him for her own.*
>
> *The peak has risen by God's will*
> *To grace the land where love is great*
> *But how much greater, nobler still,*
> *If it had tasted love—and hate.*
>
> *In silent majesty he stands*
> *Nor backward fall, nor forward go*
> *But I—Oh give me strong men's hands*
> *And fights to win, and deaths to know,*
>
> *And love to gain, with bliss complete*
> *To drink in heaven's blessedness,*
> *All else is like the mountain peak,*
> *All white and cold with loneliness.*
>
>   S.D.Y. Jan 16, '21

Double Duty

Dilworth spent twenty-six months in the mission office, entering shortly before his twenty-third birthday and leaving shortly after his twenty-fifth. Yet he had hardly been in Independence before his father wrote to tell him he was broke and could send no more money. This was not uncommon. Elder Wride says he had to leave his own mission after eighteen months because of lack of funds. Dilworth tells of one missionary who asked President Bennion to let him to do country work during the summer, because he had no money to support himself otherwise. "President Bennion found someone in the same fix and let them go out." Dilworth had to be equally resourceful.

> I had been hearing complaints about how cold the Zion's Printing plant was. It was a large plant, all windows and high non-insulated roof and the December air was cold. The man who fired the furnace came at 8:00 a.m. when all the employees came to work. It took until noon for him to get the place warm enough to work in half comfort. I went to the President and told him I would fire that boiler (which heated our offices and the church too) from 4:00 a.m. until 8:00 a.m. and from 6:00 until 9:00 at night—a total of seven hours for $30.00 per month. He agreed and I did it until I went home in October 1922, except from May to October. Those six months I hired to keep the chapel cleaned and the lawns cut for the same $30.00. Thus I paid my actual food and room bill, but that is about all I did . . . [F]rom 4:00 a.m. to 11:00 p.m. I was busy doing something.

Relatives and friends (including Gladys) occasionally sent one or five dollar bills. On May 10, 1921 Dilworth writes, "Got a note from Hi with $5. He has been sending it for a month now. And the Lord will reward him for his generosity. Perhaps I can repay him for his kindness—I shall never forget, at least." Hi was selling insurance and may have been supporting his parents and brothers and sisters at the time. Ethel Archibald remembers the elders ate breakfast at a Sister Turner's at 7:00 a.m. (study class began at 7:30), and that most the time Dilworth didn't go.

Sometimes he would slip into the mission home kitchen and nab a piece of toast. "Bye," he would say on his way out the door. Ethel would scold, "Get out of here, Elder Young! Leave [that] toast alone." She says it never occurred to her until later he had no money to eat. Alec speculates he stayed home from some of the outings for lack of fare. By the summer of 1921, another factor keeping him home was his clothing. "My suit was so worn out that I had had two seats put in. The sleeves of the coat were so frayed that the burlap lining showed for an inch or so on each sleeve. The cuffs were badly frayed.

> The President said to me one morning. "Come with me to Kansas City." I said to him that I was too ragged to go anywhere. He laughed and said, "Come anyhow." Over my constant protest he made me go with him. We stopped, parked, got out and walked for two blocks, I in my rags, to the Palace Clothing Co. He ordered the clerk to fit me with a suit. Again I protested but he insisted. He bought me the finest black broadcloth suit in the store. It must have cost him $75.00 or $100.00. I had never paid more than $30.00 for a suit before in my life. I think it was his way of showing me he appreciated my milking his cows and feeding his chickens. I could do that between firing the furnace.

Dilworth worked hard to keep the President's trust. "I figured that my job was to make the President feel at ease when he was away and that things would be taken care of." One job President Bennion gave him was to "break up the romances which continually sprouted between the headquarter's missionaries and the local girls." Once the elder he had boxed stayed late at the family of a girl. Dilworth called him and "told him to get over to headquarters. He said, 'No.' I told him to get over on the next streetcar and when he got there I was going to beat his brains out. He could have the beating at the home of the girl or at the office. He came, crawling on his hands and knees to keep from being hit. I had no intention of hitting him, but the fear of it kept him behaving for the next six months." His journal records how distasteful he found this particular task. "I can't see why the missionaries can't wait for love affairs till out of the mission field, and pay attention to their business . . . I hate to show unnecessary authority, and then to be accused of doing it unnecessarily is bitter for me to swallow . . . but I guess I shall have to do it." The elders took their noonday meals at the Tuckfield's, a part-member family. Mr. Tuckfield had three daughters married to missionaries already—Dilworth claims that in all the years they had been coming, no one insisted they be made to follow the rules. One day a fourth daughter ran her fingers through Dilworth's companion's hair. The companion "rather seemed to like it.

> After it happened two or three times and he did not object, I said to her, "If you run your hand through Elder _____'s hair again, I'll let you have this glass of water in your face."
>
> She said, "You wouldn't do that, would you," and did it again. I picked up the glass and let her have the glassful right in the face. She gasped and ran crying into the kitchen, the mother after her. The old man swore. I said to him as he sat glowering, "You know the rules, Brother Tuckfield. I warned her and she deliberately did what she knew she shouldn't. Now I apologize for being rude, but she'll have to obey the rules or we'll have to eat elsewhere." The old man glowered for a moment and then said, "You're right, Young." So we stayed and were still friends.

Brother Tuckfield became more serious about the gospel and was baptized just after Dilworth returned home. Sister Tuckfield told Dilworth at her husband's funeral that he was the one responsible. "You converted him, Elder Young." This was the first he had known. "That was my only conversion that I knew of and I got it by sprinkling."

In the spring of 1922 Gladys apparently revived the idea of meeting him in El Paso. Orphaned at thirteen, Gladys had been brought up, first in Mexico City, then in Manassa, Colorado, by her brother Rey L. Pratt, president of the Mexican Mission. She longed to visit him and his family there. "Don't you really feel that I ought to drop school and work and everything and go to them awhile? I know I owe it to them." Later in the letter she muses, "If you could just slip over to El Paso in your aeroplane, we'd have lots o' fun. There is no passport needed now and Rey would take us down home in the car. I know because he said he would and maybe we could go for a hunt up on the 'Old Cliff Ranch.'" She brings it up several times that spring. He must have told her how little money he had, for at one point she writes that she knows were he could borrow money to come. Was he offended? She apparently did not wait to find out. "I'll forget what I mentioned in my last letter if you want me to. I did it on the spur of the moment and nearly tore up the letter several times. Of course I really, really meant it but I know your spirit and didn't want to hurt you." Instead of going to El Paso she took a summer job at Old Faithful Lodge in Yellowstone, singing and dancing and helping to stage pageants, but she continued to nag him. "I am so happy here sometimes I almost burst, until I think of how I have disappointed the folks. But if I could go and stay with them from Sept. to Xmas, how happy we would all be if just you could come. Please forgive me, Dil, but I have to express myself. Isn't that the best way—."

Dilworth had met Rey in Independence, where he came more than once to oversee the publication the Spanish Edition of the Book of Mormon. President Bennion introduced them by saying, "'President Pratt, meet your new brother-in-law, Elder Young.' I was embarrassed," Dilworth remembers, "but Rey was not like President Bennion. It was not his disposition to tease young people, and he let the remark pass by with some pleasant word. I loved him immediately." He remembers his strong, musical voice and "that indefinable lucidity of eyes which is a characteristic of that particular family. Gladys had it. Dil Jr. had it. ...One can't describe it, but it is the mark of Helaman and Victoria Pratt." Alec Archibald remembers Rey playing baseball with the elders in the evening.

In September 1922, President Bennion called Dilworth to inspect the Sunday School in St. Louis. "'It hasn't been inspected in a long time,' he said with a twinkle in his eye, 'And if you arrive on Saturday, you might be on time to see a big league ball game.'"

Dilworth watched the St. Louis Browns, with George Sisler on first base, play Detroit, with Ty Cobb in left field. "Cobb was past his prime but he hit every time at bat and stole second, stiff as his legs were. Sisler as I remember got a home run." Dilworth realized the President meant only to show his appreciation. "The Sunday School did not need inspection. How does one inspect a Sunday School?"

"Finally one day in very late September 1922 . . . President Bennion called me into his office and told me I had better go home and marry that girl or she wouldn't wait much longer." Actually Dilworth had been training his replacement, Parley J. Bennion, as early as July 5. In August he writes, "I gave [him] my desk and my bunch of keys and told him to go to it . . . and it does seem odd to be a man without a country. There is yet much to be shown of course." He writes of him, "I can see in all of his movements myself as I was two years ago when I was trying to learn to keep the mission books." Gladys is busy in Yellowstone, performing and meeting tourists and having fun with the dancers and singers. She writes, "There is always a lark of some kind on and you know, Dil, I have nearly all my life been deprived of things like this, not having had college days and living so long in the mission field and I am really enjoying the carefreeness of it." She describes hikes and outings—the Park naturalist has taken a special interest in her and takes her places none of the others go. Picking wildflowers is forbidden, but they collect "specimens" for his museum. "Before I returned I had my arms so full of gorgeous flowers I could hardly hold them." She looks for a way to get out of her teaching contract so she can go to El Paso. She wishes she were a "rangeress" (Dilworth writes in the margin, "Sounds bad for me!! These Rangers and Naturalists"). "Imagine," she closes this last letter, "looking down onto a valley filled with steam. A winding river courses its way through the pines, with dashes of color on the cliffs here and there, and all the green meadows filled with flowers, and then you will know where I am."

Dilworth records his future plans in his journal. "I shall get a job when I get home and help father some to get on his feet—and to help Hi regain his happiness after the loss of Giorgia," (his fiancee, who died in a drowning accident), "which knowledge of shocked me beyond belief."

And of Gladys? Who can tell what the future will bring. I have asked her—that is enough. She may answer as she sees fit. I don't believe she will say 'no', and yet she does hesitate, but surely all the subtle encouragement she has given me is not meant by her to be foolish, but whatever my lot shall be with her I shall always regard her as the one whom lived close to the Lord, of beauteous spirit, and one in close accord with the infinite. . . . Ah, Gladys, if you knew the yearning and the heartache which goes with love and friendship, but perhaps she does—someday I'll know.

CHAPTER 5

A Job, a Family

Wooing

Dilworth arrived home on Wednesday, October 4, 1922. His family met him at the Union Depot. Dilworth spent his last dime to help pay the streetcar fare home. "I was broke. That night all we had to eat at home was bread and potato soup. Father was broke too, and for a week that is all any of us had to eat. If I went anywhere I had to walk," which was a problem, since they lived four-and-a-half miles from town. He saw Gladys, who was still working in Ogden, though his history says he can't remember how. His uncle Lee, passing him in his car one day, stopped to ask about his mission and gave him ten dollars, which he accepted reluctantly. "I think it was that $10.00 which made it possible."

Dilworth's experience in the mission office may have helped him land a job in the office of Harry Oscarson, chief clerk for Bamberger Railroad. The post paid $100.00 a month, with one essential fringe benefit—a railroad pass that allowed him to make the run from Salt Lake to Ogden on weekends. The bishop of his ward had him working two callings, which kept him occupied Sundays. "I went to him and explained the only time I could court was when he had me working. He released me on a promise I would work for the ward when I got the girl hitched." From then on, Dilworth courted in earnest, using the pass every weekend to see Gladys or to escort her home if she were in Salt Lake. If he was out too late he spent the night at the McGregors, 2909

Washington, where Gladys boarded, or at the home of his old friend Merlon Stevenson, a first-year teacher at Weber College.

Dilworth writes of Gladys, "I am certain that the Lord intended for us to marry. I hadn't given up the idea at any time during the mission." His mother had a broach with seven small diamonds and had promised one to each of her three sons. The time came, and Dilworth claimed his. He paid ten dollars for the ring and setting, and presented it to Gladys one night (probably in October). "She held it up on her finger, held it up to the light and says, 'Is this paid for?' I said, 'For all practical purposes, yes.' So we were engaged." He wonders in his history what she must have thought of it, so small, and with a flaw he wasn't aware of at the time. "But it was a ring, and a diamond, and I thought it was okay. Wasn't it my mother's? Wasn't there sentiment behind it?" By the next night, it had become academic. "I was sitting in the front room when the doorbell rang. When I opened it, there stood Gladys. I invited her in and she took a chair. She was nervous, I could see." Finally she said, "'Here, I can't wear this!' and there was that diamond." He asked "if this meant we should cut it off, or if she just didn't want to be engaged, or if she was willing to date, etc. She replied that she didn't mind dating but didn't want to be engaged. I escorted her . . . to Aunt Dora's house on Windsor Street and went home."

The next night Dilworth sat in the parlor with the wind-up victrola, playing "all the sad, broken-heart records I could find and was having a real emotional jag. . . . Right in the middle of all that orgy of sadness, and I was getting deeper into it, why the doorbell rang and I went to the door and there [Gladys] stood." He invited her in and they sat down. "I waited for her to talk. She had something she wanted to say—I didn't have anything I wanted to say. Finally she said, 'Can I have my ring back?' And I said, 'You bet!' And so I went ahead and got it and put it on her finger and we were engaged again."

I asked her what made her change her mind, and she said, as nearly as I can remember it: "Last night after I got home and

sat in front of Aunt Dora's fire, I wasn't asleep but I had a vision.
I thought I was in a room, rather dark and gloomy—the only
light coming from a lamp on a center table. I was sitting by the
table doing something with my hands on some material in a
basket in my lap—darning, or mending—I couldn't tell which.
From the gloom behind me there came two children, a boy and
a girl, who went to a piano. One played while the other one
sang. It was made known to me that these were my children. I
looked across the table to see who their father was, and there I
saw you sitting. So I decided I'd better come back if you would
have me." It didn't take me long to reassure her that I wanted
her indeed.

Dilworth worked through that winter, taking a job as correspondence clerk at Deseret Book. He speaks of his manager there,
a Mr. Hooper, as having a temper "not well controlled." Dilworth
had charge of the suggestion box, and had the task of reading the
suggestions at the monthly employee meetings.

The day arrived, but there were no suggestions in the box. I
thought, "That's too bad," so I added a few, some good, some
bad, some ludicrous. That evening at the meeting, when called
upon, I opened the box and read a suggestion.

Hooper: "Who wrote that?" Me: "I thought these were anonymous. This is unsigned." Hooper: "If I find who wrote that!
. . ." Me: "You'll get no suggestions if the jobs are in danger." I
read another and a third and fourth. Hooper: "I want no more
of that!" And so I stopped reading.

The new job paid $125 a month, and also included a rail pass.
So Dil and Gladys continued to see each other on weekends, alternating between Ogden and Salt Lake. He sent her poetry:

If earth is an oyster, love is the pearl,
As pure as pure caresses;
Then loosen the gold of your hair, my girl
And hide my pearl in your tresses.

A letter he sent on her birthday reads, "As I dwell in the happy freedom of your company, I discover that indeed I am just at the beginning of my existence. Have you ever climbed up a steep slope, and, panting, reached the top, only to find spread out in Panorama all of the lovely hills and vales? . . . Greater has been my happiness to have climbed the hills with you—and now—on the summit—to discover [the joy] to be found in the country spread out before us, thru which we are to travel." They decided to marry on May 31, 1923, when her teaching contract expired and before her summer job as playground director at Lorin Farr Park began. Dilworth says the reason was Gladys insisted she did not want to be a June bride. The *Standard-Examiner's* social page has "Mr. And Mrs. John J. McGregor," Gladys' cousins, announcing their engagement.

Anthony W. Ivins of the First Presidency agreed to perform the ceremony. "He was an old friend of Gladys' father [Helaman], they having been missionaries scouting out the place for the colonies in Mexico. Helaman was Anthony W. Ivins' counselor in the stake presidency of Juarez Stake. Brother Ivins told us both of his love for Gladys' father." According to daughter Leonore, Gladys, without family to help her, took someone's advice to simply rent her dress at the temple, but was disappointed at the plain uniform they issued her. Because Gladys was alone, Dilworth's parents planned the reception, inviting mostly relatives, to be held outdoors in their yard. Dilworth recalls his father taking him aside the night before and telling him, "'Remember to be a gentleman.' That is all the information or instruction he ever gave me on how to handle sex." A heavy snow began that night and continued the next day during the ceremony, dropping nine inches, which meant that the reception had to be moved indoors. Gladys wore a salmon pink dress and matching hat she had made. Dilworth describes two hundred people packed into two rooms that would ordinarily hold forty. "It was a tight squeeze. No one could move; they just oozed about." Gladys and Dilworth stood in a corner, while guests called out their congratulations.

One more disappointment for Gladys: Rey drove his family from El Paso, but the storms and the dirt roads kept them from arriving until 9:30 that night, just as the other guests were leaving. "We made them welcome the best we could. I was getting a chair for [Rey's wife] May . . . and pulled it back just as Rolfe their son went to sit on it. He went flat on the floor to his intense embarrassment—and mine." Dilworth and Gladys slept at the Hotel Utah that night, dining in the Empire Room. "The colored waiter who served us did not warn us that a portion would really serve two. We each ordered a portion, then tried to eat it all—couldn't! That waiter is laughing yet."

A New Life

They went to Ogden the next day in sunny weather, to a three-bedroom house they had rented for $25.00 a month at 540 16th. Dilworth says they liked the rent and the room and the large tree out front. Rey and his family came the next day and stayed five days. "We used every sheet and pillow case and towel we had in Gladys' hope chest to take care of them. The only regret I had was that, when they went home, I had to rub all those sheets and towels out with an old rubbing board." Dilworth made up his mind right there their first purchase would be a washing machine. They got a Savage, a round copper tub with three legs set up on big steel cups. "It was the kind where you tip it up and it'll spin dry, and you turn it sideways and it'll wash. But you had to have the clothes evenly distributed when it spun or it'd spin all over the house."

> We pushed it up into the corner of the kitchen when it wasn't being used, and, well, the landlady decided she was going to wallpaper the kitchen. So the wallpaper hanger came one day and papered the kitchen—he left a three foot space right in the corner where that tub was. And so the next day I called the landlady and said, "Your wallpaper finisher didn't finish!" She said, "Well, I'll give you his number and you can call him up and tell him to come back and finish." I called him up and says, "You didn't finish your job! You left a corner undone!" And he says, "Well, of course I left a corner undone. I didn't want to disturb your still!"

Rolfe spent the summer with them. Dilworth gives no indication of having minded. "Rolfe had a very sweet tenor voice which I enjoyed very much. Gladys had a beautiful mezzo-soprano. They sang together beautifully." Dell B. Stringham, one of Rey's missionaries in Mexico, remembers being told that Rolfe was captured by Poncho Villa and run in front of some of his bandits on horseback until he dropped and his lungs bled. (Rey and Gladys were in Mexico City when violence broke out, Rey choosing a baseball bat in case he needed to defend himself, and fourteen-year-old Gladys a twelve-inch hat pin.) Rolfe went on to become a doctor in California. Dilworth complains ever so lightly of difficulty in getting Rolfe to clean his room.

Gladys told Leonore about the first time she served Dilworth a boiled egg and handed him a knife. Dilworth's mother had always prepared his boiled eggs. He went at it clumsily, not knowing how, and grew so flustered when he burned himself that he swatted it across the room.

Dil commuted to his job in Salt Lake on the Bamberger. Money was tight, and they overextended themselves that first month. On the 26th, with four days left till the end of the month, they found themselves out of money and out of food.

> We had $1.50. Should we go to the theater or make it do? The theater featured a "Fat" Sanders Country Store at intermission. This consisted of drawing the torn half of our tickets. If we got the lucky number, we would be loaded with groceries—gifts of merchants in exchange for the advertising they got.

> We three sat there as the drawing began. A number—all mine but the last two digits—another—all mine but the last digit. Then—glory be—my number! I walked to the stage. The manager said: "Are you married?" "Yes," said I. "Any children?" "No." "Here's a bottle of 'catchup.'" The audience roared. He then took a twenty-five pound sack of flour and slapped it on my shoulder. My blue serge suit was duly covered. Then I received spaghetti and cans of various stuff.

When we left the theater that night, I staggered under the load of food. We got on the streetcar. Gladys would not sit by me and went to the front. I stayed in the rear. During the ride a can got loose and rolled the length of the car, stopping at her seat. She ignored it. We got off and I had to rescue the can. She did consent to walk with me—and the loot—the block from the car to our house, but we did eat after a fashion for the next four days until the next check arrived.

One day in July during lunch hour, Dilworth ran into Howard McDonald, the future BYU president and his Granite High schoolmate. Howard asked where he worked and told him about an opening for a scout executive in Ogden. Dilworth said, "What is that?" He answered, "It's a man who leads the community in boy scout work. He is the paid professional. There is an opening in Ogden and I'm going to be offered the job. I don't want it. If you would like to have it, I'll recommend you." Dilworth, whose experience in scouting was limited to helping his little brother Rich drill a hole in the kitchen linoleum with a bow and drill, told him he knew nothing about scouting. "Do they pay money for jobs like that?" Howard said yes, $2,400 a year to start, "and after that it's up to you how much you are worth." Dilworth told him he didn't believe he could do the job, but got to thinking on the way home on the train. The money was good. He was sure he could learn the program. The only thing keeping him from trying was "fear." "And so I made up my mind I would try."

He presented himself to Samuel G. Dye, president of the council, in his home. "I was scared stiff, and I'm sure I sounded like it when I asked him for the job." Dye, who did not seem impressed, told him to send in a letter listing his qualifications. "I did so and the letter was very short." At first he thought that was as far as things would go, but then he began to think it might not hurt to have the support of the Church in Salt Lake. (In retrospect it seemed unlikely to him that it would have made a difference one way or the other. "I suppose if they had raised enough noise Ogden might have listened," he writes, "but they had no influence otherwise.") He went to the office of Oscar Kirkham, who was president of the MIA and also the Salt Lake Scout Executive, and asked for his support. Elder Kirkham asked who sent him. "No one," he replied, "I came entirely on my own." Elder Kirkham, apparently not knowing what to do with him, told him to wait, then disappeared, returned in a minute and told him to follow. "We went down the hall, down a stair to the office of Richard R. Lyman, a member of the Council of the Twelve. There he left me saying, 'This man wants to be the Ogden scout executive.'

Brother Lyman leaned back in his chair, looked at me, and said, "So you want to be the Ogden scout executive! Why, you haven't got enough brains to be a scout executive."

I said, "You don't know me at all and therefore don't know that, but I'll give you the names of three men who do know whether I have or not, James E. Talmage, Adam S. Bennion, and Willard Ashton. Ask any of them."

He said, "I'm a doctor of philosophy and I haven't enough brains to be one."

I said, "You may not have, but I have enough to learn how to handle a program for twelve-year-old boys, whether you have or not."

He said, "You can't have it."

I was angry when I walked out and so went down the hall to the office of Brother Talmage.

Dilworth had befriended Brother Talmage's son Carl in the army, "and he was grateful." He writes of Brother Talmage, "he was a good friend to me."

I told him what Brother Lyman had said.

He said, "Did Brother Lyman say that to you?" "Yes," I said. [He said,] "Come with me."

We went back to Brother Lyman and Brother Lyman looked at us coolly. Then Brother Talmage gave him a dressing down such as I have seldom heard. In his precise English he called Brother Lyman everything there was to call him without using a single swear word, and he told Brother Lyman I had enough brains to do anything I wanted to do.

Brother Lyman looked at me with a supercilious smile and said, "If you don't make good in six months, will you resign?" I replied, "If I don't make good in thirty days, I'll resign." He said, "Then I withdraw my objections!"

That was that. Dilworth thought to ask Elder Talmage for a letter of recommendation. "He said he would not give me a letter, because the people reading it would know that I'd read it and it might not be the truth, but to give his name. If they asked him, he would tell them the kind of person I was."

The next he heard anything was August, when he received a letter telling him to come to the scout office on the 20th at 3:00 p.m. for an interview. Seven other candidates came as well. Each was asked to say what he would do if he got the job. "Each one gave considerable detail . . . and one in particular blew quite hard about his qualifications and experience."

> When my turn came, I said, "I know nothing about the job, but I have been an athlete and mission secretary," which qualified me for the office work, and that I was sure I could learn very rapidly. As I spoke I had none of my previous fear, but with confidence unusual in me I told them I could learn and could do the job. It took me only about four minutes. I wasn't worried about it at all.

Dilworth later got wind of a feud among the scout commissioners that influenced the selection. George A. Goates, the previous executive, had resigned to take a regional position. Dilworth writes that, after "five years plus" of service, Goates had somehow "incurred the enmity of the powers that be in Ogden." (In another place, Dilworth alludes to council financial difficulties.) George Bergstrom, who had rescued nine boys from a flash flood at summer camp on the North Fork of the Ogden River the previous summer, who was perhaps the strongest applicant, and who was acting as the group's secretary, was asked to withdraw his application and did so. "I think the reason . . . was because he had become involved in the feud on the opposition side—at least, the

Goates side was against him. Otherwise he might easily have had the job."

Dilworth received a letter informing him he was one of two finalists and instructing him to appear before the executive board at the Weber Club the evening of August 30 at 7:00 p.m. "I hadn't expected to get the call and yet my feeling about it all was one of peace." He had tickets for a production of Romeo and Juliet that night, but the show started at 9:00 and he thought he would be through in time. Dilworth says of the other candidate, Lyles Larkin, an undertaker, "We talked for an hour during which he told me what he would do when he was appointed. He seemed to be sure of it, and I didn't doubt it. After awhile I got tired of his bragging and switched him off on to how bodies are embalmed. If I was to be a dead number, I thought I should know the process." Lyles was interviewed first, taking about forty minutes. "The longer he was there the more I knew I was licked, and yet somehow I didn't."

> Finally it was my turn. I stood before a long table around which sat about twenty-five men, Mr. Dye at the head. He said, "Mr. Young, the board is very tired and we'll give you about five minutes to tell us what you would do if you were executive."

> I told them I knew nothing about the job but that I could learn and that it wouldn't take long to learn and that I was sure I could give satisfaction. I was never more calm and collected as at that moment. It took me three minutes to say it.

> "Any questions?" said Mr. Dye. John D. Peters of Brigham City, "Mr. Young, have you ever played golf?" I, "No, Sir, but I have played football, basketball, and baseball." Mr. Peters, "Come up to Brigham and join the old men's golf club and we'll teach you how to play." Laughter—amid which I was excused.

> I went through the curtain doorway, and nearly knocked down Lyles Larkin, who was eavesdropping, his ear to the curtain. He hadn't expected me out so quickly. He recovered, and I apologized

for bumping into him and congratulated him for having won
the job. I told him I had a date.

Lyles, jovial, took him to Ensign's Drug Store for a pop, then left
to go hear the decision. Dilworth went to his play.

When Dilworth returned from work the next night, he could-
n't find the newspaper. He asked Gladys where it was, and she said
she didn't know. She set an extra nice table and served a special
meal. "Right in the middle of it she trotted out the newspaper."
"Ogden Scout Chief Chosen," read the header, in bold print in
the middle of the back page. The subheader read, "Seymour
Delworth Young named Executive of Local Council." The article
states he was the unanimous choice, also noting that, "although he
has never been associated with scout activities as an officer, Mr.
Young has been connected with scout organizations, however, in
minor capacities." (The article also misspells his name. The
announcement in the *Deseret News* has the same misspelling. The
Salt Lake Tribune gives his name as Seymour Delbert Young, Jr.)
The last sentence in the *Standard's* announcement particularly
amused Dilworth: "Mr. Young is the husband of Gladys Pratt
Young, in charge of the playground activities at Lorin Farr park."
"Well, I *wasn't* known—," he writes in his history, "and she was—
so at the moment she was the one."

"We rejoiced together," he says, and he called on Mr. Dye the
next day, who confirmed the salary and told him to report as soon
as possible. He gave notice at Deseret Book and reported to his
new office (212 in the Kiesel Building) and secretary the next
week. Many times, he says, as the years went by, he tried to imagine what Lyles Larkin "looked like or felt like when he went back
upstairs and learned of the decision that night—blank amazement, chagrin? I don't know, but I am sure he thought he had it
cinched." George Bergstrom in Ogden and Alfred Freeman in
Brigham were hired part-time as field executives, "(I think to keep
me straight)." In contrast to Bergstrom, Freeman was a Goates
man. Dilworth suspected that "Mr. Dye arranged things so Mr.
Larkin would talk himself out of the job, and cut me off so that I

wouldn't. He probably had talked with several board members ahead of time and may have looked up my references but I never heard that he did." Mr. Dye is quoted in the *Standard* as saying, "the officials of the council believe that they have chosen a man who will make every effort to keep scouting on a high plane." He told the *Deseret News,* "Mr. Young has been selected because of his executive ability and leadership. We have a big problem in holding all factions together." Dilworth writes of the assurance that came over him during each of his interviews. "I know now that the inspiration was whispering to me, but I didn't realize it then. I didn't seem to worry—all would be right either way. . . . There was no real reason to give me the job. Yet somehow it seemed to unfold for me. I'm sure the Lord was in it. . . . All I know is that after my first great fear, I was entirely calm, self-possessed, and said the right things at the right time."

Children, and a Home

The Youngs were active in the Ogden 7th Ward. Gladys, pregnant, stayed home that winter to prepare for the child. Of his first months on the job, Dilworth writes, "When I think of the things I did as a green man, I laugh. But the people were tolerant and seemed to like me and I learned. . . . I left Gladys alone too much in learning my job, and she must have been lonely, although she didn't say so." At one of the commissioners' suggestion, Dilworth joined the Rotary club. "I didn't realize that this was the game, to use the club as a friend getter—to cultivate and use the membership." Though they were friendly and did things to help the council, Dilworth says he never felt at home there, probably because of the expense. "Six dollars a month dues plus the extras took quite a bite out of my small salary. I should have kept it and used it better."

The council had no permanent camp, but conducted summer camps at North Fork, where the flash flood had been. An announcement in the *Standard-Examiner* of June 4, 1924, advertises week-long sessions. "Tents are placed in a beautiful grove of quaking aspens about 100 feet above the stream. The kitchen is up and also the mess hall, which assures all scouts plenty of good wholesome food. An excellent camp cook has been engaged and is 'ready to go.' All the camp needs now is boys." The article also mentions a three-day training session for scoutmasters on the sight beginning Monday the 9. Dilworth's history speaks of a hike to Ben Lomond Peak that day, and returning home at night. The next morning, at 3:00 a.m., Gladys began having labor pains. Rey and his family were visiting at the time. "These were the true pains and she went through them until 11:00 a.m.—without anesthetic." They summoned the doctor to the home. Gladys had a difficult delivery. Speaking of her labor, she once told Leonore, "Now I know that when pain gets to be so bad, you get to go unconscious." Dilworth (who doesn't mention her blacking out), says "I held Gladys' hand, supported her as best I could through the ordeal." The child came breach. "Dr. Leonard Jenkins gave [Gladys] a whiff of chloroform as the baby was born—an eight and a half pound boy." They gave him the name of Dilworth Randolph Young.

Dil Jr. was blessed at home around June 22 by his father and grandfather and Uncle Rey, then again (officially) by his father and B. P. Budge August 3. Dilworth attended a training camp in September near Estes Park, Colorado. Gladys wrote him there, "Of course I would love to be with you and see all the wonderful sights, but you know I've seen mountains and valleys and rivers and lakes many times before—but never before have I seen two little blue eyes look up into mine and beam, with gratefulness to me for giving them food, comfort and care. Never before have I felt the loving caress of soft baby fingers on my breast tugging away at my heart strings." She adds a note from Little Dil, sending his hugs, promising to grow, complaining about his medicine and his nose pump, and commenting on his work for the day. "I've found some little round white buttons on my Mama's dress—and I'm just aching for the day when I can grab ahold of them." Gladys kept a notebook, jotting down the first time the baby laughed, got his haircut, had Christmas, cut teeth, found his hands. Trying to drink from the spray of a hose when a little older, he says, "See, Mama, I'm drinking sunbeams." She describes him at camp, "brown as an Indian all over his body," making echoes from the cliff, lying flat on his belly to drink from the creek, chasing birds and squirrels and running up and down the hills. She hurts herself on a sewing machine at home and cries out. "Dil came running over—'Don't cry, Mama. Did you pinch yourself? Are you sleepy? Don't cry, I'll take you.'" He puts his hands on her and tries to lift. "'Am I big enough?'"

Gladys writes in the baby book:

> A dear little baby boy with eyes of blue
> A dear little mouth to smile at you.
> Two little hands that play in the air,
> A little round head with lots of hair
> Two little ears that are just a dream
> The dearest nose you have ever seen.

"I can just hear Dill laugh when he reads this, but I am quite proud of my poetry. Ha ha."

Gladys put on plays and small pageants for the 7th ward. With Dilworth gone so many evenings, they hired Louise Arbon, a neighborhood girl, to babysit by the month. Later, Gladys did short pageants for the annual balls of the Daughters of the Utah Pioneers. She and Dilworth became interested in marionettes and began to put on puppet shows. The most successful of these was *Peter Pan*, which they preformed for children in various places, "especially the Primary Children's Hospital." Harlan Y. Hammond, a young cousin, remembers being amazed at how the puppets could fly, and also at one of the pirates who played a harmonica with his hands sawing back and forth in front of his face. "I wondered how they could make a harmonica that small, and how they could get that puppet to blow it." Dilworth drove a Model T Ford, but had his eye on a little red Essex. "Gladys warned me not to get it, but I thirsted and finally did. It was the big mistake of my life. It broke me." He says he had the car in the shop more often than out. "I learned that cars when they first come out are full of bugs." The council finally bought him a used Dodge, with cargo room and a "low-low that climbed the steepest hills." It "really served me well and was just the kind of car for me to drive."

Earl Wright, a contractor, offered to build the Youngs a little house with a full basement on a small lot at 2318 Eccles for $3,200.00, and they agreed. While waiting for the house to be completed, they moved in with Jim and Georgia McGregor on 33rd Street west of Washington. Dilworth, noting that neither they nor Gladys were happy with the situation, sums up: "It is a mistake to move in with people." They moved into their new house in the autumn of 1925 and found it cold enough to be "hard on the baby." Dilworth tried to get a loan through First Security for $150 to buy a furnace. "George S. Eccles said the bank could not loan without security, but that he personally would loan it to me. So he loaned me $150.00 plus a twenty percent discount which made it $180 plus the total of the interest." The discount made the interest higher. Dilworth took home $150 but had to repay $180, plus interest on the full $180. "That is where I learned about usury."

> One day Mr. Wright, the contractor, came and said, "You paid $100.00 down on that house?" "Yes," I said.

> "Would you have any objection if I drew a new contract for $3,600.00 and showed you having paid $600.00 down?" "No," said I. "It's as broad as it is long."

> I signed the new papers and thought no more of it until one day two men informed me that the First Security Bank owned my mortgage and would I pay them in the future. What Wright had done was to increase my house cost, credit me with more payment, and then discount the note for as little as possible to the bank. He may have had to discount it $500.00 and thus made $100.00, or he may have dropped the full $600.00 but would have been rid of the mortgage. Anyhow, George Eccles met his equal at discounting, and I learned a little of the art of finance.

They entertained Rey and his family, who slept on the floor of the basement. "It was all we had to offer. I tried to get them to take the bedroom but they would not." They attended the 13th ward. "We were gregarious. We ran with the 12th Ward crowd, the Weber College crowd, and our own ward." Gladys' reputation apparently preceded her, for she received a call to put on one play a month for the ward. Dilworth at different times taught Sunday School and the priests quorum and for a short time was president of the ward seventies. J. Golden Kimball spoke once to the seventies of the stake. "His approach to the problem of finance for the First Council was about as follows:

He said, "How many of you would go on a mission if you were called?"

Nearly every hand was raised.

"How many would give their lives for the gospel?"

Nearly every hand went up.

"How many will give fifty cents to the seventies' fund?"

Hardly a hand went up.

"He was a most interesting character."

Dilworth took his young family along on a scout trip to Southern Utah. When they were in Cedar City, Little Dil began to have abdominal pains, so they saw a doctor, who diagnosed a telescoped bowel. Dilworth, who had the scouts' money, rushed ahead to overtake them, while a Dr. McFarlane operated and saved Little Dil's life. "Gladys had a look in her eyes I shall never forget. I had put the money for the boys ahead of the danger to my own child." He writes, fifty years later, "I have been poor at putting my own emergencies ahead of the requirements of the scout job. I suppose there is no use in regretting now, but I have a bad conscience about it." A letter from Gladys describes the busy little hospital, and Little Dil learning to find things in magazines. "The man that had glasses on was Daddy—and he tried to pick the glasses off." She talks about possible plans for staying in the area. "If you can get someone responsible to stay with me, I believe the canyon is the best place for another month. . . . If I can just make the next two days pass quickly I will be glad. I am about as tired when night comes as if I had done a good days' washing trying to keep baby quiet and happy."

Little Dil took ill again in the winter of 1926, with Gladys nine months pregnant. "He had lobar pneumonia in which the fever comes up, then subsides, then higher, then down, higher still; and if the patient survives the highest climax, he lives." The doctor said to get him to drink. "'How?' I said, 'He won't swallow!' 'Use an eyedropper.'" Meanwhile a terrible storm howled outside. "In all my days I've never seen a worse one."

> So we took turns putting water in an eyedropper. The night of the climax Gladys said, "You've got to do something!" "What can I do?" I replied. She said, "I don't know, but do something." So it occurred to me to give a blessing, which I did with oil. Gladys laid on her hands too. The fever broke and he was past the crisis. She was sitting by the bed putting in water. . . .

> She looked up at me and said, "You are going to be a father in about fifteen minutes." I called the doctor but could not get him. I called his partner Roscoe [L.] Draper, who somehow got through that storm to the house. How he found his way I'll never know. Ten minutes later Leonore was born. It was December 26, 1926. We wrapped her in a blanket. In the morning Leona McGregor came and bathed the child. Amy Pratt [Romney], Gladys' sister, came up, gave up her Christmas holiday, and helped us for the week before she had to go back to school. I'll be ever grateful for that assistance.

This was all their children. Leonore can remember her mother wondering aloud why she never had more—apparently that was all that came. Dilworth did want a girl. Leonore remembers him telling her more than once that "when the doctor said I was a boy, my father accepted this calmly; but then the doctor said, 'No, it isn't, it's a girl,' [and] my father danced a jig all over the room."

Little Leonore cried constantly. Gladys took her to the doctor, who said, "This baby's hungry; your milk must be no good." She tried cow's milk, which the baby didn't take well. According to

Leonore, "They had a terrible time. Nothing agreed with me. I have memories of what I ate that finally agreed, and I still like those foods, smashed bananas and tomato soup." Once, when Leonore was a little over two, she told her mother she wanted to make a "balentine." Gladys said she would show her how as soon as she finished up the dishes, but Leonore grew impatient. "She said that when she came to help me, I had already cut out a fair valentine. She found out that I was quite independent."

> Mother believed in putting her babies in the sun. One day when I was six months old, she put me outside in a carriage; then she went into the house for a minute. She said that after that she knew I would be athletic because when she came out I was swinging on the handlebar of the carriage.

In fact, Leonore showed unusual skill at dancing. "Mother started me on . . . lessons at age four. She says I showed an aptitude for it then." Leonore says most of her dancemates dropped out at age twelve "and only the serious students remained. It was after this that I became a dancer."

As a small girl, Leonore had recurring infections in both ears. When the pressure became too great the doctor lanced them. With no penicillin, there was little else to do. Gladys spent three months in 1930 with the children in Santa Monica in hopes that would help. She rented a small beach house. Rey, serving in the mission presidency in Southern California, was nearby. A terse letter from Dilworth encloses an article on swimming in the ocean. "You can stay afloat for several hours," he adds, "by paddling on your back." A letter from Dilworth's father Seymour to Little Dil notes, "We see your Daddy every two or three days and he seems lonesome for that fine young man named Dilworth Randolph Young." Leonore remembers a story about Little Dil misbehaving for his mother in Santa Monica, until Gladys, in exasperation, said, "Dil, what am I going to do with you?" "Well," he answered, "Maybe we should have Daddy sit me down hard in a chair and say, 'Straighten out, there, Young Man!'"

"We were quite happy in the new house" on Eccles, Dilworth

writes, but with only one bedroom they were crowded. Leonore remembers sleeping in the same double bed as her brother until she was perhaps four, with her parents in another double bed in the same room. She was moved downstairs next, to what she remembers as cement floors and unplastered frame walls. Two cousins, Margie and Jean Pratt, from Colonia Dublan, Mexico, recently out of high school, lived with the Youngs in the basement at the same time. Leonore says Jean worked as Dilworth's secretary, and he sent her out on errands. Jean, a country girl, at first would walk out in the street in downtown Ogden looking for addresses, terrified of the passing cars. Perhaps the Youngs would have finished the basement, but for a friend, J. Bryon Barton, who "told us of the big old house on Taylor and 24th which was for sale."

> We said we could not afford it. He said he thought it could be bought for about $4,200.00 to $4,500.00. Mrs. Beck, the owner, was old and alone. The roof leaked and the lot needed lots of attention. She did not have money for the repair. Her children except one boy, Gilbert, were scattered. So for a lark that evening we walked and passed the place. We were in love with it at once.

The house in question, for a number of years on the National Register of Historic Places, was one of the first houses above Harrison, not quite a mansion, built by Augustus B. Patton in 1891. The nomination form describes a "four day carnival" conducted by "William Hope 'Coin' Harvey . . . to entice people to come to Ogden and buy land. It is reported that 14,000 people came." Patton, who may or may not have participated in the event, but who bought and developed more than one parcel that year, put up this house for himself in the "Nob Hill Addition," all alone on the bench. (Paul Bieler, who moved into the neighborhood later, characterizes the "carnival" as an attempt by "a group of Mormon-hating promoters from the East" to attract enough non-Mormons to the town to outnumber the Mormons.) The house, two-and-a-half stories high, featured four spreading gables with a green roof spilling down between them to the first story with its veranda. Constructed in the Victorian "Shingle Style," a rarity in Utah, the house's walls, except for the brick first story, were covered entirely in wood shingles. Mr. Beck had been an official with the railroad, which made Dilworth wonder whether the boxcar red paint on the brick and shingles hadn't come from the work site. Maples lined the frontage, already large, and on the other side of the sidewalk towered a row of blue spruces, already old. Inside, the first-story rooms had been done in hardwood: two in cherry and one in oak. The second floor had five bedrooms and a bath, with five more rooms in the basement and ample room for storage in the attic. "We looked through the front window that night and saw a fire burning in the fireplace at the far end of the living room."

"Bryon Barton introduced us to Mrs. Beck. She was suspicious of him so he withdrew." Gladys loved each little thing, and raved, and stressed how she wouldn't change anything. There was much to love in the house. In each of the bathrooms stood six-foot long cast-iron bathtubs on legs. A three-paned bay-window in the west wall of the dining room marked off winter, spring and summer at sunset. A pane of beveled glass set in hardwood separated the parlor from the vestibule. "We later learned that Mrs. Wattis (a wealthy woman) had offered her $4,000.00 but had said that when she got the place she would change the hand-painted ceiling, rip out this wall, etc. Mrs. Beck heard her and had other thoughts." The Youngs offered $4,200.00, with $100.00 down and $50.00 monthly payments. "She—to our surprise—accepted." Leonore new nothing of all this.

One day I got up for Sunday School, and they said, 'Leonore, we aren't going to live in this house anymore. When you finish church, go to this address.' So I got one of my good friends Faire Jones to come with me, and we finally found it, and we walked in, and in the front is a large hall with the stairs going up, and we walked up the stairs, through another long hall, and up [more] stairs to the attic. And the attic was a great big open space. You could have even play basketball up there. And it had an old victrola, and there was a big trunk. And Faire and I got into that trunk, and there were the most wonderful costumes.

Needless to say, Leonore was enchanted. This was 1934. The neighborhood was so unpopulated at the time that Leonore's five-block walk left her in the same ward and the same school.

The price of the house included much of Mrs. Beck's furniture, and they also moved in several pieces from the Eccles Avenue house. Dilworth nevertheless writes of not having enough places at the house-warming party to seat their friends. "Most sat on the floor in front of the fireplace and enjoyed the atmosphere of the place." They rented rooms to nurses at the nearby Dee Hospital to help meet house payments. They sold the home on Eccles and mortgaged the new home for enough for a new roof, "(no more pans in the attic)." Gladys worked teaching elementary in a Washington Terrace school for defense workers' children to pay for Persian rugs for the house. The grandchildren remember their plush wool and rich color, also the way they bunched and would not lie flat on the floor.

Paul Bieler notes that many of the lots purchased during the "carnival" went into orchards, irrigated with water from Taylors Canyon. "But when the Railroad took over the Taylor[s] Canyon water, this benchland dried up, orchards were abandoned and lots lay unused for many years. Some were sold for taxes. This is how 'Dil' Young had secured a number of them." Dilworth, who wanted a scoutmaster for his home ward, sold Paul a lot for $100, much less than its market value. Dilworth lived on two lots, and had four others that he later donated to the Scouts for training purposes, partly to preserve Gladys' view of the mountains. He found city water too expensive for watering his property.

In the back lower lot was a wet spot, so I dug a sump about five feet deep, and it filled with water in about two hours. I got a pump and pipe and installed my own water system. Until Pine View Dam was built we watered all the land from that sump with that pump. We had a regular park out of our half acre," he writes, "and many happy times."

Leonore remembers Dilworth getting up at 4:00 or 5:00 in the morning to care for the yard, then driving up the canyon to run camp all day and well into the evening. As for his little free time in Ogden, Leonore's friend Martha Johnson Barney says, "It seems like he was always cutting his lawn. He'd do it in sections, you know, because there was so much yard there." Dilworth had a gas mower. Once he got far enough behind that he mowed it early on a Sunday morning. Paul Bieler came out to complain as he passed, Paul standing on the property line. The second time around Dilworth said it was none of his business. Paul waited for a third pass and said it was, because of the example to his children, who wanted to swim on the Sabbath. Paul doesn't say whether he stopped, but remembers Dilworth later telling the story in stake conference as an example of how one's actions affect others. According to Leonore, Gladys got flower starts from friends and neighbors, because of little money, things like tiger lilies and phlox that spread easily. She says both Dilworth and Gladys gardened, but that Gladys was often ill and so he did the brunt. Dilworth never could quite keep up yardwise, except the summer Parker Pratt, a cousin, attended Weber and gardened in exchange for board. The yard was immaculate that year.

CHAPTER 6

A Scouter

Kiesel

In early 1925, Wilhelmine Kiesel Shearman, daughter of prominent Ogden merchant Fred J. Kiesel, made a gift to the Ogden Gateway Council of $3,500 for a summer camp to be named for her father. The council had been holding camps on the North Fork of the Ogden River but jumped at the chance to have its own. Dilworth and George Bergstrom scouted for land that spring, first on North Fork, but then on South Fork, parking one day near the Narrows and hiking up Causey Creek on a sheep trail to the point where Dry Bread and Wheatgrass Canyons meet. Dil writes, "After we had walked to the big spring on Causey Creek, we knew . . . we had found our spot." Mrs. Shearman knew the place and was pleased, as it had been a favorite of her father's. Dilworth's history recalls an act of Congress deeding the land—eighty acres—to the council, though a note in the paper in 1936 attributes the gift to Mrs. Fred J. Kiesel, Mrs. Shearman's mother, with a later addition of fifty acres by Frank M. Browning. In any case, the council was able to use Mrs. Shearman's gift exclusively for the cabin. As A. Russell Croft, later council president, says, "You could build a lot for $3,500 in those days, especially if you could get some volunteer help to go along with it." Dilworth did, and by June of 1925 they had their lodge.

Besides Dilworth and George, the camp employed a cook, a naturalist and a handicrafts teacher that first year. The boys slept in cots in pyramid-shaped army squad tents on wood platforms. These were soon replaced by a row of nine bunkhouses, each with four bunks, enough for a patrol. Dilworth says, "Sometimes the pack rats would come in and entertain the boys by jumping on them." A pipe from Little Springs supplied drinking water. Eden Beutler tells of going with Dilworth to repair it in the springtime, the two of them standing in the ice cold creek to cut, thread, and splice the pipe where it had split from freezing, then following it down to the next break. Leonore recalls the kitchen had a primitive refrigerator: "They had cold ice water running down a canvas that covered this wire cage, and that kept the food cold." James Oka, a scout at Kiesel, tells of a natural swimming hole on the way to Big Springs. The scouts had contests staying in the water. "Everybody gave up except two, and neither one wanted to give up out of those two. And finally Dilworth had to make them get out because they were starting to get blue." In 1935 the council built a small dam above the present site of Causey Reservoir, providing a waterfront big enough for eleven rowboats and two canoes, also a swimming pool with diving board, fed by a canal. Leonore remembers moss on the pool's bottom. She says the practice was to drain it on weekends, which meant the water would warm in the sun and be nearly bearable by Friday. Russ Croft says the council used Civilian Conservation Corps labor. He recalls a controversy when it was discovered the dam was on Forest Service land. N. C. Wood, the regional forester, was a friend of the scouts (and later president of the council), and helped to smooth things over.

Days began at 6:30 a.m. with reveille, played on a bugle, or sounded with a whistle, or beat out on a "lali," a hollowed-out log, from Samoa, or, one year, according to a hint in the *Standard-Examiner*, shot from a "toy cannon." After flag ceremony, the scouts reported to the lodge for breakfast, then returned to their camps to prepare for inspection. From 9:00 to noon, scouts attended merit badge and handicraft classes. They learned to identify plants, made leaf collections, and visited fossil beds. Bob Buswell later kept caged rabbits, squirrels, porcupines, snakes and a pair of trained chipmunks he took home in the fall when he let the other animals go. The boys made bridges, packs, and model airplanes, and took casts of tracks as well as their own faces, finishing these off with bronze-colored paint. For leatherwork, scouts brought the tops of old shoes for practice. By the end of the week they were ready for the virgin stuff and made braided and beaded belts, boondoggle, moccasins, axe heads, and stamped wallets and purses. Dilworth, holding a stamp for one of the instructors, once had his finger laid bare to the bone. The scouts learned rope making, first-aid, and semaphore. Gus Becker donated a number of .22 rifles that first year and inaugurated the range with a speech on safety and honor. Boys made bows for the archery range from ash, planing and whittling and sanding them down, then finishing them with linseed oil. They tied their own arrows and twisted and waxed their own flax bowstrings.

At 1:30, after lunch in the lodge, the boys had hobble-leg races, fire relays, water boiling contests, and water fights, and played games like barnyard golf (horseshoes), wall scaling, steal-the-flag, volleyball, spud, red rover, three leap, streets and alleys, night raiding, and baseball. Shower time came at 4:30, originally with buckets, though from 1926, Kiesel had a bathhouse with warm water and flush toilets. Boys worked on the trails and campsites, attended Sunday services at the base of Organ Loft, and took day hikes. Dilworth writes that on a campout in Bear Wallow in about 1930, "we happened to glance up and saw the entrance to Bat Cave on the south wall of the canyon. It proved to be reachable and was the object of many hikes thereafter." He says there was "some danger if one slipped" climbing up, which from his way of thinking was "good for the boys." Eden Beutler remembers the bats "hanging on the ceiling like grapes." Boys hiked to Big Springs or up Wheatgrass or followed the Skintoe trail around the east side of Causey Creek, then dropped down into the Narrows. They came back wet to the waist from that one. Martha Barney, Leonore's friend, remembers boys wearing sweaters upside down over their legs and waists because their clothes were wet—Dilworth always, but especially now, ordered the girls to keep out of sight.

After a 5:30 retreat, dinner was served in the lodge at 6:00. More games carried them from 7:00 until the 8:00 p.m. campfire at the central, cement amphitheater. Martha Barney and Leonore remember skits. In one, four boys play the wheels of the car and a fifth the driver. Each tire goes flat in turn, with the driver jumping out to pump them up, then all going down at once. They sang songs: Alouette, Yippie-Ki-Yi-Yo, Eiry Olly Olly Aee. A note in the *Standard* on June 21, 1925, advertises, "Let us get busy and write some new songs and new yells for Camp Kiesel. We need some stirring words for the camp song. Why can't some scout write them?"—and such songs were written. Dilworth became a storyteller. He told fish stories. In one, he caught an eighteen-pound fish in a particular hole, knocking his lantern into the water as it slipped away. Three days later when he pulled the lantern out, it was still alight. A man in the audience would then claim to have caught a twenty-five-pound fish in the same hole. Dilworth said that if the man would cut ten pounds off the fish, he would blow out the lantern. He told wolf stories, too. In one a timber harvester rides a sledge in a blizzard on Monte Cristo, pursued by a pack of starving wolves. He shoots the lead one, which its brothers promptly devour, then take up the chase again. So he shoots the new lead, and once again he's cannibalized, and so on, until there is only one wolf left. "And you should have seen his sides flap as he came around the bend!"

Dilworth said, "Every boy scout camp has to have a ghost," and Kiesel's was Jim Sanders, (or Jim Saunders, depending on who's telling the tale). Sanders was an old trapper, the last of the breed, known to Jim Bridger and Kit Carson, who worked a line up Bear Wallow, onto Little Monte, back down Dry Bread toward Big Springs, then onto the west ridge and home. His cabin still stood a mile below Kiesel when the camp was first built. Sanders would outfit himself each fall, then work his line on skis or snowshoes through the winter, and come into Huntsville with his furs in the spring. Once, on the night of the full moon, when he was delayed on his line, he heard the wolves gathering for the hunt. Before long he realized they were after him—Dilworth made this part longest, supplying all the sounds. Sanders cached his furs in a tree and made down the mountain. When he didn't come into Huntsville that spring, a party went looking, finding his cabin with the door shut. Later someone came across his rotting furs, then finally someone found a human skeleton amid the bones of several wolves, and built a cairn.

Dilworth told of sending boys to see his grave, but "they never were able to find it, because they never knew where to look." In 1925 he and forty boys sat on the hillside by the cabin watching the cliff as the full moon rose. Dilworth dozed, awakened by a boy stammering, "Look," and pointing up the hill with a shaky hand, where, sure enough, something white descended. "I said, 'That's all I want, boys,' and I started to run for camp, [with] fifty kids all on my coat tail going up to that cabin—I couldn't get rid of them." He says they did this for about five years. "Kids always thought it was one of the camp men, so they'd rush on ahead to camp and see if it was, and they were always with us or in bed." Leonore remembers a standing challenge to the boys to spend a night in the cabin. An article in the *Standard* describes Jim as having "a long grey beard and a surly disposition," and warns those seeking him that "old Jim has neither bathed or shaved since he became a ghost." The cabin burned down one year. Dilworth says, "Well, ghosts have to have a place to go, and they figured it might adopt Camp Kiesel." Then, in a blizzard, George Edwards and Troop 1 saw the white, indistinct, face of an old man through the lodge window, and went out to help, only to find he had disappeared, leaving no tracks on the ground.

Jim Sanders was a fixture at Kiesel campfires, the story ending abruptly when DeVere Childs appeared in the background draped in a sheet. The boys saw just a flick of white in the darkness beyond the glow of the campfire, and the junior officers jump, and that was invariably enough to clear the site—they'd all come laughing back. In another version, related by George Lowe, Jim Sanders was lonely, a friend to boys and men in the out-of-doors, and the scouts were encouraged to look for his form in the mists falling over the cliff or for a hint of his face in the ashes or the flames of the fire. George says that Dilworth in later years didn't like the story to be told, perhaps because of the supernatural element. His family heard him tell it, but always with a caveat at the end: In the 1960s a *Standard-Examiner* reporter doing a feature on old time inhabitants of the county asked if he could tell him anything about Jim Sanders. "Of course I can," said Dilworth, "I made him up!" The reporter was duly disappointed.

The idea in campfires was to start with skits and songs and funny stories, then finish off with the scary ones so the boys would be settled by the 9:30 taps and ready to go to bed. So after the tall stories, Dilworth told bear stories, perhaps of Old Ephraim, or Old Nephi, or other famous bears. He told One Head Well Done, and the Wendigo. By all accounts he held them spellbound with this last one—drawing the boys along with the monotony of canoeing and fishing and making camp, then letting the tension mount with talk of the beast, ("No one's seen him, but when he calls you, you gotta go.") Then night would fall and the wind would rise, then came the terrible stench and the monster's blood-curdling howl, "Défaaaaagooooooooooo," and, "Oh, my feet, my blistering, burning feet of fire," poor Défago's call. Dilworth preferred to tell the story when he had water and pines, probably because he knew his listeners would startle and shake every time the breeze whooshed through the boughs.

He tells of an overnighter in Bear Wallow in the early days, and a campfire, where they told "some wolf stories and a couple of coyote stories, and one good bear story, and then we had prayer and dismissed them and went to bed." He and Loo Roberts made their bed on the lee-side of a log, with his nephew George on the other side. (Dilworth taught the boys that the wind blows down the canyons at night and up in the day. Sometimes they listened, sometimes they didn't.) Loo Roberts had his knife out and was honing it on his boot.

Up over the log came my nephew's head. . . . "Whatch'ya doin',

Mr. Roberts?" "Oh, I'm sharpening my knife." "What for?" "Well, you have to be ready for emergencies." "Oh," says George, and down he went. . . . Loo was still sharpening. And finally he says, "Any danger?" "No-o, no. We'll protect you." Then Loo stabbed his knife into the ground and it just quivered there. Then we lay down a few minutes, and pretty soon the head came up, and George says, "[Uncle Dil], don't you think we better have prayer?" "Well, we prayed at the campfire a few minutes ago, George. No, we don't need to have any more prayer. You have your individual prayer, where you are, just kneel down and pray." He said, "I know, but don't you think there are prayers for special occasions like this?"

Dil finally invited him to sleep by them, and he did.

Dil later delighted in recalling a bear story of his own. The boys would snipe hunt on Causey Creek. Two tenderfeet would be placed with sacks and lanterns where the older boys could drive them down to them. Then of course the older boys would all make a little noise and slip quietly off to bed. "Causey Creek's no place to take boys snipe hunting," Dilworth says. "It's just dangerous. It's rough, and the water tumbling down over those rocks, and it's narrow, and you can't get up the stream itself. . . . I told them to cut it out, quit doing it, and they didn't pay any attention to me. I stayed up late, but they always outwaited me." One afternoon he stood talking to John Grow, the government trapper, on Dry Bread Pond.

> I says, "Mr. Grow, I've been in these hills a lot, I've tracked for the last ten years, and I've been told there are a lot of bear here, but I've never seen a bear. I've never even seen a track." He said, "You haven't?" I says, "No!" He said, "Well, look down at your feet." And right down there by my foot was a great big track . . . of a front paw of a bear. . . . I said, "Thank you!" and away I went. He must have thought I was scared.

Dil jumped in his car, sped down the mountain, and returned with plaster of paris. He made a cast and allowed it to set, took it to camp, then sat on the front steps of his cabin, carving off the dirt and making it smooth. That night he planted two tracks on a sand bar by the creek where the boys came to get water. He rose early in the morning to listen. Soon a boy came down the trail, swinging his bucket, talking and singing to himself. Then came the yell:

> "Whew!" Up the trail he came, without his bucket. I says, "What's the matter?" He says, "There's a bear!" I says, "Where." "Down there!" I says, "Oh, you didn't see a bear down there." "Well, I saw his track!" I says, "Oh, you didn't either." "Yes, I did!" And I said, "Let's go see." So he took me down and showed me these two tracks. I said, "Sure enough, they're certainly bear tracks alright. Let's build a fence around it so all the boys can see it." So we built a little fence around it with willows, and all the boys in camp saw that bear track. Never a boy left camp after dark after that. They stayed put.

No one noticed the bear had two left front feet.

Of the early Kiesel, Dilworth writes, "I soon learned that boys don't learn much at camp if it is conducted like a school, which ours was." He didn't like the boys sleeping in cabins, or the fact that meals were prepared. Percy Hadley, one of the scoutmasters, recalls that in the early times all the boys did for themselves was wash their own dishes in a pot of suds and a pot of hot water the cook prepared, and make their own beds. Dilworth says, "We had a half day of games, in which the men got bored and more and more they slept. . . . I wasn't happy about it but didn't at the time know how to make it better."

Dilworth Leads

In the winter months, Dilworth held training sessions for scoutmasters under some lean-tos on the four lots he owned above his house, and also took the sessions to small towns around the council. Percy Hadley describes Dilworth's method as follows: "He wouldn't try to do all the teaching himself. He'd get me and Eden [Beutler] and guys like that to be the patrol leaders, and . . . he'd tell us what he wanted us to do, whether it was rope making or first aid or fire building . . . and then we'd teach the other guys to do it. And then they in turn could go and teach their boys. That was called the patrol method." Dilworth believed that boys learned best by doing, and since it was the scoutmasters who taught the boys, he had them learn the same way. Percy describes a fire building stunt. A string was suspended between two sticks eighteen inches over a fire pit. "You'd do all you want until you light the match, and after that you can't do any more, and then the idea is to burn the string in two." Dilworth's lots had small, artificial lakes, used for mapping. Paul Bieler writes of Dilworth loading the scoutmasters onto city buses for practical training in giving up seats and doing other good turns. The Becks had left a cider press in the basement of the new home, so Dilworth and the patrol leaders made cider, and Gladys cooked doughnuts and cakes for the men to eat afterwards.

The "patrol method" dates back to Lord Baden-Powell, and is one of the central features of his program. Boys were organized in groups of six or eight with a peer leader. Patrols met weekly or more often to practice skills and stunts, and less often with the troop, where patrols demonstrated what they had learned. Scoutmasters watched, encouraged, and invisibly guided the troop through the boy leaders. Dilworth tried to get his scout-masters to organize their troops this way. Many failed to motivate the boys. Others did everything themselves. The LDS troops met with the MIA, always a thorn in Dilworth's side. He complains in a 1939 speech that troops "meet in general assembly, then go to a classroom, then have thirty minutes of a manual, then thirty min-utes of scouting in the same room, and dismiss with the Mutual at 9:00 p.m. . . . And for a scoutmaster to take the troop anywhere on Tuesday night would [require] chloroform and a kidnapping." He laments how little hiking and camping some troops did, how much scouting was conducted indoors. Paul Bieler was one who tried to make the patrol method go. The bishop wanted to keep him in the recreation hall. At one point Paul had the boys build-ing campfires indoors on beds of sand in boxes, using "dry wood so there wouldn't be any smoke." He acknowledges this "might have been dangerous," but says, "we were careful." He took advantage of competition for the recreation hall in summer to move the boys outdoors.

> We discovered a dense patch of tall oak brush east of the Ogden City Reservoir just east of our Ward boundary. We cleaned out a twenty foot area of these trees in the center of it. We constructed a good size fire pit here, and used the area as an assembly circle for the troop. From this center we cut seven trails radiating like spokes of a wheel. At the end of these, about 20 feet away, each patrol cleared out [a] 12 foot area as their patrol camp, which included a cooking fireplace and other conveniences. . . . Believe me, in such surroundings we did real scouting.

Boys sometimes stayed overnight after troop meetings. "Dil thought that was a very good idea and . . . had us write it up to send it to New York." On the other hand, "the bishop didn't like [it] at all, because he said we were pulling the boys away from the ward."

A generation of men grew up calling Dilworth Uncle Dil. This had its beginning with the Uncles Club. Dilworth records being approached by a scoutmaster who asked if he would like to associate himself with an exclusive, highly respected, international order. "Who's in it," Dilworth asked, to which the man replied, "If you sign up, that'll make two." The only requirement was you had to have hair on your chest. Dilworth qualified, and he joined. Eden Beutler says the club involved scoutmasters from all over the council. One man was refused admittance for two consecutive years because of the hair rule. The third year he appeared with rabbit fur glued to his chest, and they let him in. Club members called each other by the first name, preceded by "Uncle," as did their boys. The Uncles may have been inspired by the example of Uncle Dan Beard, one of American scouting's founders, or by Baden-Powell himself, sometimes known as scouting's uncle. Or maybe they simply thought it was better to be called Uncle than their first names, as boys sometimes wanted to do.

Dilworth disciplined the boys at camp, and could be gruff with them. A note in *The Evening Breeze*, a camp newspaper, suggests, "For those of you who are suffering from the heat, come to camp and do something you shouldn't. If the look you are sure to receive from Mr. Young doesn't cool you, it's a very bad case." Tom Feeny recalls arriving at camp, completely unexperienced, and being instructed to take a mattress tick and fill it at the straw pile. "At first I said I didn't know what a tick was, and he went and got one, and he says, 'Now go to the straw pile and get it,' and I said, 'Well, where's the straw pile?' And I guess I was getting under his skin a little. He just picked me up by the back of the neck and carried me over to the straw pile and dumped me head first in it and said, 'You'll remember it now.'" One evening Dilworth was walking along the back of the row of bunkhouses when he heard some boys swearing up a storm. He slipped silently into their dark cabin and stood unseen between the bunks to listen. One finally said, "I wonder how old man Young'd feel if he could hear us talking like this." Dilworth reached out and took him by the hair—didn't pull, just held, and the boy stiffened. "He didn't say a word, he didn't let out a yell, he just kept his mouth shut. They said, 'What's the matter, can't you talk?' He didn't say anything. The other boy that was talking, I just leaned over and put my hand over his mouth. They were the scaredest kids you ever saw. Old Jim Sanders had them that time. I said, 'Now listen, boys, this isn't half what you're going to get if you don't quit this dirty language.'"

Dilworth wanted the boys to have adventure. James Oka remembers a time when he and a number of others skipped a hike on Monte. "Dilworth Young was so upset at the rest of us that stayed in camp there that he said, 'Well, we better take you guys for another hike.'" He lined them up and said, "You follow me," and they did, on a hike through the Narrows. But it turned out some of the boys hadn't brought extra clothes, and so ran around in underwear for a day or two, and even attended flag ceremony that way. "And it worried Dilworth a little bit because he started wondering whether any of us got colds." Dilworth tested his boys.

Jack Davis, an eagle scout on the Kiesel Staff, tells of a time Dilworth challenged his mapmaking abilities. "I'll bet your first class map wasn't worth anything." Jack said he thought it was, so Dilworth said "I want you to show me," and sent him mapping up past Big Springs and over the mountain and around. "It was a big area. It took me all day. I left at 8:00 o'clock in the morning, and I didn't come back for lunch, and it was 6:00 o'clock that evening before I came back, and all I did was gather my data, make my notes. I spent the rest of the week drawing the map. I presented it to Dilworth, and he said, 'Well, that's pretty good.' And from him that was a great compliment." He says he sometimes had his feelings hurt and was often frightened by Dilworth's gruffness, but he echoes other scouts when he says, "I knew I'd be back for more. I had to go prove myself to him. There was no way I could avoid that challenge."

For all his gruffness, Dilworth tended to be patient with the boys when they had done something really wrong. Tom Feeny remembers junior troop leaders borrowing the camp trailer for various things, and in the process putting dents in the fenders of Dilworth's car. "It's amazing, why he kept getting more bumps in that fender, and nobody ever knew who did it. But he knew. He didn't worry much about it. He was a person who accepted those kind of things." George Lowe describes eight-hour lifeguarding stints at Kiesel. "Somebody'd bring lunch down to us in the hot sun." Once he fell asleep. Dilworth noticed, and staged a fake drowning, beginning with one scout pushing another out of a boat. "I slept through the whole doggone thing." George woke up and everything seemed normal, and he only learned later what had happened. Dilworth discussed it with the boys at the campfire that night. George tells of a time he and another junior leader named Frank were sent to Bear Lake on an errand. Dilworth told them, "George, you're to drive all the way, every bit of the way. Frank isn't to back the car or anything." So they went and completed their business, but when George came back to the car, Frank was already in the driver's seat and would not get out. "So he drove home." Sure enough, Frank sideswiped a car near

Brigham. "And it did a modest amount of damage. So we pulled the fender out, and he gave his name and said his father would take care of everything." Frank told George, "'We can't let Dil know what happened.' Very adamant. Well, what am I to do. Am I to tell on him or not. You know, a young kid like that." Frank took the car to the auto club on Kiesel Avenue and instructed the mechanic to have it fixed pronto and that his father, a member of the club, would pay. He got his father to drive them to camp that afternoon. "I've forgotten what excuse he had as to why we couldn't bring the car up."

> [Dilworth] just sort of listened, didn't say anything. And I later found out that he had taken Frank off, about three or four days later while Frank was stewing with a guilty conscience, and said, "Frank, you know, I can't help but know that there was an accident." And he said, "I think you must have been driving." Frank admitted that he was. He said, "Well, you know, if you do the wrong thing, sometimes you pay a penalty for it." And Frank said, "Well, Dad paid for it."

Dil reasoned with him, but wasn't sure if he listened. George found out only after thirty-odd years had passed. "I never thought he talked to Frank. But he had the courtesy to talk to him in private about it and try to get across the point."

Dilworth was a strict merit badge counselor. Leonore remembers a boy coming to pass a merit badge. Dilworth checked down the list, asking questions. One requirement was to take apart and remount a door handle. Dilworth asked if he had done it. He said no, but he'd read through it and understood the process. Dilworth made him demonstrate, with the lock on the door, on the spot. He tells of another scout who came to pass a badge. The scout assured Dilworth he had done everything, or most everything, and wanted him to skip the test and sign the card. This was the last badge he needed before becoming an eagle. He was from the eagle patrol—every other boy in his patrol was or would be an eagle. Dilworth suspected he had not mastered the material, and in questioning him, he learned it was so. He talked to him longer and found out that many other merit badge counselors had let him slide by without doing this or that. Dilworth refused to pass him, but instead of sending him away, had him come back, again and again, over a period of months, and worked through every one of the badges with him. Then he received his eagle.

LaMar Buckner, a scout who grew up to be council president, tells of informing Dilworth he wanted to pass his cooking merit badge at Camp Kiesel. "He said, 'Do you think you can cook without killing somebody?'" LaMar said he could. Dilworth told him to send a runner up after each meal and he himself would come down and sample the food. LaMar, though intimidated, agreed. He cooked the meals, and when each was ready sent his runner up after him. "I can still see [him] to this day, his long legs coming down the trail as he worked his way down to my camp." Dilworth sampled his omelet and said, "Kind of burnt it on this side, didn't you, LaMar." LaMar said, "Well, it's just the way I like it." Another meal he cooked a biscuit in the reflector oven. "Got it a little doughy over here, LaMar?" "No, it's just the way I like it." And so on until the end of the week, with hardly a word of encouragement. LaMar asked if he had passed. Dilworth said, "LaMar, did you do everything?" LaMar said yes, and reminded him of all he had done. Again Dilworth said, "LaMar, did you do everything?" LaMar again ticked off all he had done. Dilworth asked a third time, at which point LaMar got out the book and read off the requirements for him. One requirement was to carve and serve a meal. LaMar hadn't had a roast at camp, but told him he had carved a roast many times at home. "He said, 'Well fine, you'll have no objection then coming to my house a week from Sunday and serving dinner for us.' I could have died right there on the spot. There's nothing in the scout book that said I had to go to Uncle Dil's house."

He practiced all week. "We never ate so well in our lives as we did that week. This was in the depths of the depression, but my mother had a different roast every [day]." He rode his bike up to the Young house after Sunday School, knocked, and almost got away before Dilworth and his family drove up in the car. Dilworth sent him to the kitchen to help Gladys prepare. "I've never seen a roast like it before or since," full of bone and gristle. "That's when I learned that they didn't pay scout executives very much." Dilworth had him say the blessing, and in the course of the meal sent him for bread. LaMar describes trying to cut the fresh bread with a dull butcher knife, squashing it down in the process, then stretching it out with his hands. After the meal, he asked Dilworth once more if he had passed. Dilworth said, "'Did you do everything?' I said, 'I sure hope so,' because by then I wasn't sure I wanted to be an eagle scout." LaMar says, "Every scout was important to [him], and I was just as important as the rest. And if I was going to pass a merit badge, he was going to make me do my very best, and go all the way, no shortcuts." Years later, when LaMar became a mission president, Dilworth sent him a note saying, "Got your head above water yet, kid? If not, keep cooking."

Outfitting Themselves

If in winter Dilworth was gone more evenings than not on training sessions, and on more Sundays than not on scout-related speaking engagements, in summer it was camp that kept him occupied. Some of the early years, when the children were very small, he had them live at camp, but later (perhaps when Leonore got old enough for her presence to annoy the boys), he began to commute from Ogden. Up at 4:00 in the morning, he might try to get in a little yard work, then report to the scout office to take care of affairs in the morning, before heading up to camp in the afternoon. He would be there until evening, perhaps catching a meal with the staff, or if it grew too late, spending the night.

Alf Freeman soon resigned, and George Bergstrom left in 1928 to become the scout executive in Santa Monica. Alone, Dilworth felt freer to innovate, which for him meant getting away from the school format and the "'hidebound camping one learns from books.'" Even the boys, were aware of his dissatisfaction. George Lowe says Dilworth "tried to get them out of the little cabins. . . . He hated to see the kids sleeping in there." They set up campsites in the Wheatgrass river bottom, with tables and fire pits, and eventually built other campsites. Beginning in 1931, boys were supplied with cooking equipment and tents, or slept in one of four tepees the council owned. Dilworth speaks of the camp cook Nellie Rose in his history. "We called Mrs. Rose 'Ma.' She was a gem." One of her assistants was Golda Acord, "the 'Golden Acorn.'" George remembers Ma Rose's excellent meals, mentioning in particular the hot chocolate, called "muddy water," but says, "[Dilworth] didn't like this. He wanted them to cook for themselves." According to the *Standard*, the cost for a week at Kiesel, including meals, remained $4.50 from its opening until 1930, when it rose by a dollar. That year the council advertised a camp stamp book that a boy could fill with fifty-five ten cent stamps—"Remember, 'A Scout Is Thrifty.'" But the fee for a week at Kiesel dropped to fifty cents in 1931, when boys were told to cook food they brought from home or bought, at cost, in the camp store. By 1937, the camp store no longer sold food.

The day hikes expanded into overnighters. Jimmie Hobbs remembers a blindfolded hike in 1927 that seemed to go on a long ways, though years later Dilworth let on to him they had slept only a short distance from the camp. Dilworth's history says the first real campouts were in Bear Wallow. "These early trips were poorly equipped. We took a blanket or quilt (rolled up like a horse collar) each and carried the food in flour sacks." George Lowe remembers the horse-collar sleeping rolls, sometimes with linen liners, and maybe another item or two, rolled lengthwise with the ends tied together, worn around the back of the neck, down across the front of the shoulders then behind the arms. The way was hot on one early trip, the trail bad. The boys stopped and wouldn't go any farther. Dil writes, "One boy expressed it right. I said, 'What's the matter, you give out?' and he says, 'No, I give up.'" Three men relayed forty horse collars and eighty sacks the last quarter mile.

Kiesel at different times had pack animals. Or, boys could rent horses for a dollar a day from the outfitter down the road. Dilworth's history tells of a gift of a mule, likely in 1929, and the difficulty he had in getting it to Kiesel. "I got a couple of scouts who thought they'd like the experience to take turns riding it as far as camp. They thought they'd get there in one day, twenty-five miles." By the end of the first day, they had reached Huntsville, twelve miles in twelve hours. He arranged to pasture it that night, and came for it in the morning in his little red Essex, folding down the windshield, rigging a set of reins from clothesline rope, then putting the mule in front and getting in the car. "[I] turned the engine on and honked at him, and he went. Every time I'd honk, he'd trot, till he got too tired to do that, and I'd finally just butt up against it and push it." Joe Cummings, one of the staff officers, loaded the mule once to lead a group up Wheatgrass, on or around the 4th of July. "You probably could have gone for a month on the stuff he took, like we always did in those days." A boy lit a ten cent firecracker and threw it. "That thing rolled and stopped right under that jackass. And when it went off, that donkey rose straight in the air." It came down on Joe's foot, then bucked a half mile down the trail, emptying its pack. Dilworth headed it off finally in the car. They loaded it again and went up the canyon, making camp on a green, damp island in the creek. After supper, the mule cocked his ears, brayed, pawed the ground, and jerked at his tether until they let him loose. Then he got on one of the boy's blankets and wouldn't move. In the morning when they started out, Joe glanced back and saw a mountain lion, sitting cross-legged on the cliff, watching them.

Dilworth, at a scouters' convention at Estes Park in 1926, had read of Enos A. Mills' adventures on Longs Peak, and hungered to see for himself. He and a few other executives arranged a hike. William Brazee Hawkins, who was along, says Dil was a "perfect clown for the entire trip, trying to climb up every side path and every tree." Dilworth describes no particular trouble following the markers up over the rocks, except for the altitude. "As you get above the thirteen thousand foot level, one finds out, unless he's used to it, that his legs go numb about every tenth step. . . . It took us about an hour-and-a-half or two hours to go the last thousand feet." Dilworth spotted a ridge from on top he thought he could reach and save himself time on the way down. Dr. George Hill, also present, said, "You'd better not!" Golden Kilburn echoed, "'I wouldn't do it if I were you, Dil.' I says, 'Oh, I think I'll try it,'" and down he went, over a series of four-foot ledges, like giant stairs, and in no time at all was a thousand feet down.

"All of a sudden I began to realize that something was happening." It had rained the previous evening, leaving a layer of clear ice. "You couldn't see it on the rocks, and first thing you know, I slipped. I caught myself, and then began to worry, and I could see when I got there that I couldn't make that ridge." The ledge he approached dropped a thousand feet. A grand glacial cirque arced up to one side, two thousand feet deep. He crawled over onto the other side to try to rejoin the trail, only to be met by another great cirque, just as deep, both of them covered with ice. "I was caught."

"Well, I got scared," he says. "I began to get hysterical, began to kind of laugh and cry to myself, and I thought, now wait a minute." He thought of Seymour B. Young's adventures on the plains during his handcart mission, and scolded himself:

> "Your grandpa wouldn't have done that. Now you calm down." And then I started to work my way back up. I knew I had to go back up to the top. And as I said, you climb once then rest. And I climbed very carefully, till I came to a ledge a little higher than usual. . . . And I leaped up and grabbed onto the edge, and pulled myself over and lay on my back till I got my breath again, and then I was out of the ice. And I went up that mountain, and you wouldn't believe it. I didn't lose my breath, my legs didn't go numb. I climbed up in fifteen minutes what I couldn't have done in two hours before. . . . And when I got clear of the cliffs, I thought I heard a whistle blowing up there. And [as] I came in sight of the ridge, Golden Kilburn [was] standing there blowing his whistle, yelling. When he saw my face clear up over that rock, he said, "Thank God you're back."

"He said, 'I couldn't leave. I knew you were in trouble. I decided I would not go down this mountain till I found out where you were.'" Dilworth felt he was protected, and that his energy climbing back up was evidence of it. "Now you'll say it was adrenaline, perhaps, but it wasn't." He adds, "I found out there the value of friendship, too."

"We got next to ourselves then and . . . we decided we were going to really have a knowledge of how to camp." Milton Yorgason recalls being part of a group sent north from Monte Cristo, perhaps in 1927, "in search of a practical trail to the Logan Scout Camp by way of the high ridges." Dilworth was to meet them at the Danish Dugway,

> . . . but we didn't make it as soon as we expected, so we turned off to the left and came down Curtis Creek where we thought we would soon reach the highway. It was farther than we thought and we spent the night in a narrow canyon without bedding or adequate food and at least two of the party were water logged and were half sick as a result. We met [Dilworth] looking for us on the highway the following afternoon. I have never been so exhausted before or since. That night in camp, Ma Rose and 'the Golden Acorn' sang a song to the wanderers and presented us with miniature quilts so we wouldn't be caught out like that again.

Dilworth took four men on a similar trip, perhaps that fall, two-and-a-half days cross-country from Kiesel to Camp Logan. Wayne Hales brought a jar of mayonnaise. Dilworth, in a homemade, Nelson-type pack (frame with sack attached), carried a commercial sleeping bag he describes as weighing twenty-five pounds, a box of Bisquick, and a twelve inch frying pan. They all became grease-sick on his cooking. Russ Croft made a fire six feet long and burnt it to coals, then laid on hellebore stalks thick enough that he could sleep on them. But the hellebore let off steam in the night, and finally "Buss" woke them up with his call, "Pee-yuuu, I can't stand this anymore." Dil remembers, "Just then a coyote howled over on the next hill. Buss said, 'Ah, shuddup,' and the coyote did.'" The third day out, Dilworth hung his frying pan in a tree, Wayne Hales perched his mayonnaise jar under a rock, and the party marched into Camp Logan with sleeping rolls only.

The overnighters for the boys at Kiesel grew into two- and

three-nighters. A page promoting camp in the May 1929 *Standard* (which became an annual feature) suggests trips to Wheeler and Woodruff Creek, Sugar Pine Creek, Skunk Creek, La Plata Mines and a half-dozen other one-, two-, and four-day trips, including to spots as distant as Chinatown and Camp Logan. The 1930 scout page announces a fifty cent return fare for boys going to Camp Logan who do not hike back at least to Blacksmith's Fork, "where the council truck can reach them. . . . Last year the cost of bringing boys back to Camp Kiesel after they had hiked was $2.00 apiece. This extra charge is to help pay that loss." The boys used bedrolls still. "One night Sherman Barton and I sat up all night and made a mummy-type sleeping bag out of eight 100-pound flour sacks and four pounds of kapok . . . seed fluff. This was the best filler in those days except feathers and would keep one warm down to 28°F. . . . After that we taught many boys to make these bags." Paul Bieler's troop made bags from unbleached muslin. Tom Feeny and other scouts used outing flannel.

George Lowe believes his must have been one of the first bags, Dilworth making himself one at the same time. George describes getting down on the living room floor at Dilworth's house on Eccles to trace out a pattern on butcher paper. He remembers Little Dil "scrambling over our papers . . . getting in the way," and Dilworth telling him to behave. "Then we went down to Boyles and were able to obtain some so-called down—it was mostly halfway between feathers and down—and some mattress ticking, and we made our bags out of that." George's bag, sewn in sections from vertical-blue-striped ticking ("the only thing that would . . . keep the down in"), was tapered and had a slit in the side for climbing in and out. He remembers Dilworth saying he was more comfortable in a rectangular bag, and making his that way. George later added a flannel lining, which made it "much more comfortable and much warmer." The 1933 scout page says, "Two blankets weigh 7 pounds and do not keep you warm. One sleeping bag weighs 5 pounds and keeps you warm and comfortable. Why wear out your mother's blankets or quilts? You can make a good kapok bag in two hours, after which, sleeping in the hills will be a joy." A council camping guidebook written by Dilworth and published by the Rotary Club instructs, "Baste the [bag] every two feet to hold the kapok in place and quilt the whole thing in four-inch squares with a sewing machine. (An ordinary machine will quilt the bag if tension is adjusted). . . . The Scout and his mother can make the bag at a cost not to exceed $2.50."

Longer hikes "forced us to invent cheap backpacks," Dilworth writes in his history. The 1933 scout page reminds scoutmasters that the making of packs belongs on the checklist for preparing for camp. Eden Beutler describes one early type of pack whose vertical wood posts were joined by sections of nail keg, with eyelets for lashing, the whole affair wrapped in muslin to keep the bowed frame off the back. He and some others made packs from three-eighths inch pipe. His own had snaps for canteen and drinking cup and an extension on one post in which he kept his fishing pole. Dilworth came to advocate a modified Yukon design. Plans appear in the guidebook and on the scout page for 1934. Now boards were used for the posts, broad sides facing each other, with straight hardwood or plywood crosspieces along one set of edges, and canvas or rope lacing joining the others. The guidebook says, "We like the Yukon type pack because any boy can make one out of scraps of wood to be found in any back yard. (If it isn't your yard be sure and obtain permission to take the wood.)" Paul Bieler's troop used wood from casket shipping crates from local mortuaries. "We got them for nothing, and the undertakers were glad to get rid of them, and it's all hard wood." They carved grooves in the sides to make them lighter, and obtained army surplus straps for ten cents apiece. The 1934 scout page advises that "cheap woven cotton rope" is adequate for the webbing.

Early on, the council recommended ground cloths, seven feet square, folded over the sleeping bag. These could be made from "anything which will turn water, such as auto top material, treated canvas, etc. . . . Oil cloth will only do for a week, but until it cracks it is both light and practical." The 1933 scout page adds, "We have just learned that airplane wing cloth is 35 cents per yard instead of 50 cents per yard. You can make a real tent for $2.25." It notes that, with a waterproof sleeping bag cover, a tent is not required. "If it rains, all you have to do is to be curled up comfortably in your bag and 'let 'er rain.'" Dilworth stressed tents more as time went on. The guidebook and the 1934 scout page give diagrams for one-boy, tapered-back pup tents, the mouth an equilateral triangle with three-foot sides, pitched over a rope staked to the ground on one end and on the other tied to a tree, with floor. A new wrinkle appears in the 1940 edition, a tent whose mouth measures three feet on the floor, five feet on one side, and four on the other, this shorter side folding up to form a canopy. Dilworth says the waterproofed tents "were also the covers for the bags and proved to be perfect for the purpose." He stresses, "The boys made these also."

Waterproofing involved "dipping [melted] paraffin wax in gasoline and then painting it on the muslin." The 1933 scout page advises that a seven-foot square piece of cloth requires a pound of paraffin and seven quarts of gasoline. "When articles have been waterproofed with paraffin they become quite inflammable. . . . Be sure that tents and sleeping bags are in a position at night to insure safety from the sparks." Tom Feeny, who led hikes as a junior officer, remembers boys snuggling up to the fire and kicking the coals and their bags catching fire, and him throwing dirt on them to put them out. "None of them ever blazed up. . . . [They] probably wouldn't be approved now, but it was great at the time." Paul Bieler describes painting a light coat of melted wax, without gasoline, directly onto muslin, an operation to be performed "on a hot day." George Lowe soaked his in linseed oil and dried it on the clothesline. The guidebook recommends oil, noting the cloth takes about a week to dry. Later scout pages recommend raw linseed oil or fish oil painted on with a brush, one coat on the sides and two on the floor and back.

Dilworth taught tin can cooking. A can from a restaurant garbage pail with a wire bale attached served as well as any pot. A thigh-high fire allowed to burn down provided a bed of even, clean-burning coals. The cans didn't char or blacken overly when not exposed to the flame, but even if they did, one "knock[ed] them in the head with an ax" and buried them at the end of the trip anyway, according to the scout page, or "'ease[d] 'em down a gopher hole.'" Cleanup was with "S. O. S. cleaning wool. . . . Leave the dishtowel home. You're going to sterilize your dishes with boiling water and dry them in the sun." The guidebook states that "two cans, No. 2 1/2 and No. 2, form the basis of all good cooking." It also recommends a dessert spoon, a case (i.e. sheath) knife, and a pair of pliers. Percy Hadley's scouts carried bailed Crisco cans for beans, stews, oatmeal, rice puddings, and so on. A tomato can served for cocoa and other drinks. A pea can did duty as a drinking cup. The three cans (and a soup can, if you wanted to go the whole route) slipped inside each other. The bundle, with utensils, could be rolled inside the sleeping bag. (Eden Beutler's troop made canteens from juice cans with flannel covers, with lids from turpentine cans soldered on.)

Dilworth advocated boiling over frying. "Outdoor cooking is such that the grease either is cooked too much or not enough," warns an "Old Timer" on the 1935 scout page. As the guidebook puts it, "Boiled food will not make you sick even if not quite done." For breakfast, boys cooked rice or wheat or oatmeal mush or stewed (i.e. boiled dehydrated) fruit. Recommended lunches included sandwiches (first day out), biscuits, dried beef, tuna, raw carrots, cheese cubes, raisins, nuts (except walnuts, which cankered the mouth), and, (available at the council office), orange- and lemonade. Knorr Soup Rolls went into supper noodle dishes. Boys also cooked stews, spaghetti (i.e. noodles cooked in tomato juice and cheese), and navy beans, with candy (chocolate or suckers) for dessert. "Measure each quantity," warns the *Standard-Examiner* article. "Do not take whole packages. If you are going to drink cocoa twice take four spoons full, not a ten cent can." Dilworth considered five pounds of food sufficient for two days, six meals. "Do not carry canned goods except small tuna and milk. Canned foods are heavy, and they give boys no chance to really learn to cook. Anyone can open a can. But it takes a real camper to concoct a meal out of raw materials—and then live to tell the tale." He recommended single-portion milk cans. "Nothing flavors the sox and towel in a pack so much as a leaky milk can. One boy last year surveyed a pair of sox so treated and decided the only way he could get the nourishment out of his milk was to fry his sox."

Dilworth's history says, "We decided to have hot bread every meal—this is a very good morale builder." Eden Beutler says some of his boys made bread twists, cooked on a stick and pealed off when done. He describes a bread cooked in the bean can, spaced with twigs inside the tomato can, so that the inner can acted as the pan and the outer one as the oven, the whole placed in the coals. Dilworth's favorite was "hike bread," invented by Horace Kephart, "the old woodsman." The 1933 scout page warns that "ordinary baking powder biscuits made with shortening will upset a boy after a meal or two, but not hike bread. It tastes almost like a yeast bread mother makes at home." The recipe, repeated in the guidebook, in other scout pages, and in his history, contains one of each thing: one cup flour, one teaspoon baking powder, one tablespoon sugar, one pinch salt, water, and butter to grease the pan.

> Stir rapidly into a sticky dough, spread this [on pan] and bake until done. . . . One-half this recipe was enough to make a good sized biscuit for one meal, enough for the butter and jam which keeps boys from getting homesick. . . . One could add cocoa and sugar and have a cake. Or he could add an egg and have muffins, or raisins for raisin bread.

The dough was baked in a reflector oven, which became standard equipment. The oven consisted of two sheets of tin, 8 1/2 inches by 6 1/2 inches, with corner pieces to hold them up at an angle facing the fire. This gave more or less even heat from three sides. For packing, the stove folded up around its own, inch-deep pan. Paul Bieler points out that, while he made his from tin, costing less than a dollar, if you didn't have a dollar you could make it for nothing with flattened-out No. 5 tin cans. The only way to go wrong with the recipe was to stir too long, in which case the bread came out like sweet hardtack, or else to "drown the miller," as

Eden Beutler put it, when boys added too much water. He always carried extra mix for such occasions. The recipe concludes:

> Watch the butter melt into the bread. Then add a half inch layer of jam—and eat. Heaven is in your hands—and home was never like this. Wipe your hands on the seat of your pants."

(Boys carried butter in new, half-pint paint- or other pressure-top cans.)

By 1934 Dilworth's program was in place. Kiesel was a hiking camp. Boys were equipped with homemade packs, tents, sleeping bags and reflector ovens—total weight, less clothes and food, thirteen pounds. A letter on the 1931 scout page states, "In the past, camping has been done for you." This article, signed by each member of the fifteen-man council camping committee, omits Dilworth's signature, but echoes his emerging philosophy. "We are at the beginning of real Scouting for the first time."

CHAPTER 7

Into His Own

Money and Travel

In the 1970s, while advising a young relative on becoming a scout executive, Dilworth pointed out that most of what executives did anymore was raise money. Russ Croft says that, even in Dilworth's day, fund-raising was a big job. There was no United Way (though the *Standard* refers as early as 1937 to the Community Chest). "We got a little money from the wards, but not much. . . . We had to get out and raise every dime we got." Russ recalls that one of the council committee's fund-raisers was city judge Jack Hendricks, well known to the proprietors of the honky-tonks on 25th street. "All he had to do was go down and rap on their door and say, 'I've come down, I want some money for the Boy Scouts,' and boy, they shelled out in a hurry." Dilworth courted benefactors and was conscientious about showing appreciation. He paid special attention to Mrs. Shearman. "When it was Christmas time, he'd have a bunch of scouts there singing Christmas carols to her. If it was her birthday, they'd be there with roses." The *Standard* in 1928 reprints a letter from Fred G. Taylor, retiring chairman of the council court of honor, who had moved to New York, describing a party of scouts lined up on the loading platform at his departure, unexpected, saluting him while one of their number pinned a badge on his coat. Jack Davis recalls being sent, in full uniform, with a scout statue and commendation written on a scroll, to the office of Matt Browning in the First Security building, where he made the presentation alone.

Things were all the more difficult during the depression. George Lowe remembers looking at a sign in the scout office that said, "Prosperity is just around the corner," and asking Dilworth, "Really, do you think it is?" Dilworth, typically blunt, said, "I haven't seen any sign of it." Russ Croft remembers him cutting his own salary at one point. "He didn't wait for the council to do it. He didn't wait for us to run out of money. He saw things coming, so he just [drew] his paycheck [for] less than he was authorized to take."

George Lowe tells how Dilworth landed a contribution of canned goods from a wholesale grocer for Camp Kiesel. "We opened the first case, took out about two cans—split bottoms. And about three fourths the cans in there were bulging. . . . I said, 'Well that dirty so and so.'" Dilworth, he says, was charitable. "'Well, he's done a lot for scouting, and I'm sure he didn't realize that these were spoiled.'" The service clubs did their part. The American Legion in 1929 had a project to raise $10,000 "to carry on boy scouting," with a special appropriation to send twenty boys to camp. The Rotary Club presented the council with a Ford truck. Dil says, "[The] truck was so heavy the load it carried had to be very light." Once Little Leonore fell down and got her leg run over by it, but it wasn't broken. Dil continues, "We wrassled that truck all over the country, wherever we went camping, for as long as the truck held up. Finally however it wore out and wouldn't go up the steepest hills anyhow, so we finally had to sell it." A car dealer bought it. A while later, a potential buyer called and asked if the odometer had kicked over. Without giving it a second thought, he told him it had kicked over twice. The salesman called and bawled him out for making him lose the sale.

Dilworth always maintained that if you had a reputation for honesty it would save you many times. Once the council auditor showed him a receipt in his handwriting for $500, with a bank deposit that day for $300, which left him $200 short. He wracked his brains but could not remember—it had been nearly a year. They visited the president of the council, where Dilworth said, "Sir, I can't account for this. But I know one thing—I didn't take the money. There is an error somewhere and I don't know what the error is. But I suppose you will want my resignation and so I shall write you one. You can do with me what you will—if you want to prosecute me, go ahead. I can't tell you more than that. I don't know." He wrote his letter, and two days later stood before the finance committee. The president said, "Dil, we know you didn't take the money. We are instructing our auditor to find out how the mistake occurred." He writes that he could easily have been ruined on that occasion. The auditor never could completely explain it, but because of Dil's reputation, "it never was brought up again."

Dilworth says, "The council sent me to all the scout executive conventions that were ever held, either on the East or on the Pacific Coast." He mentions specifically Estes Park, Hot Springs, Cornell, Breton Woods. He attended all the Region 12 conventions. In February, 1925, this meeting came to Ogden, attended by national dignitaries including James E. West, Chief Scout Executive, who spoke in the Ogden Tabernacle. Dilworth liked to tell about a time at Estes Park that he and Dr. George R. Hill slipped out of a presentation. Dr. Hill was David O. McKay's brother-in-law and a long-time Superintendent of the Sunday School. This particular afternoon, "The meetings were dead and the teachers were poor, so I said, 'Let's go up on the ridge and see where Enos A. Mills walked.'" They drove to the trail head, then hiked to the ridge. Dilworth was cold in his sweater, while Dr. Hill stayed warm in his mackinaw. They got to talking about evolution.

> And I said, "Dr. Hill . . . over in the Museum of Natural History in Chicago, they've got a series of pictures or skeletons . . . showing an animal about the size of a cat, then about the size of a dog, then about the size of a calf, then about the size of a cow, then it has a horse. The evolution of a horse, it's called. Do you believe that?"
>
> He says, "Yes, I do."
>
> I said, "Well, I wish you'd tell me what you feel about Man. Did

Man come up from lower orders? Didn't Adam come out of the Garden of Eden?"

"Oh," he said, "I think Adam came out of the Garden of Eden, alright, but here's how it happened. . . . The Lord by evolution created bodies, and when he had evolved a body that was fit for Man to enter," and this is the way he said it, "he whisked the spirit of the animal out and put the spirit of Adam in, and Adam became a living soul."

I said, "You don't believe that, do you?"

He says, "Yes, I do."

Thirty years later, Dilworth ran into him on the street and asked if he remembered their climb. He said yes, he remembered. And did he remember their talk about evolution? Yes. "And you remember you said to me that when Adam was created, the Lord whisked the spirit of the ape out of the body and put Adam into it?" He remembered. Dilworth asked, "And do you still believe it?" Dr. Hill answered, "More than ever!"

Dilworth took the family to a convention in April of about 1935. On the road back, they reached Salida, Colorado, at dusk, where it began to snow. They pressed ahead, thinking to cross Monarch Pass to the west side of the mountains. The snow got deeper and deeper as they drove, but there was no place to turn around. Dil writes:

> We came to a stop, not knowing what to do. Just then we saw a light, a small light, over to one side. I got out and walked about fifty yards across a seeming flat and came to a cabin. I knocked. A man came to the door. I explained our predicament. He said that he was up there that one night to get his cabins in order for summer camping. We could come in and stay with him. He gave us a little supper from what he had. We put the children down on a couch with our two lap robes and sat by his stove the rest of the night. . . . Undoubtedly had he not been there with his light showing as we passed we would have frozen to death on that high pass.

In the morning, the sky was clear and the storm had passed

through. They tried to pay their host, but he would take nothing.

Dilworth led a group of scouts to what was to have been the first National Jamboree, in Washington D. C. in 1935. The boys, from Ogden and Logan councils, had their uniforms, and all the travel arrangements had been made, when the jamboree had to be canceled due to the polio epidemic of that year. In a meeting with the boys and their parents, the council decided to go anyway. They left by train from Ogden, stopping in Omaha and Florence, then to Chicago, where they saw the Field Museum of Natural History, then to Rochester for a tour of Eastman Kodak, then to Albany. Here they boarded a riverboat, stopping at West Point for a tour, then continuing to New York City. The boys kept the hotel elevators occupied between their rooms and the basement swimming pool. In Schenectady, they toured General Electric, arriving early enough for breakfast in their cafeteria, with all the hotcakes and oatmeal and coffee and juice and ham and eggs you could eat. Percy Hadley remembers that "out of a hundred and eighty-six people, nobody took a drink of coffee, not one. Those people'd sit there, and they were just [flabbergasted]. They couldn't believe that many people and nobody took coffee." They toured New York City, and saw Loretta Young in "The Crusades." Both Cecil B. deMille and Lord Baden-Powell, a very old man, were present and addressed the group. They attended church along the way. Tom Feeny remembers Dilworth taking him and the few other Catholic scouts to St. Patrick's in New York City, Dilworth standing in the back in his scout shorts. Tom remembers people giving the LDS scouts a hard time. They "wanted to know about all the wives and so on, and they made some pretty ribald and stupid remarks. [Dilworth] never said anything bad about it. He always had a good answer for them." Before coming home they visited Arlington National Cemetery in Virginia and Mount Vernon.

The council sent a delegation to the 1937 Jamboree, also in Washington, though this time Dilworth stayed behind. Don Buswell, who attended this one, remembers visiting Niagara Falls and Palmyra, New York, where they attended the first Hill Cumorah Pageant. The council was asked to supply a scout to give the opening prayer, and Don was assigned. "I worried about that all day long, and finally I . . . told them I just couldn't do it. I was just shaking. And that's one of the things that has bothered me all my life. I could have given the opening prayer at the first Hill Cumorah Pageant." Eden Beutler attended as an adult leader. He remembers orders to make sure the non-Mormon boys got to their church, whether he got to his or not. He remembers lots of short stops, and a longer visit to the Smithsonian, where they used the buddy system. Back on the bus they had the boys count off. Leo Loll, son of a prominent Ogden citizen, was missing. His buddy and five others went back, two for each floor, making the loop, but no Leo. Eden had a loud, two-fingered whistle that he used to gather the boys, four descending notes, then "'You're a horse's neck,' . . . They could hear me for a mile, and they'd just come a-running." Eden let out with his whistle, but Leo didn't come. They took the scouts to the YMCA, where they would be spending the night. "When we got back down there, here was a telegram from Uncle Dil. 'Eden, don't let Leo out of your sight. Take ahold of his hand and keep him with you.' So from then on—brother. He'd sent a telegram home to his dad or called him on the phone and told him about it, and boy, he called Uncle Dil and just give him the devil. We'd run off and left his son."

Real Scouting

The council held annual May Fiestas, gatherings where scouts competed against each other in first class skills: fire by friction, water boiling, trailing, mapping, scout's pace, whittling, height-judging and hot cake cooking (flipped with the pan). Star, life and eagle scouts, referred to as merit badge scouts, competed in their own events, in addition to which there were patrol events, such as bugling, tent pitching, wall scaling and first aid. The 1924 event, an overnighter in the river bottom just west of Ogden Stadium, featured buffalo sandwiches, with meat from Antelope Island. In 1926 the Fiesta, held Saturday in the Coliseum, included an exhibition of Japanese fencing and a fly-casting competition, first prize a $10 fishing pole. By 1931 this had become the May

Circus, commencing at the mouth of North Ogden Canyon, with the tests at stations a quarter mile apart. The boys camped at the spring near the top of the divide, finishing up at the Chard Store in Liberty "at some hour Saturday Morning, according to the speed of the hikers." The modern term, "Camporee," occurs in the announcement for 1934. Though held in the stadium, the itinerary reflects the new emphasis on camping: "Patrols of scouts, the best in their respective troops, will camp overnight in the ball field. . . . The boys must cook three meals, make camp, pitch tents, arrange gadgets for storage of food, etc." Jack Davis remembers Dilworth at camporees. "He'd actually come and camp for the night. He'd bring his sleeping bag and his reflector oven and his own food and he'd be right there cooking along with the kids. . . . He'd be on their program, he'd be their official judge, and just go off in his own camp and invite anybody to come that thought they could go in there and do business with him."

Dilworth writes in his history that the earliest three-day hikes at Kiesel were on Monte Cristo, two days out from Kiesel, then one day back. A note in the *Standard* from July 5, 1928, records what must have been one of the earliest: "With dusty clothes, horse collar packs, and happy smiles, 48 scouts of Camp Kiesel came into camp after a three-day trip into the headwaters of South Fork Canyon. Each scout carried a pup tent and a small supply of food." Milton Yorgason recalls a group that left without cooking utensils. Dilworth sent Milton and another boy after them, with "instructions to bawl the leader out good for his negligence, but . . . I was never good at that." They caught them at the head of Wheatgrass, then accompanied them to Monte and came down Dry Bread Hollow. Max Wheelwright made the trip up Dry Bread with leaders who had not been over the trail and became lost. "We hiked all day along that hollow. Hot! and we didn't find any decent water." A truck had been sent out to meet them with supplies for supper, which they didn't find until the next day. They slept on a hillside that night, then got up on the ridge and figured out where they should have been. "We were a little bit on the hungry side, but I don't remember that hurting us."

By 1929 overnighters were expected of all scouts, with a whole list of longer hikes proposed. The number of adult staff officers dropped, with scoutmasters expected to make up the slack. "Finally we went out the first day from home to a starting point and then hiked into camp," reads Dilworth's history. "We took three days for small boys and five days for larger boys. . . . This gave them experience—four nights sleeping out, fourteen meals to prepare, fifteen fires to set and put out, five days experience in hiking, caring for feet and bodies, etc. . . . Out in the hills one could imagine that bears were near and could get the thrill of the night noises." Dilworth or Sherman S. Barton led the hikes, or else sent one of the junior staff along. The 1932 scout page warns: "On its week in camp, no troop will be expected to arrive at general headquarters at Camp Kiesel until it has been out at least two nights." The scout page lists a variety of drop off points and routes, as far away as Skunk Creek, Blacksmith Fork, Bug Lake on Randolph Divide, and Lost Creek. Troops arranged for their own transportation, and boys brought their own food, made cheaper, the *Standard* notes, by raids in the pantry. The 1930 and 1940 scout pages include maps, listing ridges, cliffs, roads, trails, streams, draws and springs. The article accompanying the 1940 version notes "the trek will test the boys' ability in map reading and in hiking by means of a compass."

Percy Hadley made the trip from Liberty Divide up Davenport Canyon and over Sharp Mountain to La Plata, a ghost town. Percy says only a cabin still stood, which the boys used, besides the remains of a log saloon and a broken-down corral. Dilworth warned the boys not to go in the abandoned mines. Worth Wheelwright remembers taking that route in 1933. An airplane dropped candy on them at La Plata, which the scouts chased all over the hills. They were resupplied after two days at the head of Beaver Creek before continuing on. "Every night you'd see Brother Dil going around checking on every scout" to make sure none were homesick or just plain ill. A boy cut his leg open with an ax, so they patched him up as well as they could and packed him out.

Eden Beutler started his boys in Cottonwood Canyon at Small's Ranch and onto Ogden land and livestock land, sleeping in one of their cabins, up Lightning Ridge, over Airplane Ridge and down Skull Crack Canyon. These were "Starvation Hikes," as prescribed by the council. The hike began with the ritual of making the boys throw out all their canned goods on Eden's front lawn. One mother protested, "He'll starve to death! You don't know how he eats!" But Eden said if he wanted to go he had to go by the council rules. Boys carried no food. Eden doled out a daily meal: two pieces of cheese an inch square, four walnuts, and an inch square piece of chocolate. Beyond that, they could eat all the food they could find. They ate thimbleberries, wild currents, service berries and service berry leaves, thistle stalks, miner's lettuce, wild mustard, boiled sego lily bulbs, and chokecherries. Eden says, "At first, they didn't like service berry leaves. Then three days out, and boy, they were just running from one patch to another." They caught fish with their hands at the top of the canyon. They came into camp hungry but full of vigor and, Eden claims, weighing more than when they began. (Mothers would say afterwards, "You mean those kids ate all [that] wild stuff?" Eden answered, "Yeah, don't they look good?") They spent the remainder of the week doing traditional crafts and tests at Kiesel. "They was ready to settle down then."

Max Wheelwright remembers five-day hikes, in particular to Camp Logan and Bear Lake through Round Valley. George Lowe took supplies to groups hiking from Bear Lake to Kiesel. He himself made the trip in the opposite direction in forty hours once by walking all night. He says Dilworth "just encouraged this sort of thing. He loved to have that happen. And the more we suffered I think the more he enjoyed it." In addition to the three-day hikes, in 1933 the council sponsored two special troop camps from Chalk Creek to Mirror Lake. The Kiesel portion of the weekly camps was described in that year's scout page as simply "a rest before coming home. Hot showers will take off the dust and dirt and great campfire programs will finish off a week of adventure to remember and tell your grandchildren."

That year Dilworth revived the old style of camp briefly, cost $5.00, with bunks in the cabin and Ma Rose and the Golden Acorn doing the cooking. The week of August 21 was set aside "for scouts who like to go to camp for a vacation where they have no responsibility other than fun, pleasure and the improvement of their summer tan." This became the pattern, with "vacation" camps scheduled the last week or two of summer. The 1942 scout page stresses that troops planned their own program once off the mountain, whether crafts or tests or hikes, with open boating. "The official pool at camp will be used again this summer by the more hardy of the scouts. There is probably no pool in Utah which will give boys a greater kick than does this one." The 1945 version notes, "Expert guide services will be provided for nature hikes in botany, forestry, geology, bird study, astronomy, animal life, insect life, and weather, whenever a large enough group registers."

Tom Feeny remembers Dilworth as a fast hiker, when he wanted to be, though he often brought up the rear. "When people'd get discouraged, Dil would have a good word for them"—or a gruff one. "I saw him boot a few along that couldn't keep up on the trail, and he'd pat 'em on the behind; they couldn't go another step, and he'd tell them that they had to do it." Once Dilworth announced a race, in pairs, from Monte Cristo to Camp Kiesel. John M. Limburg, slower than the others, wound up without a partner. Dilworth told him to stick to the ridge, knowing that the other boys would head for the canyons. They did, and he did, and he won. When Tom was a tenderfoot, he and the others put rocks in one picked-on tenderfoot's sack. "He already couldn't carry what he had." Dilworth would pick it up and tote it for awhile to give him a rest, which Tom and his buddies thought was a pretty good joke. Tom remembers Dil "coming into camp carrying four or five packs besides his own because people'd given out. He was nice about it. He would even give them back their pack just before they came in."

Dilworth, in his guidebook, warns hikers to get permission before crossing private property, and not to tramp through grain or alfalfa fields. "A good camper does not borrow. He is on his own. A good camper cleans his campground. A good camper extinguishes his fire until he is sure it is out, by running his fingers through the ashes." Tom Feeny can vouch for his campground ethics. "I never have left a camp in bad shape because I can still remember him policing the camp . . . and if it wasn't perfect, we all came back." Dilworth once asked the boys at lunchtime if they had got their breakfast fires out that morning. "Yes," they assured. Had they run their fingers through the ashes? John Limburg finally admitted not having done so. "You'll have to go back—," he said, the boy's countenance falling. "But I'll go with you." The two of them returned to the campsite, and put out, not just his, but several of the other boys' as well. They slept there overnight and caught up with the others on Monte Cristo next morning.

The Carson Men

Dilworth records that at first cub scouting did not go well in Utah. "We did have two or three cub packs in the Protestant churches. The LDS Church had of course its Primary program and was not at that time interested, but we did a little cubbing." He says that "during the early period of my experiences as a scout executive, the LDS Church became alarmed over the lack of appeal scouting had to older boys." Dilworth served on a committee with George R. Hill and Oscar Kirkham and the other Utah and Idaho scout executives. The committee came up with the "Vanguard program, which the Church adopted and used for some years. This Vanguard program was the forerunner and the basis upon which the Boy Scouts organized their original Explorer program." The *Standard's* scout pages first mention them in connection with the first Carson Hike in 1932. "The council has been asked by a group of vanguards to hike from Camp Kiesel to the Lake Ruth camp [i.e. Camp Steiner] of the Salt Lake scouts, a distance of about 90 miles."

Russ Croft says of the Carson hikes, "That was one of Dil's innovations. . . . That was Dil's baby." It must have seemed a logical extension of the hikes the boys were already taking. Max

Wheelwright attended the first one, arriving Sunday night at Camp Kiesel with the others and sleeping in the cabins in order to get an early start Monday morning. Max smashed his thumb in the shutters in the sleeping cabins, but didn't dare tell anyone for fear they would make him stay home. "In the morning my thumb was so swollen I could not tie my shoelaces, and I had to get a buddy of mine to tie [them]." The first day took them up Skull Crack Canyon and down Guilder Sleeve to Lost Creek. Max remembers Dilworth became confused on the ridge about which canyon was Guilder Sleeve. "So he said to a couple of us, 'Come on along, and we'll go down here, and we'll just hike faster than the others.'" If it proved the wrong one, they could hike up and tell the others before they got too far down. Max remembers Dilworth's long legs heading downhill. "I took about three steps to his two." It proved the right canyon, so they camped, making their way up Toone Canyon next day to Chinatown. This bowl, on private land, is cut by a wash into the side of the ridge through loose, red conglomerate rock, into a forest of spires and balancing, teardrop boulders, much like Bryce Canyon in southern Utah. "I had never been to Bryce Canyon, and so to me it was just fantastic. But a couple of the fellows . . . went, 'Oh, I've been to Bryce. This is nothing.'"

They descended to Echo Canyon next. Max remembers hiking up the highway two or three miles before cutting into the mountain again. "That was the hardest part of the whole hike, hiking on that blacktop road." From here they traveled to Chalk Creek, where they were resupplied by truck. George Lowe remembers three boys went home early, "partly homesick and partly really sick." He and a couple of others were sent ahead to a town (perhaps Upton) to call Ogden and arrange rides for them. "But that was a hard, hard hike. [Dilworth] never had another hike like that one. . . . I know I was in good condition, and I was exhausted every night." They climbed onto the divide with Weber Canyon. George Lowe remembers camping by a lake when Dilworth was confronted by the landowners, who were staying at some nearby cabins. "They came down and were quite unhappy that we had camped there without asking their permission. He was very apologetic and very nice and the people were very angry, but . . . he said, 'Well, we'll be glad to leave, we don't want to inconvenience you.'" They were finally impressed enough with his politeness and the boys' behavior that they let them stay. The party crossed the west fork of the Bear and Hayden Fork, arriving at Camp Steiner Friday afternoon, their fifth day out. George remembers a great welcome at the hands of the Salt Lake scouts. "They thought it was quite an achievement." Dilworth told the Wendigo in a little cirque behind the camp "where there was a lake and a cliff that would echo," and a good moon that night. Tom Feeny says one boy got so scared by somebody startling him afterward that he jumped into the lake.

Dilworth summed up the hike as follows: "We crossed seven deep canyons in the going, blistered the boys' feet and learned that the shoes they wear every day are best for hiking." He warned regularly against boots after that. The guidebook states, "In general, you'd better wear the thing to which you are accustomed. One boy hiked clear across the Grand Canyon barefoot. He was used to hiking barefoot. Do not get the habit of wearing high boots. They are: Too hot. They sweat the feet. They are too heavy. Shoes are much better—Oxfords are better still. A good pair of thick soled Oxfords with wool sweat socks are the best possible combination." Dilworth treated blisters by opening them with a sterilized needle at the lower edge, painting them with an antiseptic such as Gentian Violet or Mercurochrome, then covering them with tape. "It takes about 2 yards of tape per man on the average to tape blistered feet on a 6 day hike," reads the scout page for 1933, the year after the Mirror Lake hike. "Last year nearly all of the 67 Carson men developed at least one blister. Some had as high as 6 on each foot."

In 1933 the Carson Men went for ten days in Yellowstone. The Log of the Carson Trail lists seventy-four boys and men from the Ogden Gateway Council, with sixteen more from Cache Valley, Timpanogos, and Teton Peaks. This trip was "70 sheepherder's miles," distributed over ten days instead of five. The Ogden scouts traveled by train through Logan and Oxford, Idaho, where they took on boys from the northern councils. At Ashton, trucks ported them the thirty miles to the Bechler Ranger Station. The Log says of this section, "Enough dust is acquired . . . to fill the quota that scientists declare a normal person should assimilate in a lifetime to remain healthy." Dilworth led out on the trail, with Sherman Barton "herd[ing] on the maimed and weak and slow that lagged behind." They followed the Bechler River upstream to where the trail crossed Boundary Creek. Some shimmied across on a fallen pine, while others took off pants and waded through. (Ock Deming, in a cartoon in the Log, calls these the first "bares" seen on the trip). They had to cross the cold river next, with sharp, obsidian sand to make the going hard. Those who didn't fish that evening visited Ouzel Falls. The next day brought more fordings, as the trail led past Bechler Cascades and Colonnade Falls to Three River Junction. Paul Bieler's patrol and one of the others spent an hour working on a bridge, only to see it wash away. At day's end, "'Uncle' Dil's voice booms through the camp the unexpected discovery of the warm pool." The boys bathe, Preston Pond, the Cache County executive, "loll[ing] and roll[ing] in its delicious warmth until the stars come out."

Next day they began to run across hot pots and made their way onto Pitchstone Plateau. Here the black and red obsidian rock suggested itself as the source of the Bechler's sharp sands. Dilworth proposed a cross country route across the plateau to Shoshone Lake, so they pushed through the pines. "'Uncle' Dil sets a warm pace, in keeping with our eagerness to reach the shore. . . . To our left plays a small geyser, to our right is the lake, ahead of us is Shoshone Creek; and on all sides . . . mosquitoes. 'Uncle' Dil stirs them up in clouds as he pushes forward." The boys fished the shoreline, warm from geothermal heat, with no success that evening. A fisherman offered to take the boys out for a fee in his two boats. Dilworth consented, declaring, "One hour of fishing for each boat load." Fishing was very good. Max Wheelwright says, "I caught three Mackinaw trout, nineteen, twenty, and twenty-one inches. They were by far the largest fish I'd ever caught in my life." He ate one that night and carried the two others the next day through the Shoshone Geyser Basin, past the "bear dump" to Old Faithful, sleeping beside the picnic table where he laid his pack. "That night a bear came along and got in the pack and got the fish out and carried them off, and you know I never heard the bear." They rested here the Sabbath. The scouts were obliged to organize a bear patrol to keep the animals out of pack and larder. The Log describes the patrol's activities: "Bears are allowed to approach the very edge of the camp and then the whole howling pack of picket men chase bears far into the timber with a deadly barrage of rocks and clubs." Tom Feeny and Ward Willis threw a rock at a moose to get it to leave the trail. The moose "didn't understand the rules, and he came right at us." They spent three hours in a tree.

Dilworth picked huckleberries to make a pie from hike bread. Of all the boys, only Charles Petty would help, and only Charles Petty got to share. Monday they walked to Madison Junction along the highway, where "the continual jar of leather heels on hard road causes an outcropping of foot trouble. . . . Every stream is the scene of bare-footed scouts cooling off the 'hot dogs.'" At least as much trouble were the parents who had driven up to meet their boys and now wanted to give them lifts. Tom Feeny remembers Dilworth telling them, "'Nope, you don't pick them up. If they're going to become men, they're going to complete the trip.' And there were some pretty upset kids and pretty upset parents, but he prevailed." One of Ock Deming's cartoons has a trembling, sweating scout yelling at a motorist, "Get thee behind me, Satan!" (Dilworth told of one boy, tired and discouraged, his parents trailing them in their sedan along the side of the road, reasoning with Dilworth, trying to get him to give his blessing for him to ride. Dilworth asked him finally what he was going to do. He said, "I guess I'll walk." Later when the scout became a missionary in Germany, he wrote Dilworth a letter explaining how bad things were and how discouraged he was and how much he wanted to cash it in. Dilworth wrote a few words about self-reliance and dependability and received in reply a note reading, "I guess I'll walk.") Two more days of hiking brought the troops to the West Entrance and the train ride home.

The next Carson Hike was through the Grand Canyon, north to south, then south to north. In Zion Park afterwards a ranger put a rattlesnake and a king snake together, and the boys watched the king snake kill and swallow the rattler. Then came consecutive years, 1935 and 1936, in which the Carson Men hiked the Uintahs. These were the first ten-day hikes where the scouts could not be resupplied. (The scout page invites "Explorers" for the first time in 1936.) Dilworth notes the Carson program was successful enough for the other area councils to copy. "Logan got its Bridger Men and Salt Lake had its Sourdoughs." The Sourdoughs hiked the Uintahs at the same time as the Carsons in 1935, and the two camps met for one day. In 1936 the Bridger Men came as well, and according to Lynn Crookston, the "Indians" from the Provo council. This encampment was billed as a rendezvous, and included contests in hatchet- and knife-throwing and knot-tying, and a battle of tall tales. Don Buswell says, "We didn't see those kids before that night and we didn't see them afterwards. It was so planned that they came in from different ways." The Carsons next returned to Yellowstone. Dil set the scouts loose with map and compass on the leg to Shoshone Lake. When he and Emery Wight arrived, they found not a soul, and Dil thought to himself, "Now I'm going to have to go find ninety boys." "Then suddenly, with a Comanche yell, the whole horde was upon us. Springing from behind rocks, trees, and bushes, the whole troop performed a perfect ambush. Not a boy was missing." Next the Carsons hiked Glacier, the Middle Fork of the Salmon, the Wind Rivers, then the Uintahs again.

Paul Bieler developed a diet for the longer hikes that required little or no cooking and only weighed one pound per day. This consisted of "condensed, dried, ready-to-eat raisins, prunes, apricots, peaches, figs, and rye crisp, parched whole wheat and corn, chocolate, peanuts, malted milk tablets and peanut butter, jam, salt, sugar, limes, and carrots. . . . At meal time we would stop at a stream and drink lots of water as we ate our food. The water swelled the food inside our stomachs, and the 'full' feeling stayed with us several hours." Paul and his followers came to be known as the "Birdseed Boys." Don Buswell's mother was afraid he would go hungry on his first Carson Hike, and so weighed him down with canned goods. "My pack weighed about eighty-five pounds, more than I weighed I think." He linked up with a couple of boys on the "birdseed menu," who agreed to carry a portion of his canned food in exchange for the privilege of eating with him. The boys climbed Kings Peak the years they hiked the Uintahs. Dilworth says, "A thunderstorm came over and enveloped those kids, and their hair stood on end, and you could take your knuckle like that and get that far from a kid's nose and pull a spark." Sherman Barton told them, "'All you guys lie flat and don't you move till I tell you.' So they all lay down and the rain soaked them but they didn't move, and the storm went on over, and they didn't get hurt. We learned about lightning on that little trip."

Yacht Club

Through his scouting career, Dilworth undertook a new project every three to five years. In 1928 it was hiking, in 1932 the Carson Men. Kiesel got its pond and swimming pool in 1935-6. In 1939, with the filling of Pine View Dam, Dilworth launched Camp Browning, also known as the Explorers' Yacht Club. Leonore believes he may have gotten the idea from a near-accident Young Dil had on a boat. "Boys will swim," reads an announcement on the 1940 scout page. "They'll do it secretly or openly, with or without permission. The Explorers' Yacht club offers its facilities to satisfy the desire for swimming in safety. Boys like all types of boats. Here, in our state, there is little chance to satisfy this desire. The Explorers' Yacht Club offers sailing, canoeing, kayaking, rowing, all with safety." Boys joined by paying a yearly fee of fifty cents, after which they could come and go at will, and stay an hour, a day, or a month. "Here, young men, their leaders, their girl friends, and their parties may find clean fun." Boys could bring male guests fifteen or over or female guests fourteen or over, as long as they could swim. Boy guests who were eligible to be members could come once, but afterwards had to pay the fee.

Dilworth records that the camp was open "from daylight to dark and on moonlit nights. . . . We had six catamarans, two sail-boats, a dozen canvas-covered kayaks and a canoe at first. . . . Later on, because of the war, newspaper print went high, and we collected a lot of newspapers and sold them for more than a thousand dollars and about nine canoes." In addition there was a diving board and swimming area roped off along one of the docks. George Petty and Aaron Ross were to staff the camp that first year. But this was 1939, and when George was called up into the service, Dilworth brought Dan Bradshaw down from Kiesel. Then Aaron Ross was called up as well, so Jack Davis, one of Kiesel's junior officers, came down. A farmer named Wilson planted and harvested hay on the land, and Dilworth had the boys help him. Jack remembers things starting slow. "That first month Dan and I were there, we didn't see anybody. All we did was farm work and build [the] cabin and take care of ourselves, and we had to paint the catamarans. They were brand new and they needed certain treatment before they were water-worthy. So we spent most of our time just doing plain labor." He remembers Dilworth coming up to check on them, sometimes working alongside them. "Uncle Dil used to pride himself on . . . being able to handle a pitchfork." Jack remembers, "The compensation [for farming] came in that Mr. Wilson had a lovely vegetable garden, and . . . Dan and I had garden privileges." Slowly but surely, he says, word of the club got out. "By the end of that second summer, we were having people every day."

Dilworth used the *Standard* to generate excitement for the club. "Camp Browning on Pineview Lake opens on June 8," reads the 1942 scout page.

> On that happy morning any Scout or Explorer over 15 years of age may "put to sea." He'll drive into the campground and check in, then he'll chose his "weapon" with which to brave the deep. There may be no wind, so he'll want to try out a Kayak— those slim, light bits of canvas and wood which glide so

effortlessly through the sparkling water—or if a breeze whips up, the breaking white caps will warn him that the age-old contest between wind, water, and man is much more fun. In that case, he'll try to sail a Catamaran over to the new log safety boom and back. Bet you can't do it, sailor. Perhaps he knows where the biggest trout in the lake is lurking, and with canoe he sneaks up to it, only to find a carp on his hook. By noon he's tired, but a quiet lounge in the new easy chairs in the club room of the new building freshens him, and he finds strength to fill the inner man via the brought-lunch or cooked meal route.

He takes a sun-bath on the roof. He tries swimming, and if he stays all night, he joins the rest of the gang in song, story and reminiscence at the campfire. Camp Browning is a camp for older boys. It is the only camp of its kind in the world. There is none like it. And it's the property of all the Explorers of the community.

The issue announces an arrangement with the Ogden Cab and Transfer company to take the boys as far as the "'corner' one and one half miles north of camp on the Eden-Huntsville road" for the simple Ogden Canyon fare. One-way was twenty-five cents, round trip forty-five. The bus left downtown Ogden at 9:00 a.m, noon, and "(for night hawks)" 12:30 in the morning. The ride lasted forty-five minutes, "putting you in camp at ten a.m. and six p.m. if you do the last mile at Scout's pace." In 1940, "boys coming to camp on bicycles or afoot" were ferried across the lake "for 2 1/2 cents each way" (two passengers minimum). Jack Davis remembers the two-and-a-half horsepower motorboat, "that most any of us could beat in a kayak, but it was good for towing stranded catamarans back to home base when the wind died or when we had sailors that didn't know how to get them back." Was that very often? Jack says, "Every day." (Evans Ray tells of monkeying with a friend on a sailboat, rocking it back and forth, and finally swamping it. Dilworth came out and got them in the boat, saying simply, "Well boys, we've learned two things today. Boats can be tipped over—and boys can be saved.") Dilworth made sure Jack spent Sundays in town so he could attend church, then he would hitchhike up the canyon early Monday. "Sometimes I had to hitchhike all the way around, and sometimes, depending on where my ride went, I ended up hitchhiking a ride across the lake on somebody's motorboat." Dilworth insisted the boys fulfill their religious duties. "Members staying over Sunday must observe the Sabbath," reads the 1940 scout page.

"Things were in good order," Jack states. "Uncle Dil was there to check" two or three times a week. "He always looked in the cupboards to see if the dishes were clean and in good order, to see if the food was packed and arranged . . . and he checked to see if our beds were made, the floor was swept, our clothes were clean, and we were clean and shaved, hair washed. He was interested in our characters and our appearance. . . . He wanted sharp looking leaders." Jack and Dan returned the second year, then the third, this time with the addition of Dilworth Randolph Young. "Uncle Dil insisted on his son performing in accordance with the direction of Dan Bradshaw, and Dan put him through his paces." Because the explorers brought dates, Jack says, "we had to learn how to behave around young ladies, and to help them . . . have a good time. And to implement all this, we were commissioned to learn to sail. We had to learn what was port and starboard and fore and aft and what was the jib and what was the mainsail and how to make the darn things really go and give demonstrations." They learned how to swamp and unswamp canoes in deep water, how to paddle properly, how to row with feathered oars, and were instructed to pass along the rudiments to the people checking out boats. "Our last ritual at night was to go down" to where the old highway ran into the lake, and build a fire on the asphalt "and make some hot chocolate and go swimming late at night. . . . Dan was a great storyteller, and a fun person to be around, and he made me learn some stories and try to tell them, so that was our evening entertainment" for explorers who stayed overnight.

To Dilworth's consternation, Camp Browning did not survive the raising of the dam. "It was a good project but my successors didn't think so and after awhile the camp was abandoned by them.

To my mind that was shortsighted," he says, because of the good it did. Jack and Young Dil attended a regatta, winning the sailboat race hands down. Later, by arrangement, the two of them paddled their canoe out a ways, "and [Young Dil] stood up and started acting crazy, and I said, 'Sit down! sit down!' and I wrestled with him and as we went we just tipped the canoe over." They heard screams from the shore—not that the water bothered them. "We were in the water all day anyway." In less than three minutes they had the canoe free of water and were back in it, to the applause of those on shore. The stunt bears Dilworth's mark, but it also illustrates his concern that the camp teach skills. "Camp Browning was a respected element on that waterfront," Jack says, "and people knew this, and they could come there for help, and we would know some first aid. They'd know that if there was a problem in the lake, that we'd go out there with our old chug-chug motorboat and stick with whatever the problem was."

Dilworth on Scouting

Character has always been one of the central issues in Scouting. Max Wheelwright remembers hearing Dilworth speak on the subject in the '50s: "He says, 'You know, it's interesting, we work with scoutmasters, we work so hard with these boys, and we encourage them to go to church, and we take them on hikes, and we teach them all these scouting skills, and we try to breed into them the scout oath and law and being good citizens, good members of the Church, and when it's all done and said afterwards, nine times out of ten they turn out just like their dads anyway.'"

Just prior to Dilworth's first year running a camp, the *Standard* printed a statement by the council camping committee: "In planning the summer activities of your boys we desire that they should come under the influence of good, wholesome, sturdy men; learn the value of time by well planned activity; eat well cooked meals, and sleep in clean beds." One of the striking things about Dilworth's camping program, as it evolved, is how thoroughly it violated these standards. He eventually reduced his adult staff to a bare minimum, made classes optional, let the boys plan their own days, and tried to get them outside and eating what they themselves prepared. The 1934 scout page points out that:

1. A scout who makes four camps in a week is learning to be a better camper than a scout who makes only one.

2. A scout who cooks ten meals will become a better cook than one who cooks but one.

3. If a troop hikes, the scout is forced to learn to pack, to watch weights, to learn to be comfortable.

4. A scout makes a pack, a sleeping bag, a tent. He employs his fingers and his head.

5. He learns to use his equipment, and thus develop self confidence and self mastery.

(After his retirement, Dilworth often complained that scouts no longer made their own equipment. "They buy the modified Nelson pack from camp supply stores or from the B.S.A. Boys buy everything and learn very little about camping.") Though rejecting the classroom model, Dilworth was determined to teach character.

6. Good character is not built in a day. If a boy at 12 develops into good character at 18 he must actively practice doing things to develop character. A week camping on a real troop hike will contribute most to the development.

Scouting taught skills boys would need as soldiers, and the government specifically asked that scout camps remain open during the war. The 1942 scout page notes, "The Scout office has had a great number of former Scouts testifying how much easier it is to be a soldier because, as boys, they knew scouting. . . . Soldiers need to know mapping, signaling, simple cooking, camping in rain storms, pathfinding, care of the feet, stalking, use of the compass. . . . But we don't do it because the boys become better soldiers. We want to make them better citizens. Camping does that too."

Dilworth prized adventure, but unlike some later wilderness programs, his didn't aim for a cathartic experience. Fun was of the essence, and Dilworth pulled his punches. Boys were resupplied by truck. The hike from Monte was mostly downhill. In 1936, the scout page quotes the camping committee as stating that the policy at Kiesel was "to give the boys a maximum of shelter and protection in equal ration to a maximum of romance and adventure." Still, Dilworth believed in putting a little stress on the boys. Wally Brown, who attended two Carson Hikes as a scoutmaster in the '50s, remembers one boy, small enough to make his pack look large. "At the beginning of the hike [at] the first campfire, they'd have each boy get up and say why he was coming on the Carson Hike and what it meant to him, and so on and so forth, and most the kids'd get up, and say a few words, 'Well, I hope we have a good hike, and I hope I make it, I hope I get to be a Carson Man, and everything.'" That was what this boy said. "And [he] did alright, of course, but that last night when we had this last campfire . . . this one little kid got up there and says, 'You know, that first night when we started out, I said I sure hoped I'd make it.' And he says, 'I found out you gotta make it!'"

Part of Dil's genius was his ability to see through the boys' eyes. "Can you remember when you were 12 or 13 or 14?" read his notes for a speech on scouting in Logan in December 1939. "Don't confuse it with when you were 9 or 10. You were ordained a Deacon. You came to Mutual for the 1st time. . . . You were in the 7th or 8th grade. . . . Do you have the period clearly in mind?

> Home was only a filling station. "Ma, can I have a piece of bread and jam?" . . . Mother says: "Just one piece." "Just one, Ma, just one?" And then we happily fare forth with one slice one and 1/2 inch thick with a quarter inch of butter, and jam—well, by licking fast we got most of it in before it dripped off—and in addition we could lick our fingers.

> What did we fare forth to? Winter: Sleigh riding, skating, catching on delivery wagons with sleds, snowball fights. Spring: Baseball, marbles, tops, hikes over the next hill into valleys

beyond. Summer: Evening games, kick the can, slip, run sheep run, stink base, steal sticks, pomp shady, daytime games like tippy and spats and spurs. Fall: Fire building and cooking spuds and football until too dark to see. All in never ending succession. Each belonged in its season. No one thought of playing marbles in the fall, nor football in the spring.

Rainy days—when a mother had her 12 year old boy in the house all day by night he could have her saying: "I could thrash you within an inch of your life." Just why, no one knows except that pent up energy of boys does explode in unexpected ways. At about 5 p.m. when clouds lifted—what an explosion as boys and girls alike burst forth from the house like so many miniature eruptions. . . .

Remember how much fun you had when your dad, or uncle, or other adults came out and played twilight games with you. They didn't boss, they just played. And when they quit at dusk and went inside, most of the fun stopped and went in with them.

He concludes: "Boys would rather play with adults—if the adults will play according to children's standards. Boys love the shadows of evening for their fun. . . . Boys love to build fires and cook simple things. . . . Isn't it difficult to remember? The fact is, you can't remember clearly—It is hazy at best. But if you can't remember at all you cannot hope to do anything for boyhood."

He asks about character:

Where did you learn to be self reliant? Where did you learn to play fair. Did you learn anything about chivalry in those days? What were the circumstances? Did you learn to love religion? . . .

Would you say that character is Caught or Taught? . . . Can we teach character to any boy?—No. We can only expose the boy to a situation—and to get much effect the boy must want to be [there]. . . .

You will say to me, "Scouting is a character-building and

citizenship-training program for boys administered by men to the boys"—and I say to you that is just what's wrong with it and you. . . . I say Scouting is "the sum of its activities and where those activities take place."

"If you know," he concludes, "or remember anything about your own boyhood, don't you now believe that these activities all belong out-of-doors?"

He taught reverence. An excerpt from the 1924 camp newspaper has "Mr. Young" giving "an interesting lesson on the creation of the earth" in Sunday School. Leonore remembers him holding a service for her and her friends at Organ Loft at Kiesel, introducing the lesson by pointing to a grove of aspens on the opposite slope that resembled a letter "I," and telling them it stood for "Immanuel." Jack Davis says, "He always carried a Book of Mormon. He always quoted it. . . . He says, 'When I go, this is my personal life, and anybody that'd like to talk to me about this, I'll be glad to talk to you.' . . . He would see a situation, and it would be appropriate, and he would say, 'This reminds me of the—,' and he'd quote a story in the Book of Mormon." He allowed others to interpret reverence in their own way. He defended Tom Feeny in his eagle court of honor when a man objected to him not going to church. "I could hear in the outside room the debate going on. And Dilworth just told him, 'I don't care if he goes to church or not. He's better than some that do.' I'm sure I got my eagle badge just for his trying." George Lowe remembers Dilworth "was very firm in his beliefs. Things were pretty well, like on evolution, black or white. Either it was or it wasn't, and he believed it wasn't." They argued it back and forth over the years. "And yet [we] always got along beautifully, and I'm sure that neither one of us looked down on the other." Referring to differences of belief and practice, George says, "He was very tolerant of that sort of thing. . . . He was rigid, but at the same time he didn't force his rigidity on other people."

Dil wanted good leaders for the boys. Eden Beutler remembers countless controversies with the bishops. "They'd just get a scouter, and as soon as he was a good man, the bishop'd take him in the bishopric." Eden remembers, "He'd cuss the bishops for doing it." Dilworth insisted, in his blunt way, that boys give the whole measure. Talmage Nielsen tells of a speech he gave to a group of servicemen in El Paso, asking how many had passed their scout pace for their first class badges (nearly all had) and how many had practiced in advance (hardly any). "And he said, 'Well that's were you got your first lesson in getting something for nothing. Nobody can do the scout pace without practice.'" Talmage continues: "He was not concerned about outward appearances. He wanted something to happen inside you." Dilworth wanted the whole program. He insisted on the patrol method. Troops were to own sufficient equipment. Boys were to do good turns. His speech in Logan culminated with this advice: "All should remember that Scouts learn to be Scouts after about 5 years of practice—but that they'll never be Scouts unless they do practice."

All told, Dilworth was a scouter one might "catch" character from.

CHAPTER 8

Rosemont

Young Leonore, Young Dil

Leonore, like many of her ancestors, was of an independent mind. Gladys recorded Leonore at age four listening many times to the popular song, "Give Me Liberty or Give Me Love." "One day, out of the blue, she said, 'Mother, what does liberty mean?' I said it means you can do about as you please.'" Leonore thought for a few minutes, then said, "Mother, I believe I'll take liberty." When Leonore was around ten, she began to resist going to sacrament meetings. Dilworth wanted her to go, but finally gave in, saying, "Well, okay, Leonore, but when will you start going?" Leonore answered, "When I'm twelve." For the next two years she attended Sunday school and primary, but not sacrament meeting. At twelve she remembered her promise and started to go. "I've gone ever since," she says.

Leonore remembers Dilworth joking with her and tickling her. She remembers playing in the old, red carriage house on their property on 24th Street, climbing the ladder along one wall to the loft, where there was an ancient desk. Dilworth eventually tore the carriage house down and built a carport in its place. Leonore remembers Dilworth, never Gladys, playing with her and the other neighborhood children on summer evenings—hide and seek, kick the can. She remembers "slip"—the child who was "it" would search for all the others, who when found, joined in the searching. Leonore hid in the lucerne field in back of the house, where no one could find her. Finally all joined hands to cross the field together, but still missed her somehow.

Gladys called the big, red house "Rosemont." Leonore remembers it full of people, including the boarders: Dee hospital nurses, a Japanese live-in helper, teachers, Hill Field employees, and Weber College students. Leonore remembers these courting on the Young's covered front porch and among the peach-cot and crabapple trees. With the renters, Dil and Gladys rarely slept in the master bedroom. Leonore and Dil Jr. as often as not slept in the attic—cold in winter, hot in summer—to open up more rooms. The Youngs loved to entertain, and Leonore herself often had friends over. When Leonore read of a "Live Five" club in the *Children's Friend*, Gladys agreed to help her sponsor one of her own. So she and four friends would gather in the Young home to do cooking, crafts, make-up—"There was something exciting every week." They caroled at Christmas and went skating at various ponds, including the one at Kiesel. The group staged *Peter Pan* in the parlor, making the curtains, preparing costumes and sets, rehearsing, and finally inviting all the girls' classmates at Lorin Farr Elementary. When it came time to fly, they leaped out a window, where Dilworth caught them and wrapped them in blankets, because it was snowy outside.

The size of the group grew to ten, so they called it the "Live Double Five." Then they invited two more friends, to make "Double Five Plus Two." Dilworth got some lapel pins of calves kicking up which he gave to the girls, so they became the "Double Six Mavericks." Dilworth often had them up to Kiesel at the end of the year, or earlier, during the first part of the week when the scouts were out on Monte Cristo. Leonore remembers making sarongs out of neckerchiefs, and pestering the boys on the staff. Once she jumped on good-natured Dan Bradshaw's back while he was painting a cabin, making him spill the paint. "That's the only time he ever got a little aggravated at me." The young men took extra care of the girls. Once when they slept over, Seaman Mills "kept coming into our room during the night to put more blankets on us. It was icy outside, but when we woke up we thought we were on fire." Leonore remembers hikes to Big Springs and Monte Cristo to meet Dil. Once she and Gladys disagreed on the trail. They separated finally, Leonore following her father's instructions to keep to the bottom of the canyon. Leonore and the girls with her met Dil in a couple of hours, Gladys trailing in with her girls some time later.

The club put on a large Halloween party each year. With Gladys, preparation was half the fun. Leonore and Martha remember waxing Rosemont's hardwood floors—Gladys had them skate across it with rags on their feet to do the polishing. Leonore says that the old, red house

> could look spooky anytime—not just on Halloween. Several rooms in the basement had dirt floors, low beams, cobwebs. . . . Sometimes stray cats would even get in there and live without our being able to catch them. The kids had to enter through [the coal chute]. They couldn't just crawl in. They had to sit on the ledge facing out, then fall backwards in—trusting that someone in the dark would catch them.

Dilworth did the catching. Each club member was allowed to invite ten guests, but more came. Leonore writes, "The last year Daddy swears that he caught over three hundred kids falling through that window." From there the guests went through the different rooms: "feeling peeled grapes for eyeballs, macaroni for intestines, shaking hands with a ghost whose hand (glove) came off in yours. . . ." In one room, beneath a dim, blue lightbulb, a skeleton in a coffin-like box rose up as the children approached— Dilworth had borrowed the skeleton from the anatomy classes at Weber College. Afterwards, there was dancing upstairs and games in the yard, like blindfolded pie-eating contests and bobbing for apples, with a fortune teller in the doll house Dilworth had made Leonore.

Dilworth built an outdoor platform above the fruit cellar. Leonore remembers sleeping there under the stars practically every night all summer. Brownie, their setter, would want to climb up on her, but she kept him off as long as she was able.

"Every morning my legs would be numb because Brownie would jump on me and curl up on my legs after I was asleep. If I opened one eye he was there with a stick for me to throw, and he would give me no peace after that." Brownie was a high-strung, nervous dog, that Leonore thought fit right in with her mother's and brother's sensitivity. He loved everyone but the mailman and the newsboy. Once on a hike, Brownie chased a porcupine and came back with a noseful of quills. On another, Betty Peterson Baker remembers, he fell into a cesspool, then came lopping up to them with a stick, dropped it, and shook. Brownie died of poisoning—they never learned from where. Gladys told Betty how sixteen-year-old Dil found him. "The dog was all puffed up from the poison, and he came carrying him home in his arms, just sobbing, carrying that beautiful red Irish setter. Oh, he was pretty."

Leonore loved to put on costumes from the attic and dance through the house. Once she made a great flying leap in the basement and cracked her head on a beam. She says, "Mother and Daddy saw that I got all the advantages, even though they couldn't afford it." She took dancing lessons, singing lessons, and "every other kind of lesson." She danced in her mother's programs, as well as filling in wherever her mother needed an extra—hazard of being the director's daughter. In high school she sang in a trio, also in pep club, and in the a capella choir, did yearbook, was elected Vice President of the Girls' Association and nearly wore herself to the ground. She took ballet from Sophie Reed, "the best there ever was," Dilworth writes. Leonore "became one of the best in Utah—we thought." Leonore danced in all kinds of programs, including many at the Bushnell military hospital in Brigham.

> I saw many heart-rending sights there: boys with blown away faces, boys paralyzed, shell shock. Once I danced in the psychiatric ward. I did a Spanish dance using castanets. The noise was too much like gun fire. One of the patients screamed and ran out of the ward, with the attendants in full pursuit.

Once she and a friend double dated two soldiers in wheelchairs. The soldiers insisted on hitchhiking home after, so Dilworth disguised himself and picked them up in his car. The two of them in the back seat complained how Leonore and her friend hadn't seemed to want to go with them to the bedroom after. Dilworth, under his hat and raincoat, fumed. One boy Leonore danced with had a shattered leg nerve, but he so loved to dance that he did it in spite of the pain. It proved good therapy. After the war, he returned and regaled her and her fiance Blaine with an afternoon of dance—he had become an instructor for Arthur Murray Dance Studios.

Leonore remembers hand-me-downs from Marjorie Tanner, a cousin. When Leonore was seven, Gladys wanted her to wear a particular green silk party dress to school. Leonore resisted, until Gladys got flustered enough at it and her that she grabbed it and tore it from her back. Gladys made clothes from whatever was at hand—Leonore remembers in particular a red skirt with a green, uncovered zipper. "By the time I was twelve I learned to sew all my own clothes." As a young woman, Leonore wanted a black velvet dress with beadwork on the collar for a prom. The price was beyond reach, so she got her mother to help her make one like it. Leonore sewed, and Gladys and Dilworth both spent more than one night stitching on all the crystal beads by hand. Dil promised Leonore a gold wristwatch when she was eighteen if she stood straight. "I got the posture but the wristwatch was forgotten." Dil described Leonore "walking up the street from school, erect, graceful posture, cheerful face, developing young soprano voice. . . . How I was stirred with pride."

Leonore remembers her brother Dil at Kiesel, "running through the beautiful meadows on the way down from Big Springs, throwing cone weeds—looking more graceful than a deer in his movements." She remembers sledding with him on a five-seat flexible flyer. In the summer, Dilworth got out the old coaster wagon from his own childhood and fixed it with a plank long enough for six or seven kids. The house had two sets of indoor stairs. Leonore played tag with her brother, chasing up one set and down the other. They used a set of side stairs outdoors to go to school, though more often they hung over the banister and dropped. She bickered—more or less in fun—with Little Dil over the supper dishes until their mother was ready to strangle them. "Stop bantering, you two." One time when they'd done something, she bent them over a table and spanked the two of them at once with a mop handle. The harder she paddled, the harder they laughed, until she gave up.

Leonore remembers Dil Jr. didn't advance far in scouting, she thinks just to First Class. Perhaps he felt too much pressure, being the scout executive's son. Yet he liked what scouts did. He was on the staff at the Explorers' Yacht Club. He and Jack Davis learned Indian dances for Gladys' pageants, and then performed them all over town. Young Dil, as he came to be known, was a Mount Ogden hiker. One year he and Jack and Stan Hurst went on rope-bound skis. Jack says, "It took quite awhile to go up there, but it was sure worth it coming down the other side." Young Dil was a punster, with an inexhaustible supply. If someone groaned at one, he would protest, "Well, u-pun my word." He sang in the a capella choir, and loved Mozart and social dancing. Once he and Betty Baker, his classmate at Central Junior High, attended a dance at Lewis Junior and won the waltz contest. She remembers the good-natured cat-calls when the crowd found out where they were from. Leonore danced with her brother at an after-school "stomp" in the eighth grade. "I could see all of the faces of the eighth grade girls drop with wonder and envy that a handsome tenth grade football player had asked me to dance. When it became known that I was his sister, a lot of tenth grade girls managed to become my good friends."

Young Dil was an athlete, strong at fullback at Ogden High. One day Leonore mentioned she didn't like watching football. "He literally tackled me and then explained the game and some of the plays on paper. I really enjoyed watching after that (if he was playing)." Dil Sr. writes that his son "got to fumbling the ball during his senior year. Instead of assuring him, the coach jerked him out so he did not do as well as he should." The *Standard-Examiner* laments, "Fumbling has been a habit with Young for two seasons." Once Dil fumbled near the other team's goal—Coach Moesinger played him at tackle the next game. But he had his share of glory, too. The *Standard-Examiner* refers to him as "175 pounds of dynamite when it comes to hitting a line." "Dilworth Young is Hero," reads another *Standard* headline. "Powerful Fullback Pushes Over Touchdown and Adds Extra Point to Nose Out North Cache."

Dilworth writes of his son: "He had great moral courage. . . . One night in the locker room he told the boys if they didn't stop their dirty talk about girls and blasphemy against God, he would not play or stay." Young Dil was a good enough player that the talk ended. Social clubs were important at the time at Ogden High. Young Dil was selected to join one and invited to a cabin in Ogden Canyon for the initiation. His father writes,

> I suspected part of the initiations included some sex fooling, so I warned him not to let them fool with his sex organs. It was winter and cold. He took a sleeping bag to the party. About 2:30 a.m. I heard the front door open. It was he. I asked what was the matter. He said simply: "Dad, they tried it on me, but I fought them off and came home." He had walked nine miles in zero weather. I was proud of that boy that night.

Young Dil ran for student body president. His slogan, "Young and Independent," reflected the fact that Dil Jr. did not belong to a social club. Jack Davis served as campaign manager. He says they adapted scout skits from their days at camp. "I think that was one of the things that attracted attention for him, because we always had a good show." They got some Chinese newspapers and had a printer put on a headline announcing Dil's campaign. Jack got permission to post twelve "newsboys" at all the doors to the building just before close of school the day before the election, shouting at the top of their lungs, "Dil Young runs for student body president!" Jack and Betty both say Dil won by a landslide. Betty adds, "The boy that had run against him was just in a state of shock, because he was one of the real swinger, social-club type people." Young Dil was a strong leader, but Leonore saw his sensitive side. "I remember him . . . losing his breakfast on the way to school every time there was an assembly that he had to conduct."

Gladys

Gladys Pratt was born in Colonia Juarez, Chihuahua, Mexico, on March 24, 1895. Her father, Helaman Pratt, the son of Parley P. Pratt, was born on the road just outside Mt. Pisgah in 1846. On the trail west, Helaman was bumped from the wagon and his head run over by the wheel. The muddy ground saved him, but he carried the scar, which Gladys remembered from combing his hair in the evenings when she was a girl. Helaman, with his wife Victoria Billingsley, pioneered the Muddy, losing their first child in the evacuation two years later, and another not long after. Helaman served several missions in Mexico, both exploring and preaching. He helped locate the site for Colonia Juarez while serving as president of the mission. Upon his release came one last call, to bring his families here, acquire out Mexican citizenship, and work and live here "until released by death." Helaman became a rancher in the Sierra Madres, then a farmer in Dublan.

Mary Pratt Parrish, Helaman's granddaughter, writes that Helaman was "disturbed" by the way the Mexican haciendas treated their laborers "Their wages were so low that they could hardly buy enough beans and rice for one meal a day . . . They could charge what they bought at the commissary, but they could not quit their job until the bill was paid. This made the Mexicans virtually slaves." Helaman hired them at a good enough wage that they could get out of bondage, and sometimes paid their debts himself. "Helaman's children used to jokingly say that he bought more land to hire more Mexicans to grow more corn to buy more land to hire more Mexicans," and indeed, that became the pattern of his life.

Helaman had malaria and heart and stomach ailments. Around 1893, two years before Gladys' birth, he grew so ill he called the children around him for a few last words of advice, while a group of priesthood holders stood in a prayer circle in an adjoining room. He appeared to pass away, but then revived. He told his family his spirit had left his body and had been met by his friend

Erastus Snow, who told him he had to take up his body again. "Brother Snow," he answered, "my stomach and heart are completely worn out. I cannot go on." Brother Snow answered that he still had a great work to perform and that his stomach and heart would be made whole. He lived sixteen more years. A diphtheria epidemic struck the colonies in 1891, and Victoria lost two children nearly grown. Helaman's second wife Dora cared for the families while Victoria grieved. Gladys writes, "It was [my brother] Rey Lucero who saved my mother's life by being her constant companion during her vigil of grief. As she paced the lonely hills, mourning and grieving, he would follow her and gently persuade her to return to the cabin." Gladys, born four years later when Victoria was forty-two, seemed to her a miracle child, and comforted her loss.

Some of Gladys' earliest memories were from the Pratt ranch in the mountains, riding out after the stock, exploring Indian ruins, making dolls from acorns, swimming near the mossy cliffs of the Piedras Verdes, watching her mother cook in the cabin's stone fireplace (big enough to sit inside) and watching "Aunt" Dora in the shed making cheese. She remembers Victoria as sensitive, pretty, an exceptional cook, with a beautiful soprano singing voice. Victoria and the boys liked to sit outside the cabin on summer evenings singing Mexican and American songs to the vaqueros, the Mexican cowboys who lived with their families in a lower cabin. The vaqueros answered from the twilight with songs of their own.

Gladys lost her father at age fourteen, and her mother a year later. She spent the next years with Rey, President of the Mexican Mission, in Mexico City, where she witnessed events of the Revolution. At one point, the mission home was close enough to the line of fire that a bullet ricocheted off a beam, passed through a hat box of Gladys', and came to rest on the floor. In 1913, Rey evacuated the missionaries. Two years later he was called to set up a mission to the Mexicans living in the southwestern United States. He moved to Manassa, Colorado, with his household, including Gladys, his wife May, and ten children. Rey's daughter

Mary Parrish remembers Gladys helped with babysitting. Occasionally they heard of rumors that Gladys was not Rey's sister, but his secret plural wife. This rankled Gladys, who had feelings about polygamy. Not that her own experience had been unpleasant. By all accounts, Helaman's household was harmonious. Between missions, illness, school, and pioneering, a child was almost as likely to be living with an "aunt" as with his mother. Harold, Helaman's son by his third wife Bertha, said to Dora once, "Aunt Dora, if I hadn't been told I never would have known which my mother was." But Victoria bore some jealousy toward the other wives that Gladys apparently internalized. Leonore says, "Grandma Victoria was a highly sensitive person, easily angered, and very creative, and the other two wives were . . . calm and placid, so that if you wanted peace, you'd go to their house. If you wanted to get upset, you'd go to Grandma Victoria's house."

Gladys, Leonore says, was five foot five, with light green eyes—"not hazel, just straight green." She remembers her in pants while hiking or outdoors, which in that day was at the "frontier of propriety." Gladys' street dress was elegant, in a hurried way. Margaret Wilson Barlow remembers her wearing shawls from Mexico. "There was always something dramatic and good looking about her . . . No one else would wear a shawl, and Aunt Gladys looked wonderful in [them]." Gladys' weight went up and down. She could not afford expensive clothes. She had a mind of her own—Leonore remembers her in a house dress and a pair of Dilworth's old black socks out working in the garden. And yet, Leonore remembers, in spite of everything, Gladys struck people as glamorous. Her hair went gray in her early forties, so that at times she was taken for Dilworth's mother, again to her irritation. Margaret Barlow remembers the hair. "She'd sweep it up, and there was always a wonderful comb, like a mantilla, or something." Leonore says she never had money to have it dressed, but had a way of folding it over that struck people as elegant.

Leonore says, "Dad always got my breakfast." He fixed cracked wheat mush. Gladys ate on a porch platform Dil built her on the east side of the house amid the garden's greenery. "Mother would sleep in . . . I think because of her health." Gladys had difficulties with her heart and bowel. Leonore remembers her alternating between periods of intense creative activity and illness. "She'd do these great big enormous things like put on a play a month. That would kill a normal person. And so she'd shine very brightly for awhile and then burn out quick." Martha Barney thought she detected a rebellious streak, "like there was something inborn in her." She went to sacrament meeting, but not relief society, "and I don't think she went to Sunday school, because she'd stay home and fix dinner." Leonore agrees: "Mother was very rebellious at times." She remembers her drinking coffee. "It was a humiliation to me . . . I just was mad at her all my life for drinking coffee." She thinks she felt it helped her bowel trouble. Also Victoria partook, as did others of the Pratts in Gladys' generation. Grandson Dilworth Parkinson remembers being amazed at the coffee flowing at a Pratt gathering, when he was a small boy.

Gladys had unusually refined senses. She could tell who had been in an empty room twenty minutes later by the odor on the air. She could taste something once at a restaurant or a dinner party, then duplicate it precisely in her kitchen at home. Gladys served elegant meals, each dish with some special flourish. Leonore says she made up her recipes, often as she went along. She says she spent a hundred dollars a month on groceries, an enormous sum for those days. Martha Barney remembers making fudge at the Young home Sunday after Sunday, from Droste cocoa, imported from Holland. Leonore speaks of Victoria omelettes, in which the yolks were mixed into a batter, cooked thin like crepes, then folded over the whipped egg whites, which were sweetened and flavored with vanilla. She recalls lots of interesting conversation being batted around the table, and her father teasing the nurses. "My dad wasn't around all that much, but when he was home, supper table was a delight." She remembers Gladys holding her own with him, less inclined to joke, yet warm, vivacious, almost tense—"bursting with creative energy, was her problem." Whatever person or project occupied her at the moment got every ounce of her attention, every thought and emotion. Leonore, who sometimes felt neglected, noted it was easy to forget when her mother's focus was elsewhere, because all the times it had been centered on you.

Leonore remembers occasional, vociferous arguments between her parents. Both were strong-willed, both had well-thought-out reasons, and both said just what they thought. She says her father was the more likely to give in, "only in a very rough, brusk manner that irked her." One source of disagreement was finances. "Daddy was always fussing over bills. Every time it was time to pay bills, he was in a stew." Several times he would not let Gladys have a Christmas tree. "Daddy was very poor, and Mother would find a lot of ways to spend our money." Gladys got so aggravated a time or two that she stormed out the door. She would walk a little way down the road, then realize she didn't have any place to go—she was an orphan, after all. So she would walk around the block and come home. Martha Barney describes Dil and Gladys as "salt and pepper"—not from their hair color, but because they were so different from each other. Gladys lived for drama and passion. Dil, despite his consideration and his romanticism, was blunt and plain. Even into middle age, Gladys fantasized of being swept off her feet, and regretted that, for all Dil did for her, he could never do that. While in Manassa Gladys had been courted by a more passionate young man, later a mission president, who played the guitar. He asked for her hand. She was willing, but Rey interviewed him, found something he didn't like, and called it off. Mary remembers him asking for his guitar and leaving.

But Dil was devoted to her. Myrene Brewer, who saw a puppet show the Youngs put on for the Daughters of the Pioneers, was impressed at how Dil supported Gladys and threw himself into the role. "You know, so many times husbands don't do this. . . . I felt that they were an ideal couple from that standpoint. . . . They were in harmony all the time." Mary Wilson agrees: "They'd help each other, and nothing was too hard to Uncle Dil to move and fix it so it would be in the right position." Leonore remembers the fires used for lighting at one of Gladys' outdoor dramatic productions. "Daddy would do anything for Mother . . . Night after night he'd cut all the firewood for all those fires." Martha Barney says, "They'd kind of argue, you know, and he kind of protested, and yet he supported her. The things that [he] did to support her [were] unbelievable."

Mary Wilson remembers party favors from a dinner at the Youngs—each guest received a card with a picture cut from a magazine that more or less resembled them. Each card had a poem. Mary's and her husband David's read:

> Bathsheba was a woman who caught King David's eye.
> A bold slender beauty with regal look and high.
> King David in a modern sense has found a counterpart.
> But you see her name was Mary and she hit him in the heart.

She remembers them entertaining at the little house on Eccles, the guests more than filling its cramped dining area. People enjoyed themselves, but rather than let them sit around and think about it, Dilworth brought the evening to a close with another poem, more or less like this:

> The hour isn't late
> But we've eaten all that's on our plate
> Now there's nothing left to do
> But to bid you all, adieu.

Then the two of them stood and shooed them laughing out the door.

Dil and Gladys entertained often, and cultivated talented people to help them do it. Dorothy West, a pianist, remembers helping out a number of times, with her trio, at Rosemont or other people's homes. "She'd call me and say, 'Bring some music. We need it.'" Gladys and Dil put together a "crazy quartet" that included Young Dil and Jack Davis, dressed them in knee pants and hose, and had them sing funny songs to a violin. They performed at parties and gatherings all over town. Dil and Gladys, with several other couples, organized the Debonairs' Dancing Club, which soon grew to around a hundred couples. The original couples took turns organizing events, choosing a theme, arranging for and decorating the hall, hiring the band. This inner circle also met for frequent dinner parties. Maggie Gammell remembers one the Youngs hosted in the Twelfth Ward recreation hall, around an oriental theme, with servants carrying trays of food over their heads, and live music drifting in from the balcony. Mary Wilson speaks of the "luminaries" (candles in little paper sacks of sand) lining the walk prior to another dinner held on the Youngs' east lawn. Singers meandered down from the garden at twilight, then gathered near the house for their final presentation. Guests had been warned to be punctual that evening—at the dinner's climax, Gladys rose and said, "Now, all stand up and rejoice!" and gestured to the mouth of Taylors Canyon and the red, craggy peak at its head. There, as if at her command, rose the full moon.

Between boarders and scout training and plays and entertaining, there was always something going on at the Youngs'. Leonore remembers being disappointed at moving into a sorority house when she left home, because as exciting as that was, it didn't compare to Rosemont.

Pageants

Gladys had been doing plays and pageants at least as early as her teen years. Mary Parrish remembers Gladys putting on a production for the primary—Mary was a Dutch girl, and Gladys dressed the other children as dancing cranes. Ward plays, tableaux and mini-pageants for Rotary, at Ogden High, the D. U. P., and various places, culminated in a pageant for the Primary General Board in about 1932 in the Tabernacle in Salt Lake City. Beginning around 1936, Gladys staged pageants on the pond at Camp Kiesel. The water wound around a bend in the canyon, creating a natural amphitheater. Audiences of around two hundred sat on rows of split logs on one bank. For her stage she used the road cut into the other bank, lit with bonfires, and the entire mountainside above. A flute and a soprano and tenor singing Indian Love Call to each other from opposing cliffs set the tone.

"Moonlit trails," began the narration, "how dim, how fantastic, above in the milky way—below in the lapping waters, around us in the cragged peaks—they wind and zig-zag. As we track these trails in our fancy, we see signs of tragedy—we sense a struggle between fear and courage—and we are calmed by the sweet presence of romance.

Gladys' script echoes Dil's philosophy:

Men who know that without hard work and suffering there can be no pleasure worth having, send three boys along one of these trails, that they might develop and be made perfect.

A storm rises, catching the three tenderfeet unawares:

Suddenly the fish cease to bite, and the birds to sing, the squirrels seek shelter in the heart of their trees, and the quail venture no more to tempting morsels of falling seeds, but are hidden safely under the sheltering rocks. A flock of crows fly silently overhead and take refuge under a projecting cliff on the mountainside. All nature has suddenly become hushed and seems oppressed. . . .

Soon clouds roll up the ridges from the southwest like great piles of popcorn. . . . The wind gradually increases to a gale, the clouds become black and ominous—Lightning flashe[s] and thunder rolls. . . . Rain comes down in torrents. Great hail stones fall, breaking down the tender grass and flowers and tearing the tender branches from the trees. A bolt of lightning strikes a giant, dead pine tree across the creek and tears it into a thousand pieces . . . leaving the trunk, which is strongly impregnated with pitch, burning brightly while the storm rages.

One boy twists his ankle, and all are afraid, for,

they have not yet learned that many of Nature's finest lessons are to be found in her storms, and if careful to keep in right relation to them, one may go safely abroad with them, rejoicing in the grandeur and beauty of their words and ways.

Most the action to this point has been accomplished through sound effects. Now appears a torch on the mountain, and a voice singing out, "Wakanda de vu, Wakanda ah tonee," then other torches and other voices joining in. These are the young men of an Indian tribe, just coming in from their proving. The lights gather into single file as they make their way down to the road. Next comes a flotilla of canoes and rowboats with the people of the tribe, men and women, paddling around the bend in the water, and singing,

> Tee-bee-wendo-bon-o-guay, I-ya-bay
> Tee-bee-wendo-bon-o-guay, I-ya-bay

A dancer performs a firelighting dance, after which the head of the tribe addresses the scouts:

> Sons of our great white brothers, we salute you. You walk the trails alone, but you are . . . afraid. Your wits are dulled and your nerve is paralyzed with fear. Your courage is gone because the song in your heart is dead. Come with us to the council fire, and we will heal you.

He speaks of many things, and with his pipe prays to the four directions, while the scouts take courage.

> *Peace possesses your entire being,*
> *And serenity and strength have become your two wings.*
> *In your eyes shines courage,*
> *Power and prowess dwell in your heart.*
> *You are healed—you are healed—you are healed.*
> *Peace—Peace—Peace.*

He prays once more, and a ball of fire descends along a wire strung from the cliffs in back of the audience, lighting the council fire in answer to his prayer.

Dorothy West recalls Dilworth directing all the physical preparations, the chopping of wood, the rigging of the wire, whatever involved land or water. He provided labor in the form of camp staffers. Jack Davis remembers, "Gladys just came down and gave us our assignments. She didn't bother to inquire whether we planned to or not." Jack remembers several days spent "chiseling out terraces" on the south bank of the pond and hauling and installing the log benches. "We'd be in Ogden, we'd be on the hill, we'd be running errands, we'd be digging holes, gathering firewood, whatever she needed done." Sometimes Dil himself took over lifeguard duties. Jack, Dan Bradshaw, and Young Dil, the three Camp Browning staffers, played Indians in this and other pageants. They had learned the dances, and, Jack recalls, they required no makeup with their deep tans.

The acoustics of the spot carried the singing and voices perfectly to the audience. Leonore remembers especially the flute and song echoing from the cliffs in the prologue. She lets on it's the same Indian Love Call "that people make fun of now, but it was really beautiful then in our eyes." But the acoustics were not so good that participants could hear the narration, or each other. Gladys ran the pageant through an elaborate system of prompts, and Ena Barnes, a prompter, says her shows moved along. "You had to keep your eyes open to keep up with her, because it was happening, there was no spare time." Ena, dressed as an Indian, cued the dancers from on stage. A signal from a flashlight brought the fire down from heaven. Once Young Dil's headdress caught fire as he performed the fire lighting dance. Ena, thinking quickly, danced up behind him and clapped it out before it could flare up. Ena says the audience never knew the difference—her clapping might as well have been a part of the dance.

In 1939, under the auspices of the Drama Club of Ogden, Gladys staged an original play on the west lawn at Rosemont, *"Apachurreros De Huesos,* (The Crushers of Bones)." The name "apache" is thought to be a Zuni word meaning "enemy," but the title of the drama plays on the Spanish verb *apachurrar,* "to crush," referring to the practice of breaking the bones of a fallen enemy. This "pageant drama" retold a story from Gladys' family past. In 1892, three years before Gladys was born, Helaman moved his family to a ranch lower on the mountain and rented the Pratt ranch to a family named Thompson. Apache Kid and a band of renegades left over from Geronimo's flight had terrorized the Sierra Madre ranchers for years, and continued for several more. Mostly they pilfered from camps and killed stock, but this day they approached the cabin while the father was away and shot the mother and two sons. A small girl and one of the wounded boys saved themselves by crawling into a chicken coop. One of the renegades finished off the mother by breaking her skull with a rock. Gladys' version had the Apache women following after the men to crush the bones of each of the fallen—this is how she had the story from her mother. The production featured a cast of more than fifty people, also horses and riders, a variety of effects, elaborate costumes, and dances, including the Apache devil dance and Mexican hat dance. Leonore remembers it was cold the night of the production, also a donkey in the show that kept braying out of turn. Myrene Brewer recalls ropes used to shake the trees to simulate the wind.

In 1934, Ogden, which had no founders day or other annual fete, inaugurated a Pioneer Day celebration. Then, as later, Ogden's festival developed into a tug of war between sacred and secular elements in the community. The festivities included multi-day parades and rodeos and, the first three years, historical pageants in Ogden Stadium. Gladys helped direct the 1935 pageant, "Three Day's Journey." This wordless spectacle showed the pioneers enduring various hardships, "including an attack of the wagon train by Indians, the burning of a covered wagon, [and] a chase by mounted redskins." A prologue depicted "the coming into the western states of the early Catholic missionaries and explorers, of the trappers and trailblazers," and a finale showed the development of "modern science and the growth of the west." Leonore says this was a "very unhappy experience" for Gladys because of creative differences with the director, who "was very dominant and made Mother do what she wanted." The secular elements of the celebration—parades, rodeos, and the carnival—grew in importance after 1936, while the pageants dropped out of the picture. In 1938, ten LDS stakes protested the rodeo held on Sunday. "You may be assured of our whole-hearted co-operation in any of your activities which are legitimate and proper," read the letter. "In return we ask that you . . . confine your program on the Sabbath day to those features that are in keeping with Christian practice." Mayor Peery in response asked the stakes to revive the historical pageants. "I am sure all our people missed this feature very much this year." Apparently nothing got off the ground until late 1939, when the celebration committee retained Gladys Pratt Young to direct three productions, to be held 1940 to 1942. (Illness kept her from doing the third.)

Gladys' pageants had narration, which she herself wrote. Leonore says, "She always wrote very, very flowery [language], and much too much, and my father was the one that cut them." Preparations began as early as November for the July shows, which involved hundreds of people. Ena Barnes remembers Gladys' ability to manage the crowds, assigning each his job. She controlled the groups through Ena and her other prompters. "I could almost read her mind, because she had it so . . . organized." Ena says Gladys was "soft and kind and gentle. . . . She could correct you, but it wasn't a harsh tone when she corrected you, and she'd always smile when she was telling you and explain to you what she meant and why," in contrast to Dil, who was sharp at times. Of the pageants, Dorothy West says, "Nobody ever refused to go the second time. . . . People just kind of fought to be in those things." Martha Barney recalls some marriages came out of them. Dilworth Parkinson, who as a boy visited during preparations for Gladys' last production, remembers her running from one mini-rehearsal to another, flanked by artistic people who were devoted to her, Gladys continually in a tizzy over people who couldn't, or wouldn't, do their jobs—exactly like Leonore, when she grew up and directed shows of her own.

The 1940 pageant, called "Thither Go We," acted out the arrival of the Mormons in the valley. Again Indian life and dancing were depicted, with one group putting up some resistance to the pioneers. A quadrille typified pioneer recreations. Leonore remembers Heber Jacobs' boy gave him a swat as he descended from his wagon. Heber gave chase until the child took refuge beneath his mother's skirts. The Mormon Battalion, (descendants of actual soldiers), marched onto the scene with guns and cannon. More trains came, some of teams, some of handcarts, some, according to Ena Barnes, falling by the wayside. In one poignant scene, a baby was buried on the prairie. "Fact is," Ena says, "we had people that called us and wanted to know why we left that child buried in the dirt. It was a doll, but it was so beautifully done, you couldn't tell the difference." Ena says Gladys knew how to grab your attention, where to take your eye. "She had something going in that stadium every single minute. . . . You couldn't just guess what was coming next." Each group entered the arena from a different direction, acted out its tableau, then served as backdrop for the others.

Gladys, and the city, went all out for the 1941 pageant. The pageant committee hired Gladys a housekeeper, who cleaned up and fixed the children's meals. Rosemont was, more than ever, a flurry of activity. Dorothy West, one of Gladys' principal aides, moved to the house for the summer. The pageant committee budgeted $12,000 for the event. Dilworth recalls that "the W. P. A. had a big sewing project to give women work. That group was turned loose on it." The *Standard* speaks of 40,000 watts of special lighting, in addition to the regular Ogden Stadium lights. "Lighting effects can be compared favorably with the system employed at the Golden Gate fair's pageant production, according to the officials in charge." This year's pageant assembled a cast of one thousand five hundred, recruited from the Daughters of the Mormon Battalion, Daughters of the Utah Pioneers, C. C. C. boys, mutuals, choirs, and organizations all over town. Dorothy West recalls the Catholic youth borrowed the bishop's robe and miter for a processional. She speaks of Gladys' ease moving in the local Mexican community, describing a meal served on the kitchen floor in one humble home. "She was right with them. She loved those people, and she could talk their language." Betty Baker remembers Gladys getting so angry at her and a friend for missing a cue in rehearsal that she bawled them out in Spanish, of which they understood not a word.

This pageant, called "The Trail Breakers," depicted the discoveries and exploits of Columbus, Balboa, Ponce de Leon, and Cortes, meeting Caribbean, Florida, Iroquois and Pueblo Indians.

Next came French and English explorers, Cartier, Marquette, La Salle, Hudson, and finally Americans like Lewis and Clark and Fremont. Trappers and traders filled their role, together with the Mormon pioneers gathering at Council Bluffs, and the Mormon Battalion in dry camp on the Santa Fe Trail. Gladys staged scenes from village life from each culture, Indian, Spanish, French, Pennsylvania German. Dorothy West remembers the flourish and mannerisms of a male dancer from Charles the Second's court. "Of special delight to the audience," the *Standard-Examiner* reports, "was the snake dance and sacrificial ceremony of the Aztecs, the conversions of the Indians of Florida and California and the spontaneous gayety of their fiesta." Before their conversion, the Florida Indians burned a Jesuit at the stake. The actor had an Indian costume under his robe, and simply danced off with the others. Concealed in the pile of brush and straw in the tableau's center was a papier-mâché manikin, for the actual burning. The Aztec snake dance used a long, plumed serpent, for which Gladys used an old hose from the fire department. Montezuma wore an elaborate cape, to which the W. P. A. women had glued thousands of tiny feathers. The scene's climax came when the shadow of three crosses fell across the pyramid, arresting the human sacrifice just before it could be completed.

Ena Barnes remembers how stinky and smoky the Jesuit was the first time they tried to burn him. Ena had the idea of making the manikins, (four in all), by pasting paper over a man wearing knit stockings, then slitting it so he could get out. The head forms came from a hat shop. "They were so real-like, after I got them made . . . I took these guys up and laid them on the bed. One day I went dashing upstairs there and here I about scared the wits out of me." Dorothy West tells how Gladys tried to get the painters to give a certain effect she wanted on the Aztec pyramid. "And the painters did everything they could do and it still didn't quite please her." The dress rehearsal (which had a paying audience) went off alright, but then in the night it rained hard. "She went home crying that night, because everything was going to be wrecked," but next day they discovered the rain "had done what the painters couldn't do. It had aged that stuff. . . . It was as perfect as anything could ever have been, and nature did it." Gladys insisted on authenticity: songs, dances, and costumes had to match the period. Dorothy says Gladys had her "going through *National Geographics* until I was nearly blind hunting for certain patterns for the costumes" for the Aztec scene. "It wouldn't be any other Indian at all. It had to be the Aztecs." She says, "Even if she'd have had to leave out some part because she couldn't make it authentic, it was left out, rather than have something substituted." Ena kidded Gladys about the amount of effort she put into things, telling her such and such a detail only lasted a for minute. Gladys stopped and told her, "The sunset only last[s] for a minute, but it's one of God's most beautiful creations." Ena says, "I never will forget that one forever."

Dilworth thought the pageants were his wife's "real work. . . . She was a genius at it no doubt." The 1941 pageant he calls "a magnificent production, . . . as good as anything Hollywood could have done." Afterwards she took to her bed for more than a year, as Leonore remembers it. "I think she had . . . angina, which hurt a lot, gave her a lot of pain." One suspects also a case of physical and emotional exhaustion. Leonore recalls, "I did most of the cooking at night." She remembers going in to keep her mother company, telling her all that was going on in her life. "It's the first time I ever talked to my mother at any length of time."

Dil

Dil was six foot one, with broad shoulders, light blue eyes, an elongated jaw, pointed nose, and protruding ears. His hair was coarse and brown, like a buffalo robe. In his forties it thinned and developed a wave, but did not gray until he was in his seventies. Dil was busy, focused, sometimes irritable, but also quick to laugh, with a ready grin. Dil's long, malleable face served him in his storytelling, as did the snorts, chirps, and howls he could bring up from his throat. His voice was homey rather than melodious. As an older man, his dentures muted his s's into a whistle that added to his distinctive spoken style. To the scouts, Dil projected confidence, manly vigor, and strength, carrying their packs, pressing out in front of them with his long-legged strides.

Dil was active at church and in his seventies quorum, though Leonore remembers him being gone as often as not to speak in sacrament meetings around the council. Martha recalls him substituting in her Sunday school class when Ralph Oborn's job kept him away. George Frost tells how Lou Fleming, their seventies quorum president, would come by with an interview booklet, asking worthiness questions. Dil, after they had talked a minute, said, "Lou, let me look at that book." Lou complied. Dilworth scribbled across the form, "None of your business." Lou, who himself thought the questions a trifle personal, was amused. Leonore says Dil ran with a group of college professors in the '30s, some of them doubters. Dil later spoke of friends, perhaps the same ones, who criticized the Brethren, and how he found himself joining in. Leonore remembers he told of listening to general conference on the radio when "the Spirit came over him and witnessed to him that these apostles and the Prophet were the true spokesmen of the Lord." He did an about face. From that time Dil's stance was to defend the Brethren.

Friends speak of Dil's easy way around the neighborhood. Mary Wilson remembers him throwing apples at her husband David while he watered the lawn. Myrene Brewer tells how, driving up the canyon on his way to Kiesel, he would stop in at her summer home. "He never came empty handed." Always he had bread, lollipops for the children, honeycomb. "It wasn't very much, but he always had a . . . tidbit." Margaret Barlow, Mary Wilson's daughter, remembers honeycomb too, as part of Christmas cards. "He didn't believe in sending cards . . . that you couldn't eat." She remembers her family pooling dinner with the Youngs. Dil "would come over and say, 'Gee, what's in your refrigerator. Ours looks just awful.'" Whatever they found they would put together and share, "and so we would have sort of a banquet out of not much meal."

Dilworth loved practical jokes. Leonore tells how he brought home a box of chocolates one April Fools and offered her some when she was little. "I wouldn't touch them," she writes, suspecting soap or cotton inside. She watched as Dilworth, Gladys, and Young Dil ate them all. Once Dil bought a toaster on time, advertised to cost a nickel a day. Dilworth brought in a single nickel, day after day, until he had paid for it in full. Dil traded jokes with his neighbor Leland H. Creer, the historian. Once the Creers invited the Youngs to supper. When the hour came, the Crofts, mutual friends, arrived at the Creers. "Dil and Gladys couldn't make it, so they sent us in their place." Five minutes later the doorbell rang again—another couple with the same story. Five minutes more arrived another couple, and five minutes later the Youngs, carrying a big pot of soup for them all. On another occasion Dil had a letterhead printed for the "Historical Research Society of Weber County," and, writing under the name of Mrs. S. D. Yoking, invited Leland to lecture at the inaugural meeting in March of 1937. "It is our thought that the Daughters of the Pioneers are too social for the objects they profess. [Our society] is organized purely for business." Creer's assigned topic was the history of Weber County prior to 1847. Dilworth, aware of how little history there was in Weber County prior to 1847, watched his neighbor's window, where sure enough Professor Creer burned the midnight oil. He let him work up until the very day before letting on.

Dilworth read incessantly. Martha Barney remembers, "We'd ride along in the car, and when we'd come to a red light, he'd [have] a book here, and he'd pick it up and read." Leonore adds, "If he ever had to walk anywhere, he'd walk while he was reading. . . . Most people get motion sickness doing that, but he didn't." (Leonore picked up the habit, and passed it to her children.) Dil took a year's worth of classes at Weber College with the idea of completing a degree, but lost interest because the work was so easy for him. Leonore remembers him saying, "If I have to do this for four years, I don't want to do it." Blaine Parkinson, his son-in-law, with a doctorate in Educational Psychology, considered Dilworth as knowledgeable as most PhDs he knew. Leonore says Gladys hated to go to the in-laws, "because every time they visited

Grandma Lou, [Dilworth] reverted back to his sullen childhood,"
sitting around, reading whatever book was available, and ignoring
whatever else might be happening. Leonore remembers him visiting the library weekly, always coming home with a stack of books.
The Youngs' lawn was full of tiny purple violets. "Every spring,"
she remembers, "he'd pick a big bouquet of violets for the librarians."

CHAPTER 9

On Trial

A Juryman

On Monday, March 13, 1944, Kent S. Bramwell, Ogden's mayor, resigned abruptly. Bramwell, thirty-one, had been elected the previous fall on a platform of cleaning up city government. The *Standard-Examiner* reported the resignation the next day, stating that Sunday he had resigned his calling in the LDS 24th Ward bishopric as well. The war was on—D Day just weeks away—and Bramwell's resignation removed his deferment as a minister. Bramwell met with the draft board, where he waved all procedure, and by the 14th was out of town and in uniform. Rumors flew. A *Standard* editorial that day alluded to secret meetings with special interests intent on setting up a Huey Long style political machine. The state attorney general's office investigated, eventually calling for a grand jury. The city commission attempted to get Bramwell back from Fort Douglas to set the record straight. One of the commissioners talked to Bramwell's commanding officer, who said Bramwell could attend if he requested permission. Bramwell replied to the commission by cable: "Detailed to K. P. duty Saturday. Impossible to leave post. Awaiting shipping orders. Consider resignation final."

On April 4, John Charles Meyers, owner of a game room in the Eccles Building called the Playdium, was arrested for paying Bramwell a $500 bribe. In Meyers' April 7 preliminary hearing, Bramwell admitted to receiving a $600 loan from Meyers, part of which he and City Attorney M. Blaine Peterson had used for a trip to California. When he had difficulty repaying the loan, Meyers told him to keep it, that there were other ways he could repay him. Bramwell said he met with Meyers three times, during which they discussed a scheme for 25th Street tavern owners to pay into a fund, on the order of $300 to $1000 a month, in exchange for the police not enforcing anti-gambling laws. According to Lyle J. Barnes in his Utah State University master's thesis, high stakes poker games, slot machines, and "marble" or pinball machines with payoffs, not to mention prostitution and bootlegging, had been tolerated on 25th Street for some time. "To make them think I was playing ball," the *Standard* gives Bramwell's testimony, "I told them I could fix the chief." He said he found five hundred dollars in an envelope shoved under his door one morning, and that Meyers later wanted to know why the laws were still being enforced. "He asked me if I had received the money. I said what money and he said the money the boys had sent and I said that I had received $500."

Next day, April 8, Meyers, in a long, unsworn statement, told of the loan and of schemes by Bramwell to pay it back. Meyers was going into the war surplus business, and he claimed Bramwell gave him a list of items the city would be putting out to bid, with figures penciled in as to how much had been budgeted for each. He said he offered to have Meyers purchase two cars for the city and mark them up by the amount of the loan before resale. He said he offered to have the fire department buy some tarpaulins Meyers would be manufacturing from surplus blimps, condemning the fire department's old ones if necessary. Meyers said he later got into a conversation with Captain Clifford Keeter of the Ogden police at a restaurant counter. Keeter described a visit by the mayor to the police: "No one in uniform was to take even as much as a package of gum from anyone." Meyers said, "I stated that the mayor had a lot of business talking to the police department in this manner when he was trying to pay me a $600 debt in every way but the right way." He said Keeter asked him for help, "as he would like to find out if Bramwell was crooked.

Meyers said he attended the meetings with Bramwell, but stated, "What I there said, and all I there said was with the intent and for the purpose of provoking conversation by Mayor Bramwell . . . in furtherance of [Captain Keeter's] investigation of the corrupt conduct of Kent S. Bramwell as mayor of Ogden city."

Keeter also testified, concurring in the matter of the meetings. He said he, Meyers, and Warren I. Cassidy had obtained a "dictagraph" from a supplier in Salt Lake, and hidden a microphone in room 902 of the Ben Lomond Hotel, and later in room 303 of the Eccles Building, where the meetings took place. Meyers' counsel tried to introduce into evidence vinyl records made of the meetings. This was sensational news. "Let the truth be told through the voice of science," said defense attorney Arthur Woolley. John A. Hendricks, district attorney, replied, "Let us be sure that science has not been tampered with so that we shall be certain that what we get is the truth." Keeter had not told his superiors what he was doing. He had told A. L. Glasmann, owner of the *Standard-Examiner*. At one point, Glasmann had possession of the records. The prosecution strongly objected to the records being played in court, but Judge Gladwell finally allowed it. The *Standard* called the playing an "anti-climax because the recordings were so indistinct." Woolley apologized for the poor copies and offered to produce better ones.

Things looked bad for Bramwell. There was the matter of the $600 loan, plus the fact he held on to the $500, telling no one until his wife turned it over to a representative of the state attorney general's office a week after Bramwell left town. Peterson had made the California trip with Bramwell, so also benefited from the loan. Chief of Police T. R. Johnson, whom Bramwell offered to "fix," was Bramwell's political appointee. On the other hand, Meyers and the 25th street operators were hardly above suspicion. Whether they intended to set up a fund, or whether they meant to frame Bramwell, either way they stood to gain. In addition, these operators in the past had enjoyed a cozy relationship with elements in city government. Lyle J. Barnes writes that the previous mayor, Harman W. Peery, preferred to have vice out in the open.

Peery never attempted to hide his motives, and prided himself that the revenue of government from property taxes was low . . . and that the city obtained money for governmental service from the fees and forfeiture of bail received from vice. It was his further contention that prostitution, gambling, and liquor couldn't be effectively combated, and that harassment would only drive these operations underground.

This sort of collusion was exactly what Bramwell was elected to stop. But if Bramwell did not know whom he could trust, the same must be said of Keeter. Did he fear his superiors would quash an investigation. Or was he on the take, collaborating with the operators to get rid of Bramwell. Bramwell pointed out in Meyers' preliminary hearing that Keeter had been passed over for the chief's job, and Woolley, one of Meyers' lawyers, had been passed over for city attorney. Then there was Glasmann's role. Glasmann had a reputation as a back-room operator. Was he just trying to preserve the old order. Or did Keeter come to him as a member of the press in its watchdog role.

On May 2, Judges Cowley and Adams of the second district court ordered a grand jury investigation. Grand juries are made up of citizens, like trial juries, but their duties are investigative in nature. They do not judge guilt, and are not bound to hear testimony for the defense, but rather bring indictments where they think there is sufficient evidence to convict a person. They are sworn to secrecy, and have broad powers to subpoena and question witnesses under oath without representation, whether it be mayor, criminal, bureaucrat, lawyer, or ordinary citizen. "Often the mere announcement that a grand jury will be called," the *Standard* observes, "is enough to cause persons to get out of town in a hurry," and sure enough, players began to disappear. A grand jury's probing powers, and the fact its members are drawn from the community, suit it to the task of ferreting out corruption in public office, but also of keeping public officials from unjustly charging ordinary citizens. According to the *Standard*, this was only the third grand jury in the history of Weber County. The second, in 1917, also investigated corruption in gambling and liquor enforcement. Few indictments came, and no convictions, but, according to S. P. Dobbs, the district attorney, it did help clean up Ogden. "According to a rumor, now of 27 years standing," he is quoted in the *Standard* as saying, ". . . about 200 persons left town, and scores of couples rushed to the county clerk's office to get married."

Forty names for the grand jury were drawn from a box on April 14, among them Dilworth's. Dil was trying to cope with the wartime manpower shortage and get Camp Kiesel ready in time. Prospective jurors were notified by registered mail. Dilworth states that when he read his name,

I thought to myself, "I won't have to serve. Camp opens in sixty days and the judge won't keep Camp Kiesel closed. If it is to open, I must get it ready. There is no one to hire. . . ." Thus I thought and as I thought I seemed to have a feeling the excuse would not be granted and I would have to serve. The closer the time came for the decision the more it seemed to me I would have to serve. On the morning of the jury call I walked over to the courtroom with Bill Diehl, the manager of the newspaper. . . . As we crossed the city hall square, I kidded him a little. I said: "Bill, have you ever seen a prophet?" He: "No!" I: "Would you like to see one?" He: "Yes (with an oath)." I: "Look at me; I'm one." He: "Oh, yeah?!" I: "Would you like to hear me prophesy?" He: "Yeah." I: "I prophesy that I'll end up on that jury." And then I heard myself say what I had never thought any time. "And what's more, I'm going to be its foreman!" He looked and acted incredulous, and we entered the judge's courtroom.

The names were drawn from the shuffle box and it was no surprise when my name was lifted out first. I rose and offered my excuses, telling the judge that if I went on that jury there would be no camp for seven hundred boys that summer. He smiled and motioned me to enter the jury box. After six others were chosen, the judge asked us all to arise and we were all sworn in. Then he said: "It is in the province of the judge by law to choose the jury foreman. I choose you, Mr. Young!"

I looked over at Bill Diehl and put my thumb in my ear and wagged my hand at him. He had a peculiar look on his face. His mouth came open wider and wider, as the full impact of what I had said struck him. He shook his head from side to side. I grinned at him.

The grand jury met May 2 through June 30. Members were paid for their time, according to Cecil K. Parker, one of the jurymen. "They'd go two hours, maybe, in the morning, two hours in the afternoon, sometimes maybe not that long, then they'd skip a day or two." In addition to their work on the corruption charges, they were required to review pending criminal cases and to investigate the jails. One of the jurymen took minutes, and apparently had difficulty. The jury's report suggests future juries be assigned "a competent court reporter to take down the testimony." Dilworth writes of listening to testimony:

> I learned a lot . . . about men's perfidy and a lot more about the false standards of lawyers. Some are honest and dumb, others honest and bright, still others dishonest in both categories. I learned, too, that people will tell the truth as long as their own interests are not at stake.

There was some fear of underworld reprisal. Leonore, seventeen now, disappeared one night, and Dil and Gladys, fearing she had been kidnapped, called the police. Actually she was sleeping at Joan Allred's and had left a message with a visiting cousin, which didn't get through.

Leonore remembers talk that the "back room" powers, including the LDS Church, had attempted a cover-up, that Bramwell ought to have been exposed and excommunicated. The *Standard* on April 20 had reported on a meeting between A. L. Glasmann (a non-member), Ralph Duvall of the chamber of commerce, LDS stake leaders including Samuel G. Dye and Earl S. Paul, and at Glasmann's insistence, David O. McKay of the LDS First Presidency. Glasmann played the recordings. "Everybody hoped that the matter could be solved without a scandal. It was thought that probably the best thing for the young mayor to do was to enter the army." (Bramwell, in Meyers' preliminary hearing, alluded to a "mandate" to join the army and get out of town, from chamber, press, and church, in the persons of Duvall, Glasmann, and Dye. Bramwell stated he wished he had stayed "to clean out the pressure groups, the rackets and the rats.") Duvall, one imagines, was thinking of Ogden's image and business climate, which was, after all, his job. Like Duvall, Glasmann may be accused of hastiness, but criminal conspiracy? His editorial of March 14, the day after Bramwell's resignation, is more concerned with the propriety of partisan interests setting up a political machine than with any criminal activity, but nevertheless alludes to the meetings and the secret fund. The Church had an interest in protecting its good name by distancing itself from the appearance of impropriety, which it did by accepting Bramwell's resignation the day it learned of his troubles. The Church also had a responsibility towards Bramwell as a member, though any disciplinary action would have had to take place privately, and with more confidentiality than Glasmann's meeting afforded. Leonore's sense is that Dil was fearless as a juryman, and followed leads no matter where they led. She said he told of questioning David O. McKay privately, who according to the story said, "Kent lied to me." She says Dil became convinced the rumors of LDS complicity in a cover-up were unfounded, and defended David O. McKay in and out of the jury room.

On June 30, 1944, the jury returned fourteen indictments involving twenty-five people. Some of these were routine criminal cases, some had to do with unrelated police corruption (two officers were brought up on morals charges). Some involved officials of previous administrations, including Harman W. Peery and his police chief Rial C. Moore, for conspiracy in the matter of licensing gambling. Another indictment accused J. C. Meyers, Warren Cassidy, and eight others, (but not Keeter), with conspiracy in the matter of the $500 bribe and fund discussed in the meetings. One final indictment accused Kent S. Bramwell of asking for and agreeing to receive a bribe.

The jury's report came down on the jails with directness typical of S. Dilworth Young, who likely wrote it. Meals were not only bland but badly balanced. "The sheriff is by law allowed 20¢ per meal for feeding these men. This method is bound, sooner or later, to result in the prisoners being fed little and the sheriff profiting by the deficiency." Sometimes garments and towels were not clean. The report criticizes especially the "tank," a windowless, unventilated room, ten feet by twelve feet, where prisoners were held while awaiting arraignment. On a weekend that might be three days, in addition to which men with short sentences often served them here. This "safe-deposit box for the human erring" featured seating for three, but had known as many as thirty-five occupants. Drunk and sober, filthy and clean, all were packed in together. "In the opinion of this Jury it would be an excellent place in the 11th Century but it is a barbarous place for 1944."

The report recommends the police department "cease to be a political plaything of elected officials," and that police chiefs serve longer terms. Police officers are criticized for moonlighting in uniform as security guards and bouncers. The report recommends they be paid enough that they don't have to. Gambling should be combated uncompromisingly. Some had suggested limiting gambling to west of Washington to protect the city's children. "The Jury confesses that it can't see any difference between children on the Bench and children on streets west of Washington." The report is critical of the Corrupt Practices Act, with its one year statute of limitations, which amounts to "a huge joke perpetuated upon the citizens of our state." One wonders whether, if the law had had more teeth, there would have been more indictments. The report recommends a property tax increase, and is critical of the system of bail forfeiture, noting it adds $24,000 annually to the city treasury.

> Bail forfeiture as a corrective is a vicious practice, which does not deter but merely becomes a license. Does any honest citizen suppose that the gambler cares to whom he pays his graft? . . .

In the private graft a few become corrupt. In the public graft we all become corrupt, and our children are quick to sense the corruption.

The jury members returned to private life. Dil's history doesn't mention whether Camp Kiesel opened. There was no scout page in 1944, but the *Standard* does invite boys to Camp Browning that year. The criminal cases dragged on. Mayor Peery and former police chief Moore fought their charges until November 20, 1945, when they pleaded guilty. Peery was fined two hundred dollars, Moore one hundred. Peery went on to be mayor again, in 1948-1949. J. C. Meyers was eventually convicted of bribery, but died in late 1945 while appealing to the Utah Supreme Court. Perjury and conspiracy charges were abated at that time. The conspiracy case against Meyers, Cassidy, and the others fell to pieces when Meyers died, and none of the others would testify against each other. These charges were dismissed December 3, 1946. Kent S. Bramwell served twenty-two months in the army, including eighteen in the Pacific, before being acquitted of bribery June 8, 1946. He claimed bad judgment in his desire to be a "lone wolf" and a "an amateur detective," but of course bad judgment is not a crime. In the trial, the *Standard* says, "[T. R.] Johnson testified to frequent meetings with the mayor relative to pinball machine operations and law enforcement and stated that never at any time had there been a request or indirect suggestion by the mayor that the law not be enforced." Perhaps this, together with Bramwell's character witnesses, was what finally swayed the jury. Bramwell took a job with the Red Cross, his old employer, training in water safety in Catalina before moving to Phoenix. The last motion in the case came from his side of the aisle, requesting that the $500, which no one had claimed, be turned over to the county treasurer, which it was on May 15, 1947.

Dilworth Randolph Young

Young Dil sang his freshman year at Weber College, was active in campus clubs, and played football under Bob Davis, where, his father recalls, "he had no trouble fumbling and became a very good halfback." That spring, 1943, Dil Jr. and his classmates were drafted, and left for Fort Douglas on the same train. Dilworth Sr. writes:

> When he and Ensign Williamsen were questioned by the recruiting officer, they were told there were several training schools to which they might go: signal, first aid, etc., etc., or they could have combat. They both said, "I'll take combat!" When I asked Dil why he took combat, he said he felt if risks were to be taken, he could not ask any other man to assume his risk.

He trained in California, Texas, then near Colorado Springs. His letters to Gladys comment on concerts and movies, and are full of poetry, often to the exclusion of news. Sonorous, full of fantastic nature imagery, his verse is reminiscent of his mother's prose:

> *Strange, discordant, the challenge is thrown high;*
> *And from the wild driving clouds, screams in the sky*
> *What is the spirit kind that can catch this lawless form*
> *And swiftly translate peaceful mind,*
> *To ride fearless, lustily the storm. . . .*

He complained at army "efficiency." He worried about Leonore dating soldiers—Leonore says, "He knew what the guys were after." A "big tough" challenged him to a boxing match. "My brother had done little fighting, but because he was big and an athlete and because he didn't drink or smoke, he easily beat the tough, who had all of the vices. He gained a superman reputation in the camp from this event." At Christmas, Dil recorded his greetings and a pair of hymns, "Now the Day is Over," and "Come Thou O Mighty King," on two records and sent them home.

Dil Sr. writes,

> Gladys was filled with foreboding and said she felt like he could not come back. She became ill and was in bed with what we

thought was heart trouble. She had all the symptoms. Dr. Draper sat for hours watching her, testing, etc., and could not diagnose anything else. Yet three days before his last furlough home, she rose from her bed and by the day he got home was well and had no reoccurrence.

Dil wanted to give his son a blessing during this visit, and thought to do it during a hike to Mt. Ogden. "I thought I would like to promise him that he would come home unharmed if he kept the commandments even as I had been promised in World War I." Dil says as his son sat on a rock on the summit, looking east,

> I walked up behind him to put my hands on his head, and somehow I couldn't. . . . I walked around a few minutes more and came back to put my hands on his head, and I couldn't do it. I just couldn't feel right, and something stopped me. . . . So I thought, Well, we'll do it later. I didn't say a thing to him. He never knew I did that.

They hiked down Wheeler Creek, and Gladys picked them up in Ogden Canyon. That evening Dil blessed his son in the parlor, intending to make the same promise.

> Several times I began to tell him this thing, but each time I could not seem to do it. It wasn't a premonition. I could not seem to say the words; they seemed out of place. And so I didn't make the promise. I am sure that I was as prophetic as my grandfather, for my prompting was not to promise.

He noticed later that Dil Jr.'s patriarchal blessing, unlike Leonore's, made no mention of marriage or family.

Leonore writes of one last contact.

> Dil was given a weekend pass just before he was to be shipped overseas. He tried to telephone Mother because he wanted her to meet him in Denver for the last leave. Mother was at Monte Cristo, twenty-five miles from Ogden. She suddenly got an extremely strong impression to go home immediately. She tried to throw it off but it became more intense. She finally told Dad she had to go home. When she got there the call came from Dil.

She went to Denver and they had a wonderful weekend.

Gladys, in a 1947 journal entry addressed to Dil, writes of

> that day in August when you said, "This is goodbye, Mom.
> Maybe it will be a year or two before I see you again." Even then
> Son I knew it would be all the long years of the remainder of
> my life time before I would see you again or hear your voice and
> when our little long distance farewell was over I went towards
> the garden, but withered in body and soul I sat on the bottom
> step of the little back porch among the flowers and wept the
> desolate tears of finality . . . Your voice was wistful as you had
> talked to me and I knew that you also knew.

Leonore worked at Hill Field as a courier. Once as she turned a
corner on her scooter, a bus load of soldiers waved and called out.
"I was distracted, lost control of the scooter, and the mail bags
swung around and knocked me off. I landed running. I never did
fall down but I was over so far that I actually skinned my nose."
Later she worked at Defense Depot Ogden filling overseas orders.
"Each of us had an Italian war prisoner to help us lift things, etc.
I soon learned to count in Italian. My helper had a beautiful oper-
atic-quality voice and he would sing all of the time. . . . The pris
oners would sing opera as they marched to and from work." Jobs
went begging during the war. Dil Sr. took a part-time position as
an early-morning washerman at the Weber college gym.
Controlling the valves to the washers meant standing beneath the
chilly draft of a vent, which warmed as the day dawned, bringing
with it snatches of conversation from the showers. Gladys taught
elementary in Washington Terrace. Leonore remembers her
telling of one little girl during a Utah history lesson who said,
"Why do there have to be Mormons here." Gladys was amused—
Ogden had had a large "gentile" segment since the coming of the
railroad, but still, the war was changing the face of their little town.
Gladys also taught Spanish at Weber College. Ben Davis
remembers her walking down 25th Street to class, often late. Ben
would pick her up in his car, and so was never later than the
teacher. He remembers her as quiet, unassuming, yet with good

rapport, and a knack for getting the students' attention. He remembers Spanish songs, and a Mexican meal with all her students each term. Leonore was just out of high school, and Gladys wanted her to have a Mexican experience. So Gladys went to work for a month at Hill Field to help pay for an extended stay. Dilworth noted how nervous it made her, and wrote his son, "I don't like her to work but she will do it." Gladys was nearly driven batty by her supervisor, a Mrs. Dibble, who chattered away the better part of the day. Finally Gladys brought a sack of rags to work. Every time Mrs. Dibble started to talk, she took out her rags and cut and trimmed. By the end of the day she had a good-sized ball. Getting it home meant getting a pass, which meant explaining how she got it to the main supervisor. "Well the upshot was," she explained in a letter to Dil Jr., "that the troublesome woman was removed to another department and I am now doing a full eight hours unmolested."

On October 8, 1944, Gladys and Leonore, with Leonore's friend Ann Bailey, traveled by bus to Mexico City. They took an apartment by the central grand plaza, intending to stay for a year. Leonore had studied Spanish in school, but found she understood nothing. After a couple of weeks she began to be able to make out talks in church. She writes, "My goal was to study voice and learn Spanish dancing." They shopped around in the dark, employing finally a Russian soprano named Sonya Verbinsky. "She was everything that Sonya Verbinsky should have been." Large, forceful, red-haired, rich-voiced, with exaggerated vibrato, she would show Leonore what she wanted her to do. Leonore had all she could do to keep from laughing.

Leonore remembers being impressed in Mexico City with the elegance right next to squalor. She describes how the young men would promenade clockwise around the square, the young women counterclockwise, the men saying "Ay, qué bombita," or other flattering things. If a boy liked a girl, he might follow her home to learn where she lived, then send an intermediary to make the first contact. Never would he go himself. Gladys wrote to Young Dil,

The two girls are a joy to be with. They are so young & green and beautiful. . . . They have had starry eyes either from the happiness of unaccustomed beauty or from tears of homesickness all the time we have been here. One minute they are walking on air as they see some beautiful orchid or camellia or look & listen to symphony or beautiful drama. They are thrilled when all the young cavaliers toss them beautiful compliments as they walk down the street. They are blue or homesick when night comes on and there are no friends no home or family.

Ann wore a beret, which the Mexican boys called a tortilla. Leonore was a brunette, but as Gladys explained, both girls were "blondes down here you know, and how these Latins do love blondes."

The 104th Infantry Division boarded the Lejeune in New York August 26, 1944, landing in Normandy September 6. *Timberwolf Tracks,* the division history, records that between September 21 and October 10, Dilworth's regiment, the 415th Infantry, took up guarding "railroads, pipelines, pumping stations and warehouse docks," with orders to "shoot to kill." "Black market looters had been tapping thousands of gallons of gasoline out of the pipelines, hijackers had been raiding trains and trucks for army food and cigarettes. It was not long until the 'Old Faithful' Regiment had reduced these loses to a mere trickle." Dan Bradshaw, Dil's scout camp friend, walked seven miles to look him up for a visit. Dil met him with a smart salute, after which they got down to "some good old bull sessions." Dan said the non-LDS soldiers admired Dil, and the LDS ones looked to him for spiritual guidance. "I just won't forget how he impressed me with the facts that God lives, that he guides and directs men who live a clean life with an honest and pure heart." Dan enjoyed the company "of a man I knew had not lowered to the . . . little habits of the army so unpleasant in the sight of God." Next day Dil, just back from an eight-mile march, walked the seven more to find Dan and tell him about church services. The two of them, who had been fasting, shared Dan's rations.

The division shipped out on October 16 and 17 for Vilvorde,

north of Brussels, Belgium. Dil's regiment rode freight cars, forty men to a car, like his father twenty-six years before. Dil first saw battle the night of October 24, 1944, just over the Holland border southeast of Breda. Friends differed as to what happened. Peter T. Bardin says early in the morning of the 25th, Dil was hit lightly in the shoulder by machine gun fire. Peter talked to him and found him in good spirits, though he thought him in shock from loss of blood. Dil, bandaged, and three others, tried to crawl up on the machine gun nest when a grenade landed nearby. A fragment nearly severed his arm at the shoulder. A medic rebandaged him and, over Dil's protests, gave him a shot of morphine, then left him in the field. Dil later walked several hundred yards down the road, fainting just as the medics arrived in a jeep. He died soon after reaching the aid station.

Dil's first letters from Europe didn't arrive in Utah until November 9, and his father wrote him several times after he died. One letter, dated November 7, alludes to Dil Sr.'s loneliness in the house. "I sleep each night in your room. And I think of you when you were a little boy and I was a foolish unwise father. But I loved you in my undemonstrative way. It's hard to realize that when you come home you will be old enough to vote, 21 next June. It doesn't seem possible." Gladys wrote him for the last time on October 24, within hours of his death.

> Sometimes it seems you are a million miles away and I cannot penetrate the void and deep despair that lies between. At other times you are as near as the morning sunlight enlightening my soul with your beautiful spirit, reviving my aching heart with your contagious laughter, filling the moment you are with me so full of beauty that a complete eternity is packed into a single instant of bliss. I would give all my possessions and anything else that was asked just to know you are safe and not too uncomfortable at this moment. If I ever see your handwriting on a letter again I will know what it must be like for you when letters reach you finally after long delays.

She tells him, in her 1947 journal entry, "As you died I was struck at the same instance with a sharp unbearable pain in my abdomen and follow[ed] by hours of great physical, mental and spiritual suffering and a flood of uncontrollable tears."

Dilworth received the telegram from the War Department probably Saturday the 11th. He had written Dil that very day, and been to Guy and Delora Hurst's collecting *Reader's Digests* for him. Dilworth describes taking the telegram from the delivery woman and reading it. She asked if he were alright. He said, "'Yes, I think so.' As I do in crises, I felt no emotions. I went dead emotionally. I went [back] down to Hursts and there briefly burst into tears, rushed out of the house, drove around in the car sobbing for ten minutes, and went back." Delora remembers him returning— "he was just ashen"—telegram in his hand. The Hursts helped him dial up Salt Lake. Family members came that night to be with him. He tried to call Gladys in Mexico, but didn't reach her until the next morning, at the chapel during services. "She hung up, and I didn't know more about her until I got word she was on her way home. . . . She told me [later] that after I called she 'went black' and could hardly see to make her way to her apartment." Gladys' journal reads, "The darkness which followed was very staggering for many hours, but somehow I got back to our temporary dwelling and while in mockery a hand organ ground out the gay tunes of my homeland my heart broke."

Gladys' journal continues, "I called to you for help and beloved as you always did, you came in my hour of need and sustained me." Gladys was intensely romantic, but also visionary, and it is not always easy to tell when she intends something literally. That she refers here, not to a sense of presence, but to a visitation, is attested in others of her writings. One describes a pale light filling her dark room, and "a calm sweet peace" coming over her. She spoke from where she was on the couch to her son, "Was it so hard Dilworth—so very hard?" Now Dilworth appeared, standing in mid-air, answering with words that came into her mind, "Not too hard, Mother." She asked, "Is Ensign with you?" meaning Dil's friend Ensign Williamsen. Dil answered, "No, not yet, but he will be soon." (Dilworth Sr. notes, "We did not immediately talk to the Williamsens, but three months later when word came of Ensign's death, we went over and told them.") Gladys said, "Oh Dil, what shall I do. What shall I do?" Dil answered, "Go back home, Mother, and comfort Dad. Don't ever leave him, and don't neglect him. Go back and do the things for Ogden we were going to do together." She said, "I will, Son, I will." He sat by her on the couch

> in exactly the same angle and position he had done so many times in life—[except he did not] reach over and take my hand as was his custom in life, but with his look of deep compassion and love from his beautiful eyes and his smile and sweet expression of his tender mouth, and the noble spirit that radiated from his manly brow, I know if it had been possible for him to do so he would have kissed me and held me in his arms until my aching heart was healed.

Dil Jr. promised her Harold B. Lee, who was visiting the mission, would comfort her. Elder Lee gave her a blessing that evening. Her account of it records a promise that she "would be privileged from time to time to have the spirit of my son mingle with my spirit," that the Holy Ghost would visit her, and that she would have moments of doubt and anguish but would continue to receive comfort. She later recounts a dream or vision the night of November 16 of Dil being received in the Spirit World by his loved ones, all in white, Dil surprised at them all, Seymour B. Young Jr. in front, shaking hands, very proud, Rey L. Pratt coming forward, then Helaman, then "my dear little mother. She reached up and took Dilworth's face in both her hands, drew him down to her and kissed him so lovingly tender and so proud. He looked down at her—chuckled that sweet tender chuckle because she was so tiny and sweet." The day Dil's life insurance check came, Gladys felt as if he were standing behind her as if to stroke her hair. Calmed, she asked, "Oh, Dil, is it true that you are completely happy there. Is the place so beautiful that you would not desire to return even if you could. Is it as lovely as they try to make us believe?" For a split second, she thought she saw the room "transfigured into a golden radiance . . . [which] assured me we were not capable of understanding the beauty of the other world." Yet another time she saw him dressed in white, with Rey L. Pratt and Seymour B. Young Sr. He smiled, but then turned his back and walked away. As Leonore tells it, "She was given to understand that he had work to do and couldn't come back again."

Betty Baker remembers the Youngs consoling others. She describes Dilworth as cheerful and cordial when Gladys returned from Mexico, but Gladys told her, "when everyone is gone, that's when he just breaks down and sobs." The family held a memorial service on November 26 at the Institute of Religion. Dilworth wrote Dil Jr.'s army friends repeatedly, trying to iron out the differences in their accounts of his death. Margaret Barlow, who substituted as Dil's secretary at the Scout Office one week the summer of 1945, tells of the day Young Dil's things were returned. Solemnly, a tear rolling down one cheek, he sent her home. "I don't think I'll be doing anything else today." Gladys writes, probably a few months after Dil's death, "I have had no uncontrolled or inconsolable grief . . . except for a few hours when I have rebelled or grown angry and bitter." Leonore remembers her mother's grief as long, and deep, lasting more than a year. She took to her bed again. Leonore says, "I don't think she ever got over it, but Blaine took his place a little bit." Dil wrote to his son in 1952:

> *Last night I dreamed that you were home again,*
> *Forgot the eight long years you've been away.*
> *I watched the evening firelight on your face,*
> *Your hands entangled in old Brownie's hair,*
> *Your dog, contented, now that you were there.*
>
> *You felt the texture of the new rugs on the floor,*
> *Laughed at your sister's picture on the wall,*
> *Approved the new upholstery on the chair,*
> *Warmed to the warmth of color in the hall—*
> *Smiling and nodding enjoyment of them all.*
>
> *Then you climbed the stairs.*

I thought you liked the way we'd kept your room.
One readies rooms against a boy's return;
Imagines what he'd like to see and feel
When he comes home again—
The bed placed there, the table there, the walls
The color that he loved—and on the
Table in its leather box the schoolboy honors won.

Hours seemed to pass—I tiptoed to your bed,
And heard your gentle breathing, even, faint.
(Surely this doesn't sound like one who's dead!)
Put out a hand to touch your brow
But hastily withdrew it, lest I break
The rhythm of your being home—but now,

Today, we wander aimlessly about the empty house
Here are the roses brought in memory of you.
There is your boyish picture on the wall
(The ivy from a vase along the frame just so.)
The purple heart is in its box of blue
Beneath some lines that Joan wrote long ago:
  "So keep his heart fed with familiar things;
  No sound of tears
  Flaw the clean air where his tall shoulders lift.
  His laugh may stir
  The valleyed quite some immortal day,
  And we be easy, feeling him home again."

The Call

On March 12, 1945, Dilworth and Gladys attended the funeral of Samuel O. Bennion, his old mission president, now a member of the First Council of Seventy.

While there, a thought came into my mind that I would take his place in the Council. I paid no attention. All my life I have had a feeling that I "belonged" among the authorities but I have discounted it and paid it "no mind". I accounted it to ambition, not inspiration. The thought came to me very strong about two weeks later and this time I could not shake it. I did not mention it to Gladys, and our daily routine continued. . . . All the while I said I was "nuts" to think such a thing, but there it was.

Truman Madsen recalls Dilworth's telling of a scheme to sound out Oscar Kirkham, Dil's old scouting colleague, now in the First Council of Seventy. Dilworth had been playing with the idea of taking a scouting job in California. The big house seemed empty without Young Dil, and too full of memories. He took it up with Elder Kirkham, thinking that if he had an inkling, he would discourage him from doing something hasty. Elder Kirkham said, "I think that's a great idea. That's just the thing you should do." Truman says Dilworth "'kicked himself' back to Ogden trying to get the original impression out of his head."

> On the evening of April 5, 1945, I was restless. I seemed to know but it wasn't apparent to my mind. On the morning of the 6th I washed towels, and at 7:55 was home to take Gladys to school. As I entered the house, Gladys said: "There's a call for you from Salt Lake." I: "Did they leave an operator's number?" She: "No!" I: "Then let's go."
>
> We went to school and I left the car with her, walking to the office. I walked the streets of Ogden until 9:45. I knew what the call was. I don't know why I couldn't go to the office. At 9:50 I entered the office.
>
> Steno: "There's a call from Salt Lake." Me: "Is there an operator's number?" She: "Yes." Me: "Get the number."

Dil made the call—it was David O. McKay of the First Presidency. "All the time we talked it seemed to me that I knew just what he was going to say before he said it. It was a curious feeling." President McKay said, "Where are you?" Dil said he was in his office. McKay said, "What are you doing?" Dil said, "I am working." McKay said, "Would you like to attend conference?" Dil answered, "I would like to but I don't have a ticket." During the war, conferences were held in the assembly hall, and seating was limited. President McKay told him to report to his secretary

and she would give him one. Dil said he would have to find a way
to Washington Terrace to get his car, then go home to change out
of his scout uniform. President McKay told him to hurry and to
report to him on the stand after the morning session. Dil told him
he would do the best he could.

He made the trip, checked in with President McKay's secretary,
got his ticket, then walked to the south gate at Temple Square. "I
showed it to the gatekeeper and asked if that would let me in. He
opened the gate a foot or so, and I slid through the opening." The
policeman who escorted him to the north door of the Assembly
Hall was the first to tell him of his call.

> I slipped in and took a seat on the bench just in front of the
> door. A fist slammed into my back at the shoulder level.
> Turning, I saw Gene Hammond [the Salt Lake scout executive]
> grinning at me. Then President Clark arose and looked in my
> general direction and said:
>
> "I have just been informed that President Young has just come
> in (he didn't know me). I have the honor to inform you that
> you have been sustained as one of the First Council of the
> Seventy." I didn't move—just sat there. It was 11:45 a.m. After
> the meeting, I edged my way toward the stand and met
> President McKay in the aisle. He offered his hand. I took it. He
> smiled and said, "Will you?" I said, "Yes, sir." That was all that
> was said to me then or later.

On May 23, Presidents George Albert Smith and George F.
Richards set Dilworth apart. He began traveling to stake conferences on weekends, sometimes with other general authorities,
sometimes alone. He resigned as scout executive, suggesting to the
board that they hire Loo Roberts, his old camp associate, to take
his place, which they did. "I stayed until August running Camp
Browning on Pineview Lake, while we had a makeshift Camp
Kiesel. I bowed out of my work there and reported to the First
Council of Seventy." Dil joked about how surprised his friends
were at his call. Wally Brown remembers him asserting in a conference the calling must have been inspired, because no one else

would have picked him. It must have occurred to him that his family background had something to do with it. His setting apart referred to "blood" in his veins "of those who have served devotedly in the past." His great-grandfather Joseph Young had been one of the original Presidents of the Seventy, serving as Senior President forty-four years. His grandfather Seymour B. Young Sr. was Senior President too. Brother-in-law Rey L. Pratt served on the Council, and uncle Levi Edgar Young was currently Senior President. Perhaps Oscar Kirkham had exerted some influence. Dilworth felt Samuel O. Bennion, his old mission president, was pulling for him, and expressed the suspicion too that David O. McKay appreciated his grand jury work and had something to do with the call. Yet in 1972 Dilworth wrote, "I am sure at this moment that my life has been guided in what I should do. Every job has been a guided preparation for my present position." He mentions not going to Annapolis (which he felt would have taken him far afield), his mission (and his not challenging the change from Hawaii), his marriage to Gladys, his scout job. At each turning point in his life there was something, some help, some intimation, and often a strong premonition. This was the long and short of what he thought about the source of his call.

Gladys, when he went to get the car in the Terrace on his way to that first conference, asked what was going on. "I told her I wasn't sure. I didn't tell her my premonition." He alluded to it next day in general conference, though:

> A good portion of my life I have thought that the calls which came to those who are to do things for the Church, while officially coming from the prophets, perhaps might come as a still, small voice speaking to the person in the manner of the words of the Lord when he spoke to Samuel. He called, "Samuel." Samuel had to answer two or three times. The words which came to me sounded distinctly like those of President David O. McKay.

> I submit to you the questions he asked of me because I believe there have never been propounded, to me at least, three more innocent questions.

Where are you? What are you doing? Would you like to attend general conference?

CHAPTER 10

Second Mission

New England

Dil was forty-seven at the time of his call to the Seventy in April of 1945, a young man still. He had held his scouting job for twenty-two and a half years, and would be a general authority for thirty-six more.

Dilworth commuted to Salt Lake now to his office on the second floor of the Church administration building. Down the hall, uncle Levi Edgar Young had grandfather Seymour B. Young Sr.'s office that Dilworth had visited so many times before. Dil traveled alone or with various general authorities to Stake Conferences: Logan, Ogden, Moon Lakes, Bear Lake, Thatcher, Tucson. He toured the Northern California Mission with German E. Ellsworth, the mission president. "I slept in the same bed with him for three weeks, nearly, and he told me a lot of things about the brethren, good and bad of his own experiences. He had had a lot." Dilworth began publishing articles in the Improvement Era: a yarn about a wayward cow he heard in Arizona, an account of a visit to the Navajos, the story of one steady old couple he met in Illinois and their lifetime of simple service. Various articles advise returning soldiers to be ready for changes, to fill missions, not to expect privileges, but nevertheless to take advantage of the GI bill. In July, 1947, the pioneer centennial, appeared his history of scouting in the LDS church. In another article he pitched his own brand of camping. Boys should

make their own equipment. Leaders should pick challenging, out
of the way trails. "Plan to go where at some place or other, the
boys will let out an inward 'oh-h-h.'"

Dilworth's early general conference talks again urge returning
servicemen to serve missions, even if inconvenient, even though
they've been away. Bishops are advised to counsel with "every
clean living, righteous young man in the ward who is home from
war" about going. To parents he says, "If a boy is able to go on a
mission, he ought to be given a chance. Let him turn it down if
he wants to, but don't make his decision for him." He urges young
men with a desire to go to approach their bishop, rather than
waiting for him to receive the inspiration. President George Albert
Smith had asked for missionaries. Dil says, "I think that President
Smith wants every young man to feel that he can go to his bishop, and volunteer, saying, 'I am willing to go.' I believe that is the
way to interpret it." He alludes to the early sections of the
Doctrine and Covenants, saying, "if men desire to be called, they
may be called." In the fall of 1946, he talked on the life of a mission president. His thesis—it's not a three year vacation by any
means.

Winter 1946-47 Dil and Gladys toured the Spanish American
Mission, "from Fresno, California, to San Diego, to Brownsville,
Texas, to Denver via El Paso, Albuquerque, Santa Fe, Manassa,
Colorado. It was a hard, long ride." Gladys' brother Leon,
Leonore's namesake, died January 11. Gladys and Dil drove to
Mexico for the funeral, apparently interrupting the tour. Dil says,

> We were driving along from Cortez, Colorado south toward
> Gallup, New Mexico. . . . The thermometer was by the actual
> count ten below zero. We had a Chevrolet car with no heater in
> it. We were bundled up in blankets to where we could hardly
> move. There was a ground blizzard on, and the snow was drift-
> ing across the road. One could hardly see. . . . I was going along
> about fifty miles an hour, with the lights penetrating not more
> than seventy-five or eighty feet.

A horse loomed suddenly in front of them, crossing the road,
another behind it.

There wasn't time to stop. I don't know to this day what happened. All I know is, that horse jerked his head back as I went by on the left hand side of the road, and back into the right-hand side again. . . . I didn't do it. There wasn't time to do it. There wasn't even time to think.

Dil could not understand how he could have missed the horse, or how he avoided skidding off the road, other than the Lord's hand in it. As he points out, "At ten below zero [we] would never have survived."

They returned from the mission tour in late February, 1947. Dil writes, "I, having seen a bad situation in Texas, made an appointment to see President McKay, then first counselor in the First Presidency." A little ways into his story, President McKay interrupted, said he had only allowed him five minutes, and said he would call him back in two weeks to finish. "I thanked him and left."

About two weeks later on a Saturday afternoon I came in from Ogden to go to the Tooele Conference and found a note on my desk. It read: "President McKay wants to see you the first thing Monday morning." I thought: I'll be there and finish my story on Texas.

I went down the hall, the stairs, and toward the back door. As I opened it, I seemed to say to myself: He doesn't want to talk about Texas; he is going to call you to preside over the New England Mission. As I thought it, I knew it was so. There was no doubt. Sunday night I said to Gladys; "How would you like to live in Cambridge, Massachusetts?" She: "I'd like it; are we going there?" I: "Yes, we are." She: "What are we going to do?" I: "Preside over the New England Mission!" She: "Oh no-o!" I: "Yes, we are. Tomorrow President McKay wants to see me. I'll go in and he will say: 'How would you like to preside over the New England Mission?' And I will say: 'I'd like it.' He will say: 'You are called.' Then he will tell me when to go and instruct me a little. Then I will walk out of his office and call you and tell you that is what he said."

And that is what I did and that is what he said.

Truman G. Madsen, who heard Dil tell the story, recalls his account of President McKay's reaction: "I have called many mission presidents. I have surprised very few."

Dilworth and Gladys leased the house to Farrell R. Collett, the artist, and his young family. The Youngs left Ogden around May 14, 1947, arriving in Cambridge, Massachusetts later that month, taking up residence in the Mission Home on Brattle Street. President William H. Reeder, whom Dilworth replaced, called all the missionaries into Boston for a conference before he left. "Instead of turning things over to me [he] proceeded to instruct them for about two hours in what they were to do the next six months. I think I just greeted the missionaries." President Smith's call had indeed brought an influx of elders, fresh out of the military, to the Church's missions, with few to train them. Dilworth found his elders "low in morale with no spirit," and resolved to bring them along the same way he had been brought along. He instructed the elders to obtain hand grips, 20 inches by 14 inches by 6 inches, in which to carry one shirt, one pair of socks and garments, one handkerchief, and toilet kit, together with tracts and copies of the Book of Mormon. He met them in conferences, spending the morning telling them of his own experiences without purse or scrip in Louisiana. In the afternoon he told them it was their turn. They were to travel into the country on foot, giving up their apartments. They were to carry money in compliance with anti-vagrancy laws, $2.00 in Massachusetts, $5.00 in Maine, $10.00 in Canada, but were not to use this money unless absolutely necessary, depending instead on the hospitality of those they sought out. They were to "meet and hold meetings with farmers and villagers," "bear testimony of the Restoration of the gospel and of the divine mission of Joseph Smith," and "present the Book of Mormon as the witness of that restoration, and . . . sell as many copies as possible." No missionary was forced to go, but none physically able asked to be excused. Commencing June 22, 1947, eighty-two elders set out for the countryside.

Country Tracting, 1947

Dilworth's written instructions for "country tracting" warn the elders to contact state and local police and explain their purpose and itinerary upon entering an area. "This will save annoyance should people phone in that they are being bothered by suspicious characters." Elders are not to use the phrase "without purse or scrip" unless totally without cash. Otherwise they explain they are "dependent for their physical needs upon the hospitality of those who want to hear their message." Elders visit the members once a month and give them the sacrament, "staying over one night. The rest of the time is entirely with non-members." They attempt to contact "every house," and hold a cottage meeting "every night." "Hall meetings" in churches, schools, or other buildings are arranged as frequently as possible. *No hitchhiking is allowed,* the instructions admonish. "We advise against any kind of transportation, except walking." The missionaries send in reports each week, including an address, usually a post office, where they can be reached the following Saturday. The mission office then forwards mail, literature, and money for essentials such as clothes and haircuts. "It shouldn't cost more than $20 per month to live on this basis."

The instructions recommend an umbrella, "carried suspended from the arm hole of the coat when not being used. (Try this. . . . It is very convenient.)" They give hints on courtesy and cleanliness. "One can always retire to the woods and wash and bathe in the creeks and branches and runs. Sometimes the housewife will iron your shirt, of one does it too awkwardly in her presence. Usually the host housewife doesn't mind, if the Elders use her washing equipment. (Furnish your own soap)." The elders are to "always pray with the people; they expect preachers to do this." They are admonished, "The biggest factor in the success of missionaries in the country is the determination of the missionaries to stay out, regardless of weather or treatment, becoming dependent entirely on the Lord." Humility is the keynote. "Remember the vision of Joseph Smith in which he saw the twelve, bloody and careworn, with the Savior in their midst, but because they couldn't humble themselves enough, He could not reveal himself and minister to them."

Elder Truman Madsen and his companion Reuel J. Bawden, were assigned to Prince Edward Island. Dilworth and Gladys drove them into Canada and across the ferry to Charlottetown. "There we ate our last paid-for dinner in a little restaurant, and the Youngs drove us out into the country, shook our hands, and wished us well."

> In the early stages we were so preoccupied with our stomachs and with the question of lodging that we, in fact, failed. We were no better than glorified "bums." [One elder] summarized what he called the worst possible door approach. You went to the door and knocked, "Madam, can I have a drink of water. I am so hungry I don't know where I'm going to sleep tonight." When we got past that kind of approach and decided we would put bearing witness and arranging meetings first and not worry about our stomachs, the work began to succeed.

The instruction sheet states, "The techniques of tracting are the same anywhere." Speak to the man of the house if possible. Avoid speaking to adolescent boys and girls unless parents are present. Oscar W. McConkie Jr. noted one difference in country tracting—it was easier to get inside. "New Englanders are a very reserved sort of folk, and it was always a hard job to get past the door. When I was in cities, I would go a week of tracting ten hours a day and never get into the house sometimes." The missionaries were a novelty, twenty-five hundred miles from home. "They were anxious to see people who could speak, who could talk in full sentences," who carried themselves well. He recalls setting up hall meetings. They generally went to the deacons, or lay leaders, not the ministers. Some small towns only had circuit ministers, but Oscar notes also the strong congregational bent of local congregations. "Even the Baptists up there were very congregationalist. No matter what church it is in New England, they're really centered in the congregation." The deacons would usually let them hold their meetings in the church houses, "and if we couldn't get them in churches, we could get them in libraries" or other halls. "We'd publicize them door to door as a usual thing. If we had a week's shot at it then we would put it on the bulletin board or maybe get something in the paper. I'd go to the local papers and get our picture in the paper. 'Two Mormon Elders Are Going To Be Visiting Around Here.'" He says Truman Madsen wrote an article or two that ran in local journals.

The mission compiled comments from the missionaries' weekly reports and sent copies out to them again. In one early mailing, Andrew Kimball and Chester Hamilton note they have been out over a month, and "have had good bed each night in which to rest and since we have been actually in country tracting have spent not a penny for food. . . . Have missed a few meals now and then which merely makes us appreciate food more when we get it. Have had no casualties, except for my poor suitcase, which some dog mistook for a tree and all dogs since have done likewise." Elders Vaughn Lauritzen and Harold Redd, working in Whitingham, Vermont, Brigham Young's birthplace, were told they would get no one to their meeting, but "we had to be shown. . . . We set to work to invite people to it. The attendance to our meeting was better than half the usual attendance of the local church—fourteen people present to ours. Also we sold a Book of Mormon and received a place to stay." Grant Lloyd and Joseph Davies describe difficulty in getting a schoolhouse they had used before, "for no particular reason only that possibly our minister friends' influence has been felt here. We did sell several Books of Mormon to very intelligent people that we feel quite good about. . . . Last Wednesday it looked like we were going to have to break a record and sleep out, but about 9:30 P.M. as we were hurrying down the road, retracing our steps a man came after us and offered us a bed."

Richard Beesley and Durward Burnett helped fight a forest fire. Lloyd W. Brown and C. P. Hill found the people reluctant to hear them until they helped with a haying crew. Next morning "we found that nearly every door was open to us and inviting us in to eat and sleep and discuss the Gospel. The news of the haying

spread rapidly and people were only too willing to listen to us."
Clifton Johnson and Donald Brown write that they "agree with
our mission president that umbrellas sometimes offer good protection against the canine family." They have encountered some
enormous specimens, "but through the Spirit of the Lord and a
few good thrusts of the umbrellas we have so far emerged victori-
ous." Truman Madsen and Reuel Bawden quote the week's scripture, John 11:39 "By this time he stinketh." "We've Learned—
One can wear a dirty shirt inside out, but MUM'S the word."
They describe a mob, "soused with moonshine . . . assembled to
'drive us out.' Satan had mongered the rumor that we were 'com-
munist spies'. . . . The group 'chickened out' when one of their
number suggested we might be 'armed.'" Hospitality grew scarce
as the rumor preceded them, though

> we managed beds and food with people whose age or deafness
> (or common sense) made them immune to grapevine nonsense.
> Yesterday the Mounties who had been swamped by calls from
> fearful and patriotic citizens, picked us up and requested that
> we move on to a fresh district—also that we avoid back roads
> and people who have not yet emerged from the stone age. After
> prayerful consideration we've decided to let the Lord to boss—
> to maintain our present policy of covering every house includ-
> ing the back roads (until the farmers begin making bayonet
> attachments for their pitchfork)."

The elders stayed out until October, ten weeks, averaging two
nights out, $12.20 total spent on lodging and food, $18.75 for
other expenses, 5.7 cottage meetings, 2.2 street and hall meetings,
8.8 copies of the Book of Mormon sold or loaned, 5 investigator
families, 2 nights out. One companionship in New Brunswick
slept out 21 nights. Another, in Nova Scotia, didn't sleep out once
or ever have to ask for a meal. Two elders did "country work" in
the town of Hopkinton, Massachusetts, for a month without paying for room or board. According to Dilworth, the elders agreed
"country work is the finest part of missionary work," and that
"they'll know better next time how to obtain meetings and how to

hold them. . . . All agreed that they felt physically better and tougher, although most had lost some weight. . . . All agreed that the power of the Lord is exercised on behalf of the Elders as much now as it was in the old days, when Elders do their duty."

Sometimes the missionaries had remarkable experiences. Truman Madsen and Reuel Bawden, without food, retired to a wood and prayed. A trout leaped in the brook, which set them thinking. Elder Madsen caught six of them on an umbrella, strung with thread, with a safety pin for a hook. Oscar McConkie heard a voice, that of S. Dilworth Young, repeat the president's instructions, "Go slow, don't miss a house," as he hurried to a hall meeting. Here were two houses they had missed. They would be late if they stopped, unless they skipped a bath and meal. Finally each companion took a house, after which they hurried to the meeting. One of the residents showed up part way through, and proved the only convert from that town. More often their spiritual experiences were of the quiet, ongoing variety. Truman Madsen said the elders learned to pray "telegram prayers." Ten words or less: need food. D. Woodward speaks of little, ongoing miracles. "It's like the Lord being right [here] and you being right there. You say a prayer on that side of the ditch, and you get your answer on the other side of the ditch. He'd tell us what doors to knock on, who to ask, and what to ask them. . . . That happened to me thousands of times."

Cambridge, Massachusetts

Rex Williams, mission secretary, remembers the big, three-story mission home, with its many fireplaces. "[President] and Sister Young used to love that atmosphere, and used to roast chestnuts like the New England people did. And his wife had special Christmas parties and puppet shows for the saints around that area, and took everyone caroling up to Beacon Hill." The mission home stood on the corner of Brattle Street and Longfellow Park. In back, an access road had been converted for regular traffic, and, Dilworth writes, "The cars and trucks made a lot of racket. As Gladys said, 'The rattle on Brattle.'" The chapel, a converted house next door on the corner of Brattle and Hawthorne, had belonged to the Longfellows. The Youngs entertained often, and many of the missionaries and branch members speak of the multi-course meals. At branch gatherings, Dil told his scout stories, including the Wendigo. With firesides, sightseeing tours, clam bakes, and the ongoing work of running a mission, Dilworth writes "there was never a dull moment." A diary he kept mentions plays and lectures at Harvard, church books on quiet afternoons, and the occasional football game on the radio or excursion to see the Red Sox play.

Branch members, many of them Harvard or MIT students and their wives, came to know Dilworth's rough edges. Barbara Williams confesses she could not tell when he was joking. Once he said, "Bee, the only reason we invite you [to dinner] is because you are married to J. D." Another time when she was sick with fever, Dil and Gladys brought her roses, which, in her weakened condition, she stuck haphazardly in a vase. Dilworth said, "Well, you know your supposed to arrange them, don't you?" Barbara says, "I was always dumbfounded. I never knew what to say to him." John Hale Gardner acknowledges Dilworth "may have offended some people sometimes. He was a little curt sometimes. He didn't try to coddle anybody." Yet he came to appreciate Dilworth's plain-spoken practicality. His last year of graduate school, he and his wife struggled financially, and he says it brought some conflict to the marriage. His feeling was everything should be secondary to his schooling, but Dilworth told him, "Okay, your family needs more money, you get a job, and it'll bring in more money." Hale says, "It shocked the life out of me, but it turned out to be good advice."

Members contrast Dilworth's rough side with his tenderness. Richard Harline speaks of Dil's "sense of wanting to help people. . . . He had a very blunt way about him, in many of the things that he said and did, but when you got to know him, you knew that his bluntness was not trying to embarrass you or to chastise you but to help you grow in the gospel. Dorothy Nielsen says, "There were times that he would put his arm around me and say such warm and human things." Her husband Talmage, who was completing a medical residency, counseled Dilworth on medical matters, and remembers his concern for the missionaries. "If one of them was ill or if one of them was distressed or if one of them had a problem with testimony or a problem with a girlfriend, he was very, very personally involved with their lives." Rex Williams and his brother J. D. were both impressed at Dilworth's hobby of anonymous giving. Perhaps this went back to his scout days, the good turn daily. Rex says, "He loved to do it, and he loved to receive such remembrances and gifts." J. D. tells of a Christmas sermon of Dil's, urging his listeners to go out and bestow some anonymous kindness on a group of people, who "would then feel such a sense of responsibility, and not knowing who the donor was, . . . to cover their tracks they would have to repeat this with at least five or ten people, and so the circle of kindness would grow in a geometric ratio."

Dilworth had to learn to deal with the adulation that goes with being a general authority. Once Mary Lou Harline came up after a sacrament meeting talk to tell him how much she had enjoyed it. He looked at her and said, "What did I say." Her mind went blank. "I stammered, and I'm sure I blushed." Dil apologized. "I'm sorry. I didn't mean to embarrass you. But I've often wondered if when people come up and say they enjoyed the talk, if they ever really listened to what I said." Hale Gardner thought Dilworth a good speaker in New England. "He was to the point. He made things brief, stated things clearly. . . . He could tell a story well, and he could put together a sermon which had an artistic quality to it. . . . He kind of seemed to have an inner feeling about the fitness and the appropriateness and the choice of words." Dilworth frequently called people out of the audience to speak. At least once he lost someone out the side door, but trying people this way gave him an opportunity to see what was in them. He told Talmage Nielsen after calling on him without warning in a stake conference a few years later, "Well, Talmage, I've always looked upon you as a very intellectual person, a man with a great many important ideas. But I wanted to find out if you could get

234 S. DILWORTH YOUNG

the Spirit." Dil would occasionally "unpreach" a sermon when he thought someone had strayed beyond the bounds of correct doctrine. Once a law student gave a talk on polygamy, laying out all the low points and challenges, perhaps as an academic exercise, but then leaving them unanswered. Dilworth called someone up who had been raised in one of the old families to talk about her experience and tell another side of polygamy.

Dilworth changed the time of sacrament meeting in the Cambridge Branch to the evening, to meet Church policy. According to Rosemary Fletcher, he encountered resistance among the members, finally offering to babysit their children himself if they acted up. "And he actually did. If they got upset, he would . . . take the children, and go to the mission home and tend them." One Cambridge Branch party was attended almost exclusively by women and children, because the men were all studying. Dilworth chided them in sacrament meeting for neglecting their wives, said they should have taken the time, saved their pennies, skipped breakfast to buy them corsages. Rosemary remembers a nearby supermarket sold orchids for ninety-nine cents. At the next branch party, wives arrived with their husbands. "And as each new person would come in to the dance, we would just roar because there would be another ninety-nine cent orchid." Dil told the men in a sermon in Bangor, Maine, that they ought to be considerate of their wives and get them some of the modern conveniences. Rex Williams says, "I think the report came back that practically every woman in that branch ended up with a refrigerator in a week or two."

Hulda, Dilworth's second wife, says Dil at first resisted the Anderson Plan, the ancestor of the uniform missionary discussions, preferring to see the elders preach straight from the heart. Rex Williams remembers a visiting missionary demonstrating a flannel board. This elder, on a leave from another mission to fill a two-week naval air corps commitment, checked in at the office and showed Dil a lesson on the Godhead, with figures for each member. Rex quotes Dil as saying, "I'm really glad you came. I've always wanted to see what the Holy Ghost looked like." One day out of the blue Dilworth said, "Elder Williams, I'll be leaving you in charge, because I'm going up to New Hampshire today to visit the elders." Rex told him he wouldn't find them, as they were out country tracting. Dilworth said, "No, I just feel I ought to go up there." He returned that night, and said, "Yeah, I was right. All the missionaries were in their apartment playing cards when I got there." Gene F. Deem, a missionary who married Dil's niece, tells a story of two elders caught kissing girls in the chapel, one the caretaker's daughter, the other a sister missionary. Dil told them they were going home, either married or disfellowshipped. They chose marriage. Truman Madsen knows of three instances in which New England missionaries were in danger of losing their girls. "President Young in each case did an exceptional thing. He 'released for twenty-four hours' the elders, arranged for them to have time with their fiancees, saying, 'Take her out and hug her and all will be well.' It worked."

Rex Williams tells of Dilworth's clowning with the elders after hours, trying to get them all to crunch their celery at the same time. Saturday nights the Youngs and the mission staff had sandwiches. "He'd always say, 'We have to pull the blinds, because . . . you make 'em as big as you want.'" He remembers the missionaries gathered at zone conference forming a circle with their chairs to ask Dilworth gospel questions. "He was a real stickler about the basic things of the gospel. . . . He knew how to say 'I don't know' if he didn't know, and he sort of told it like it was always." Truman Madsen sent in four questions weekly, typed on the front and back of a page, with space for President Young to pen in answers. Some answers seem brief or off the cuff, some are thoughtful and profound. How is it we "walk by faith" when we say we "know" the Church is true? Dilworth says,

> You can only know it by the Holy Ghost bearing the testimony in your heart, and when He isn't bearing it in your heart (mind), then you know it from the memory of the testimony. . . . When you want to know, want to say it, the Holy Ghost puts it in your mind for the moment so you can say it—and

while you are saying it you feel very certain of it without being able to prove it. The memory of this experience will give you courage to repeat the process the second time, when promptly you will get the same feeling—a little stronger perhaps.

Truman was called as mission secretary, and was a little in awe of the prospect, when Dil brought him down to earth by releasing the previous secretary and sustaining Truman with a single vote. Truman remembers someone questioning Dil's not using the extra beds in the mission home attic during a mission-wide conference. Dil said something about wanting to keep the companions together, but then "paused and, in a tone of voice I will never forget . . . said, 'Don't you know we lost a son?'"

Gladys ran the auxiliaries, and Dilworth describes her as "a good leader. . . . [She] was, I believe, the first to institute home primaries (1947). She started home Relief Societies, but she got that idea from Ivie Huish Jones of the Spanish American Mission." Gladys "tried to improve the cultural abilities of the saints with tray painting, rug hooking, etc." Mary Lou Harline, like many of the branch women, took tole painting classes from her. They painted Chippendale-style trays, "delicate with roses and flowers and gold leaf and stenciling" on a black base. "She was very careful to have the authentic touches of the New England style." Gladys was nervous at times, had chest pains, grieved severely. Hale and Olga Gardner remember being aware of Gladys' difficulty. "We didn't know about the poor health, really, except that she would be sometimes not available, she'd be indisposed." Martha Barney, Leonore's friend who worked as mission cook one year, remembers Gladys in a to-do about a visit from Marion Romney, she wasn't sure why. Elder Romney when he arrived sensed he would be a burden and offered to find a hotel. "Oh, no," she protested, "I wouldn't hear of it," and she was gracious and correct his whole stay, but still managed, as only Gladys could, to fill the air with electricity. Gladys made coffee one morning, its aroma filling the first floor—Martha suspected to provoke him.

Farm to Farm

Dilworth continued sending missionaries into the country without purse or scrip from May to October, or, in Canada, from snow to snow. Hale Gardner remembers the policy "caused quite a stir" when first announced. "I just gasped. . . . People thought he was doomed to failure. For one thing, the New England people, it was said, were too cold and inhospitable." He says the older branch members, and some students, thought the idea of country work "fantastic," "laughable," but "he was very stubborn." When the missionaries began to report back, and the members saw how humble and spiritual they had grown, they began to come around. Hale says that as far as the missionaries were concerned, "that began to change the character of the New England mission." Olga adds, "—to the amazement of everybody." Dilworth got calls from worried parents. Or the parents would call the Brethren in Salt Lake, and he would hear from them. He wrote a long report to the First Presidency on October 16, 1947, the day after the elders were to come back into the city after their first summer out. George F. Richards, President of the Twelve, answered that Dilworth's report "was read in the meeting of the Council of the Twelve Thursday, October 30, and reference made to it in the meeting following of the Presidency and the Council of the Twelve. . . . Your report gives evidence of careful thought on your part and courageous effort and the results seem to be very satisfactory. The reading of your report was intensely interesting."

Harold B. Lee toured the mission that first year. Truman Madsen remembers a rumor he had been assigned

to come back to New England and tell S. Dilworth Young to cut it out. Whether that is true or not, he did tour the mission and listened to the testimonies of the elders. Some [of the missionaries were] rather bedraggled but all [were] full of dedication. In one instance as they described how they had been humbled, President Lee stood up and said, 'Brethren, it's a good thing to be humble. But, Brethren, don't be proud of your humility." He returned to Salt Lake and encouraged the brethren to support the plan.

Elder Lee wrote Dilworth, telling of his positive report to the First Presidency and the Twelve. "They were all very much interested in what I had to say because of the comments for and against, no doubt, that have been made." He alludes to a few concerns "which I have already discussed with you and which you are already in the way of correcting." He adds, "If I had a son leaving for a mission there would be no place that I would rather have him labor than with President S. Dilworth Young of the New England States Mission." That comment meant enough to Dil for him to repeat it in his history.

Rex Williams says Dilworth "used to feel I think a lot of pressure from Salt Lake, from parents of missionaries and some of the Brethren who felt it wasn't right." Safety was a concern, and Rex remembers Dilworth's efforts to reassure the parents. He kept sick missionaries in the cities. He communicated weekly with all those in the field, sometimes using local radio stations to contact them in emergencies. He tracked meals missed, and instructed district presidents to inform him if elders slept out. "They should not sleep out more than two or three nights during their entire experience. If they are sleeping out regularly, something is wrong." He brought all the missionaries into apartments in the cities in winter. Another concern was the impression the missionaries gave. Elders sometimes abused the system, slipping into cities, or asking their door contacts for food. One elder purchased a sleeping bag. Dilworth told the missionaries at every opportunity not to abuse their contacts' hospitality. "Warning: Do not stay with any family, member or non-member, longer than overnight, except when you have an invitation to spend a week-end. During that time, preach and teach as much as you can. . . . Do not visit folks who are interested oftener than about every three weeks, to eat or sleep. If it is just to preach—of course."

Dilworth's 1947 report to the First Presidency lists his "Personal Observation" that "there is only one way to do missionary work:"

a. Go without money where possible.

b. Be bold in declaring Jesus Christ the Redeemer and Joseph Smith a Prophet.

c. Present and testify of the Truth of the Book of Mormon and its claims.

d. Forget oneself and one's self-development as though they never existed—at the conclusion of one's mission these will be found to have had plenty of development.

e. Learn to depend upon the Lord completely.

He insisted on the going without money. His instructions for country tracting state, "This is not an experiment. It is the way which the Lord wants it done . . . unless there is law against it (as in cities)." He refers the elders to Doctrine and Covenants 84:77-91. Verse 86 reads, "Therefore, let no man among you . . . take purse or scrip, that goeth forth to proclaim this gospel of the kingdom." Of course the other reference to travel without purse or scrip in the Doctrine and Covenants, section 24:18, states it is the "church" that "shall give unto thee in the very hour what thou needest for food and for raiment, and for shoes and for money, and for scrip." The church can feed its missionaries as well from contributions by member parents as it can from contributions from the field. Dilworth, with his sense of drama, sometimes overstated his position. Later in life Dil advised a missionary grandson, "It is a case of which prophet is speaking. Joseph Smith was instructed to use the system. The present leadership instructs elders to receive their support from home." Christ also at different times sent missionaries with or without money (Luke 10:4, 22:36). Late in his mission, Dilworth found himself defending city tracting. His notes from a February 1951 missionary conference refer to the good "winter work" of an Elder Dew," and state, "If travel without P. & S. is the only way to get humility, the Church would have been dissolved long ago."

There can be no doubt Dilworth felt pressure to discontinue country tracting, nor that he had second thoughts, at least concerning the elders' willingness. On June 28, 1950, Dilworth wrote the missionaries, already in the countryside,

> Last March I went around the mission having about made up my mind to not have country work this summer. However, when I mentioned it, the elders all expressed their desire to do it—so I let it go on as usual. In my heart is a lingering fear that some of you would rather not do this type of work. I have never wanted to force any elder to go into the country unless he really was willing to do it of his own volition.

He asked the elders to talk it over with their companions, then write their feelings candidly on the postcard he enclosed. Most were eager to continue. Some spoke of hardship and bad attitudes on their own parts, but also of increased humility and faith—they now wished to stay. Some were neutral. It didn't matter, city or country, whatever the president chose. A small number complained, not of country work, but of the difficulty of working areas that had already been covered. Dilworth may have underestimated the role of novelty in country work's earlier success. But others told how doors continued to open, how they slept out none or few nights, how they missed hardly a meal.

Dilworth continued the program until released, defending it as the best way to cover rural areas. "The people in the country have a right to receive the gospel. They are the farmers—the choice people of the country." He spoke of his successes. Anyone who doubted need only visit the Schoonmakers in Amherst, or go "to the Abbotts in [Foxborough], where a Sunday School of 45 meets and where 3 families have joined the Church; or to Holliston, Framingham, Hopkinton area, where another group likewise flourish[es]." Looking back from the 1970s, he felt the families converted through country tracting served as the cores of branches, which then formed the cores of wards, and these of stakes. Dil was proud of his missionaries, and met at reunions with them for upwards of thirty years, one of the longer lived groups in the Church. D. Woodward remembers, "he used to brag quite a bit. He said, 'I've got more bishops and more mission presidents and more church officials out of my hard-old New England over-worked missionaries than any mission president in the Church.' And he'd remind us of that quite often." Truman Madsen remembers him saying "he would 'stack up' his elders (in terms of their faithfulness in the Church and the depth of their spirituality) against any other missionaries from any other missions in the Church." Rex Williams' view: "I think he really felt strongly that his first purpose was to build missionaries, and he felt this was the greatest way in the world to build their faith and to get out among these country people. I'm certainly glad that I had the experience." He adds, "I'd hate to do it again."

Travels

Dilworth traveled four times a year to hold conferences with the missionaries. Oscar McConkie remembers especially the training sessions. "His concept was that you don't learn by instruction, you learn by doing." If he were teaching testimony bearing, he would have them set up their chairs in a circle, then walk them through. "When you bear testimony there's certain things you do," he remembers him telling them. "First of all, you bear testimony of Jesus." He would have each think of a scripture about Jesus, then bear a testimony based on the scripture. Dilworth jotted down the programs for these meetings in a diary: hymns, prayers, speeches by "Pres. Young" and visiting authority, talks by each of the elders and sisters and how much time each used. To the side, the diary invariably lists eight or twelve points on the missionaries' talks, which he apparently used to coach them afterwards. "You have the gospel, spiritual, authority, and ethical. They have the ethical—and whatever spiritual comes from using the ethics." "When you say 'you gamble' you place the gospel on a plane which should never be done. It's no gamble—don't put the idea in his head." "Any companion, no matter how weak can open up any district if humble enough. Your very inexperience is the best recommendation." "Elder [So-and-so], you'll be more effective if you memorize the scriptures you quote, and quote them slowly, and pronounce the words—not slurring them." "Men are heads of house." "When in a town which won't receive you don't get to feeling abused." "If you don't have the Spirit of the Lord at first—keep talking. It may come." "Use of word 'God' too freely." "Don't mention churches by name if you don't want to start persecution."

Dil and Gladys traveled by train, plane and car, attending general conference each spring. One missionary died in the field and Dilworth, feeling terrible, accompanied the body home. Gladys' long journal entry from 1947 addressed to Dil Jr. notes the mission has "given Dad a new zest for life and has helped me to stop grieving for you most of the time. I got to the point where I could almost play your records.

> Oct. came 1947, and in the East the language of the Autumn if you understand it makes you forget all other languages. And though it's melancholy I knew that somehow you were disturbed and I cried and all the old grief came back.

> And then one day you came to me only for a moment with that calming assurance that all was well. And on the very night 3 years to the day the telegram of your return came to us.

Young Dil's body was to arrive in New York on October 26, and the Youngs went to meet it. A riverboat carried them and other parents out to see the ship coming in.

> We chugged out to the Statue of Liberty and then to the east out of the mist like a beautiful vision appeared your flotilla.

> A great grey ship with buff chimney trimmed in black and draped with black garland was riding slow and graceful on the crest of the very calm ocean, escorted in front by 5 spick and span river police boats in black and white. On either side of your ship rode a beautiful, slim grey destroyer and escorting you at the rear was a swanlike, all white destroyer, the flagship with colors at half mast.

> A squadron of airmen flew out to meet you and formed an umbrella overhead. A salute of 21 guns was fired from the

armory. We chugged along way over on one side and as your ship passed Dad rose and bared his head and stood at attention until you had docked. Just as you passed the Statue of Liberty, sailors threw great wreathes overboard and they bounced and glided until they touched your ship. It was an entrance worthy of a prince or a king, all due you, beloved son.

They drove to Utah for the reburial. The Colletts graciously made room, but still Gladys found it agonizing "going into the home when it was not a home at all." She fixed things as near as she could to how they had been, but didn't wish to disturb Mike, the Colletts' young son, who had Dil's room. "They brought you in a bronze casket, elegant in its simplicity and draped all over with the flag, and we placed you there under the east window where you loved the evening sunsets and the morning radiance." They looked at his photos, reread his poems and letters.

And when the embers had died to ashes, and only the moon shot a weak little beam on the flag and all the rest were sleeping I stole silently to your side and then I smelled the earth of Belgium that had so mercifully preserved you and it was sweet to my nostrils and the gasses too that once were you I smelled and thanked God He'd returned this much to me to lay in native soil. . . .

Dil spoke at the burial, (also at Ensign Williamsen's). Leonore placed ivy, mint, and roses from the yard on Young Dil's coffin. Thatcher Allred read "He Is Not Dead," a poem by Seymour Dilworth, and a male quartet under Roland Parry sang "Now You're Home," music by Parry, words also by S. Dilworth Young.

Leonore had spent that summer, 1947, working as cook in the mission home. Dilworth warned her, "If you ever look sideways at one of the missionaries, I'll send them next day to Newfoundland." Elder Blaine P. Parkinson, the mission secretary at the time, answered the door when she arrived—Leonore was immediately smitten. "I was very good. Every time Blaine came into a room and we were alone, I would leave." Still, she admits, "I couldn't help but steal some sidelong glances." Dilworth liked

Blaine for his steadiness and devotion to the work, but also because he stood up to him. Dil had insisted there be no exchange of birthday gifts in the mission home. "He made a great issue of it," Blaine remembers. It was a waste of time and their minds ought to be on other things. When Dil's birthday came, the missionaries went in on a present anyway. Blaine bought a three-inch wheelbarrow, and set the present on it at Dil's place at table just before mealtime. "He was speechless." Dilworth had told them more than once of his own antics as mission secretary, delivering Ethyl Archibald's gift from Alec in a wheelbarrow. "And of course he was pleased to get a present anyway, so everyone had a good time about it." (Dilworth's diary mentions gifts of Mounds bars from the missionaries other years.) Gladys too had been very taken with Blaine. She calls him "Kin" in one extended journal entry, writing of walks and long visits together, and of feeling happy in his presence "for no reason I could define at all." His first day in the office she had asked him to cart some trash. "And then I knew you fit, the steps were taken three at a time up and down from the basement to the 2nd floor and all the time you laughed and joked and carried boxes higher than your head. And I saw Dil again in so like manner and knew why I had seemed to know you even when I saw you first." Dozing once, she saw him "smiling at me from out the face of a dear, little, brown-eyed . . . curly-headed . . . girl. And she was you in miniature."

Leonore returned to Utah. Blaine courted her by mail until his mission ended, then in person. They announced their engagement March 28, 1948, when the Youngs were in Utah for general conference. Gladys writes of "Dad's mischievous, noisy kidding that wounded me to tears and made everyone else glad. I cried for 24 hours. He laughed for 24 hours. On these things we're always eons apart." The Youngs returned for their wedding in September, driving as he tells it "fast and furious." They brought the furniture and Persian rugs down from the attic. "We shelled about one hundred pounds of pecans by hand for the pie. . . . Helen [Olsen] made enough pecan pies to serve a small chunk to 800 guests." Dilworth had the announcements engraved on the outside, but hand wrote the invitations on the inside. When a friend stopped him in the street and asked why he hadn't been invited, "I would fish out one and give it to him then and there." Rosemary Fletcher thought part of the reason he hand wrote them was to save money, but says each contained a personal note—"No two were alike"— and that people were amazed he had gone to the trouble. Dil's history mentions the poor-man's candles at the reception, as well as the harp, flute and violin music by Sam and Louise Pratt. "Even President McKay came, and a lot of uninvited friends. . . . After the reception, we packed the furniture back to the attic, leased the house, rolled up the Persian rugs in moth proofing and stored them and went back to Cambridge."

Dilworth's and Gladys' release came by telegram on Christmas Eve, 1950. J. Howard Maughan, the new president, arrived February 14th. Dilworth greeted him at the airport with a row of missionaries holding placards spelling out "W-E-L-C-O-M-E." "It made him smile," he notes in his diary, "[a]nd I think was warming." Gladys had returned to Utah in late January, so Dil was alone. President Maughan toured the mission. "I—against my principles—toured with him. I put him up to his duty by opening the meeting in each place, then excusing myself briefly, and forgetting to come back, leaving things up to him." Gladys wrote Dilworth at each stop. Dil answered of his loneliness and plans for when he got home. He spoke in a birthday letter of his inability to grasp Gladys' emotionality, but also of his determination to keep on trying.

> Looking back, I realize that I have been extremely difficult to adjust to. My practical nature . . . which prevents me from getting deep feeling over music, etc., must have been a thorn in your flesh almost impossible to bear. I do wish that I could have realized sooner just what that attitude was really doing to you. I believe I would have tried sooner to change, for fundamentally I never have desired to hurt you or torture you.
>
> The same thing is true of me as a young father. I loved the children, yet I was emotionally incapable of being thrilled by them

when they were small. I suppose that it was the worry of [the] new job and trying to make good, etc. No one will ever know how difficult that making good was. Geo Bergstrom in the background ready to take hold the minute Gus Wright got me out . . . Yet that isn't the reason. Mostly it was my inability to feel the things which concerned me most. Anyway it gave you a lot of misery, I'm sure.

I have always had, and it has grown larger with the years, a profound respect and admiration for your many talents. But yet these have been the basis of pride—not the basis of love. I've never needed that. You've said I have a deep loyalty. Maybe so, but I maintain it isn't loyalty—it's fundamental love. Men not in love find ways to stay away from home. There has never been a night that I haven't faced toward home with anticipation, not because of the house, or the shelter from the world, but simply because you were there—and just to walk in your presence gave me complete satisfaction and fulfillment.

He speaks of "the days of exquisite ecstasy with you when fulfillment was reached," and "the days of intense sorrow, when the steel of your character sustained you when Dil was killed.

All of these things and my part in them [have] not reached the heights of your part in feeling, but I'd rather have these exquisite joys and sorrows with you than with anyone else on earth, for all the rest is dead.

Let's start anew this spring and see if I can't learn to be all you'd like me to be as a companion—a helpmate—and a lover.

Gladys, on an earlier birthday in Boston, writes, "I'm older now and still a little weary with grief and pain—but the love of a Great Man has made me live happily today."

President Maughan visited Utah one more time, which kept Dil from leaving until March 27, 1951. He covered the distance home in four days, arriving on the 31st. Leonore and Blaine had two children by now, Loraine, and Dilworth Blaine, whom Dil helped bless the following day.

CHAPTER 11

Their Long Road

A General Authority

When Dil was first called to the First Council and began commuting to Salt Lake, and he and Gladys to travel to conferences on weekends, Leonore transferred to the University of Utah in hopes of seeing them once in awhile. Now, home from New England, Dil commenced his daily drive to Salt Lake again. Gladys' heart problems continued. He writes, "I took her everywhere I went in a car." His living allowance, he found, was on the lean side. He bought gas at Heber Jacobs' station on 36th and Harrison. One day, talking to Heber, wearing his old blue suede suit, he said, "This is my nicest suit, and it's been a long time that I've been wearing it." In addition to overseeing the seventies, Dil filled an assignment as coordinator of Indian affairs for the Church with Milton R. Hunter, and another, under Harold B. Lee and Mark E. Peterson, evaluating the effectiveness of priesthood quorums. He traveled to missions and stake conferences—Alaska, Texas, Newfoundland, Central States, wherever the Church was organized. He noted the landscape and people where he traveled, and took advantage of the time to engage the older general authorities in conversation. He sometimes called former missionaries or Boston students on short notice to accompany him. Oscar McConkie, Truman Madsen, Talmage Nielsen were among those he tapped to go.

Talmage Nielsen sometimes gave Dilworth medical advice. When Dil developed a bad back, he told him he ought to put a board under his mattress. "He came back and said, 'Oh, I can't tell you how grateful I am for that advice. It makes my back feel so much better, I can't believe it.'" Dil started carrying a sleeping bag with him on his travels. "Whenever he'd go to a conference and go in somebody's home to stay, they'd have a nice bed fixed for him, and he'd take his sleeping bag and . . . sleep on the floor." His hostesses would find the bed unslept in the next day, "and they'd think, 'Oh, dear! He didn't dare get into my bed! I wonder if it wasn't clean? I wonder if it was uninviting?'" The back got better, but he developed bursitis in his hip, and so took to carrying an inflatable, donut-shaped pillow to meetings. Circulation problems kept his extremities cold, until he began carrying his own bedding again, this time an old sleeping bag lining, to supplement his blankets when on tour.

Gout gave him trouble in his toes and fingers, and his doctor imposed dietary restrictions, telling him he could eat baked fish or chicken for supper. Dilworth said he couldn't see himself eating baked chicken every supper for the rest of his life, so ate halibut instead, on Thanksgiving, at family gatherings, at home, and on the road when he could. He drew up a form letter that went out in advance of his visits to the wives of stake presidents. Leonore Brown, who received one, gives the text as something like this: "My health is not too good, and I'm on a very strict diet. In meat, I can have fish or chicken. Now I'm sorry I told you that I could eat chicken, because everybody gives me chicken. For breakfast I want five soft boiled eggs. You can have the yolks, and I'll eat the whites." She says, "He told us afterwards, 'I scared more stake presidents' wives to death, sending them that letter!' But you know, he was one of the easiest guests you could possibly have. He'd go into the kitchen and take care of himself." At breakfast he'd say, "'Let me boil those eggs,' and he'd boil them and he'd separate them." Others agree he was easy to care for, and that in fact he did not stick to his diet. One Pratt niece remembers getting the letter, only to have him urge when he arrived, "Aren't you going to fix Mexican food?"

When Dilworth was a scouter, he had taken the family to New York, where they attended a circus, with Jimmie Durante as caller, on a Sunday. Returning to the car, they found a note under the wipers from an Ogden friend. "He had seen the license plate and my name plate on the steering column . . . which proves that one cannot conceal his sins when far away; someone will see." He had this happen the other way in Idaho Falls now that he was a general authority.

> I had ordered breakfast and was waiting for it. A young man came up and introduced himself as a Salt Lake boy. I asked him to bring his breakfast over to my table which he did. As he sat down, the waitress put a cup of coffee in front of me. Almost without thinking, I said, "Did I order this?" "No," she said. "I really don't want it." If I had said I didn't order this, the young man would not have believed me . . . I have had that happen in several ways in my time.

Once when Gladys was ill in bed, Dil left things to keep her until 6:00, then attended a function in Provo, not managing to break away until 11:00. "I was fit to be tied." He rushed home, pushing the accelerator past seventy miles per hour down the hill into Weber Canyon when he was pulled over by a patrolman.

> I said, "I guess you're arresting me for speeding." He said, "Yes, you were doing better than sixty miles an hour when you passed the Hill Field Road." I said, "I was doing better than seventy miles an hour when I passed the Hill Field Road." I said, "But give me a ticket. I've got to go. My wife's sick. I'm in a hurry, and I'll pay the fine gladly, but let me get out of here. . . . " And he said, "Don't get your shirt off. Stand still a minute."

The patrolman said he would give him a warning ticket instead, on the promise he would drive within the limit the rest of the way.

> I said, "I'll do it." So he gave me the ticket, and when he handed me the ticket, it had my name on it and everything. He smiled, stuck out his hand, and said, "My name's Bybee. I used

to be one of your scouts at Camp Kiesel." And all the way in I said to myself as those wheels on my car turned, "What if I'd lied to him." . . . If I tried to hedge in any way, he'd have given me a ticket, and I'd have had no influence on that man ever again."

Dil had occasion to give blessings. He told a BYU audience he felt he had no particular gift for healing, though it was his practice to "rebuke" the illness, "because the priesthood itself contains power. One has a right to rebuke by that power, but it depends, of course, upon your faith and that of the person to whom you are administering." He told of being asked by a stake president to bless a man with an eye injured so badly the doctors told him it would have to come out. Dil bristled "because I thought that perhaps he might be one of those many people who just love to have the general authorities administer to them when they have perfectly good men, right in their own stakes or wards who could do it equally well." Dil said as much to the stake president, who offered to call the man and tell him he didn't have time. "I repented immediately of the thought . . . and said, 'No, don't call him. Tell him to come and we shall do it.'" Dil blessed him, but could not "recall having any particular sensation about that man, except the feeling of guilt for having hesitated to see him." He received a letter two weeks later that the man's eye was mending, the doctors said he would not need to have it out after all, he was on his way to being healed. "I decided that as far as I was concerned I would never again argue with the Lord as to whether I would administer."

Leonore recalls an early mission tour of Eastern Canada with President and Sister Ursenbach. Distances were great, and every time they stopped for a break, Sister Ursenbach would get out her watercolors and go to work on the scenery. Dil bought canvas, paints and brushes when he got home and began to do the same thing on his weekend travels. He wrote articles for the *Improvement Era*, on doctrinal themes, on experiences while traveling, also free verse poetry. A two-part account of visits to the

Hopis followed his earlier effort on the Navajos. Poems celebrat-
ed the solemn assembly and the dedication of the McKay
Building at BYU. He wrote books, in the office, at home in the
evenings and early mornings. Leonore says that now that Dil was
older, he found himself sleeping only a few hours a night, and so
wrote and painted to fill the other hours. He had always been an
avid reader—Gladys teased him about the writing, saying, "I
wondered when all those things you were putting in were going to
come out." Dil's first book, *An Adventure in Faith*, was serialized
in the *Improvement Era* from November 1955 through June 1956,
under the title "High Adventure." In this work of fiction, Jed
Colby, age 16, is shanghaied from London's streets, forced to
become a sailor, then shipwrecked off the coast of Texas. He
makes his way to Santa Fe, where he falls in with the Mormon
Battalion and shares their adventures. "Written for boys," this
book hearkens in spirit to two of Dil's old friends, James Fenimore
Cooper and Horatio Alger. Sometimes weak in style and charac-
terization, the best parts are when he gives the details of scouting:
signal fires, Indians disguised as trees, tripe soup, sure-footed
mules. Perhaps his most basic literary insight is that the life of a
saint is not boring. As he writes in the introduction, "the greatest
adventures have been had by those who love the Lord."

Family Night Reader appeared in 1958, followed in 1959 by
More Precious than Rubies. These are collections of doctrinal
lessons in simple language for young readers. The latter, on priesthood, filled a need for a gift book for boys being ordained deacons, and has gone through more than a score of printings. In
these books, Dil shows a knack for striking analogies. Also, over
and over, he bears testimony in simple, plain, uniquely under-
standable ways. He takes as his task to teach his readers what testimony is, and does so with unusual clarity. *Here Stand I—
Looking*, a collection of his poetry, was not published until 1963,
but gathered poems from as early as 1945. Eulogies for the most
part, mostly in blank or free verse, some of these are powerful and
subtle in the progression of their emotional imagery. Some are
prosaic, sermonesque, replacing images with ideals. All are acces-

sible, almost to the point of sentimentality, but not manipulative. If Dilworth cites ideals, one must remember how much honor and ideals meant to him. He lived by them. He talked about them in his private life. He counseled his grandchildren, "Always set your ideals high. You won't reach them all, but you'll go higher than you would have if you didn't have any."

Dilworth spoke at BYU devotionals and leadership weeks. To make his points about teaching, he used stories from his scouting days. He recounted Washington's life on that president's birthday to make the point that, if a young man is to go right, he must start right. Speaking of honor and sacrifice on Armistice Day he told of his experiences in World War I, also of a time he drove Dil Jr. to general conference at the Assembly Hall. Tickets were required to enter, but servicemen were also allowed inside. "I suppose this boy's uniform will let him in," S. Dilworth told the gatekeeper. "It will let *him* in, but it won't let *you* in." Dil snapped, "Well, who asked to get in?" The door cracked open for Dil Jr., slamming shut just as quickly, and Dil watched with a certain sadness as his son disappeared. So would it be in heaven. One's family, one's office wouldn't qualify one to enter. In another speech he used a text by Kahlil Gibran to talk about prayer, contrasting his lyrical, mystical lines with the plain and simple gospel teachings. "I can testify to you that you'll get answers, personally and privately, to things you ask for in righteousness, concerning your own future, concerning your own safety, concerning your own needs." In his speeches, he loved to dwell on the deep things of the scriptures, and lay them out for his audience. His style is humorous, familiar, rough and rhythmic, full of unexpected words and quirky turns of phrase, reminiscent of Lincoln, perhaps, or Brigham Young.

Myrtle Hill

Dil and Gladys talked repeatedly about selling the house, and once got as far as signing a contract for a home on "A" Street in Salt Lake, only to buy their way out. "It cost me $4,000.00 to do it," Dil notes in his history. "—I'm still glad." They finally sold Rosemont in 1955—"It nearly killed Gladys emotionally to do this"—and bought a lot at 575 "J" Street. Dil records the sale price as $7,000. A notebook of Gladys' refers to the decision.

It is the most beautiful lot in Salt Lake City. Dil is thrilled and anxious to work at it and to build upon it. When I saw it I was calmed, comforted & relieved from tension.

She alludes to their ease in finding a place, at Eagle Gate Apartments, so they could release the old home for sale, then to a pair of blessings.

Dil promised me in the name of the Lord that I should have the power to withstand the shock of leaving and of making change. Bro. Lee blessed me with the knowledge that I am loved of the Lord for past obedience. That I must go to be with my husband where he is available to future greater responsibilities & blessing. . . . [That] I must be where every moment of togetherness counts, not where there is wasted time and wasted effort to be together. That I would be calmed & made able to meet this change if I will keep my faith strong and doubts out of my mind.

"Only when I have doubted have I wavered. I am willing, I have faith." Of the Eagle Gate apartment, Dil writes, "Gladys could not stand the place. It gave her claustrophobia, and so we found a basement apartment on 10th Avenue directly behind the Ensign 4th Ward." Gladys calls this apartment "sunny, airy, pleasant but a basement withal. Have had a tremendous loneliness here and a feeling of being caged." She agonizes,

O God, I am humbled into the dust. Help me to accept it and to profit by it. Help me to rise above it and to sing the song of life again. Help me to conquer the emotions that have always ruled my life and have at this period gotten the upper hand. Help me to be gay, to sing and to dance with life abundant, not slump into remorse and deadpan feelings. Help me to come alive again.

Cousin Cannon Young drew plans for their new house, which Gladys refers to in her writings as "Myrtle Hill." Construction was complete enough for them to move in by May 1956, at a cost of around $21,000. This long home had wood floors and a large, vaulted living room built around Gladys' Persian rugs. Set on a steep hillside, the house had two exposed stories on the south, where the top floor windows offered a broad view of the valley reaching out to Point of the Mountain. Dil installed an elevator car in the stairwell in view of Gladys' heart—to the delight of the grandchildren, though he banished them from it when they ran it off its track. Gladys again developed claustrophobia because of the house's narrowness, which Dil determined to fix. "I borrowed all the money I could on an insurance policy and bought tools and lumber ($1,000.00). I built [a] porch addition on the south side," mostly alone, but with some help from friends. "Cannon Young supervised me." This addition is what makes the house distinctive. Set up on beams anchored in the lower side yard, the room, used for dining, features a central chandelier, cherry wood trim, and banks of large, sliding windows on three sides. When Dilworth was putting in the windows, Cannon stopped by and said, "You got your windows upside down, haven't you." Dil said,

> Yeah, but I'm not gonna take 'em out. It takes twenty nails to nail that thing around, twenty eight-penny nails." I said, "They'll go back and forth. I tried it." He says, "Well, they won't do as well, and you'll wish you had if you don't take 'em out now." I said, "Well, I'm not going to." Then it suddenly dawned on me I had a $100,000-a-year architect telling me what to do for nothing. . . . So I says, "Cann, if I was a contractor, what would you do?" He said, "I'd make you take 'em out and put 'em in right!"

Dilworth took them out and put them in right.

> I got real pleasure out of doing [the addition]. I remember the day that I nailed on the subfloor. When I started at the south end and finished at the north end with the new floor flush with the main floor in the middle room, I knew I was a carpenter.

The room, he says, "proved to be a most pleasant addition and it proved to be the cure Gladys needed to feel at home in the house."

Later Dil built a carport and patio, and added retaining walls on the upper and lower property lines.

Granddaughter Charlotte Fry remembers the Youngs' visits. Gladys carried a cherry pie with a lattice crust in a special pie basket. "The things that she did were [always] sort of a little extra special." She remembers the old ice box at their house on "J" Street with its empty slot for ice. Refrigerators had been in use for many years, so Gladys painted hers black, with Mexican motifs, and kept "goodies" inside: cakes, cookies, sweat breads. Charlotte remembers eating eggs from egg cups at the Youngs, also picking mint leaves and making mint tea, which they drank in dainty china cups, adding cubes from the sugar bowl with tongs. "Everything was like a little ceremony." She remembers acting out Hansel and Gretel for friends of the Youngs. She was Gretel, brother Dil was Hansel, sister Lori played the witch. "Grandma and Grandpa were the mom and dad . . . [little sister] Annette might have been the sandman or something."

Elder Lee, in his blessing, counseled Gladys to befriend and cultivate the wives of the other general authorities. She fretted that by moving away from Eagle Gate she was failing to do so. He told her she "had every right to seek after the beauty and culture" in Salt Lake. "It was what was needed to broaden me so that I could express myself through writing. This I shall do again. I must develop this talent if I can do any good with it." Her papers, going back as far as New England and as late as 1960, are full of free verse nature poetry, lush descriptive prose, family history, memories of Dublan. The *Improvement Era* published one of her poems, "Desert Whirlwind," in June of 1956. Letters to her grandchildren tell of Spanish moss in Louisiana, pirates through the Golden Gate, a chair-shaped bathtub, a trundle bed, blackbirds dancing in the wind.

Dilworth's date books from the 1950s have the Youngs going to symphonies and plays frequently, dining at the Knife and Fork Club, attending scout functions, funerals, and weddings, entertaining and being entertained by Salt Lake and Ogden friends. Gladys was called to put on plays for the Ensign 4th Ward, after which, Dilworth says, "she found herself again." She did a road show, and in March of 1958, Bernard Shaw's *Pygmalion*. This production was featured in an article on drama among the Mormons in the magazine *Theatre Arts* in December of that year. Gladys went at it with her usual eye for authenticity, combing the libraries, "in the end referring to issues of *Harper's Bazaar*." She got ward members and others to search their attics. *Theatre Arts* quotes Gladys: "There for a while it seemed as though all of us were going through old trunks. We found two outstandingly beautiful dresses from an eighty-three-year-old lady who had been the bell of Salt Lake City and had saved some of her most elegant outfits." British missionaries provided frock coats, bowlers, toppers, spats. Others loaned fans, parasols, jewelry, beaded and velvet bags, and old artificial flowers for Eliza's flower basket. A lumber yard provided used lumber for sets. A hardware store loaned the lighting. Gladys used the talents of English immigrants living in the ward. Her Freddy had been born in a slum area and lived in London. Alfred Doolittle came from Lancashire, the housekeeper from Bristol. One English Salt Laker, not a member of the Church, coached Eliza in Cockney speech and mannerisms. Nearly every ward family helped in some way, and eight hundred people attended the showing. "Among the most interested guests," reports *Theatre Arts*, "were English people from all over the city who came to hear the music of their own dialect spoken again."

Stroke

In December, 1958, Gladys put on one more pageant for the ward at Christmas time. A real mother and infant portrayed Mary and baby Jesus, and the little shepherd boy attending carried a real lamb. Dil's history records, Gladys "was on her way to becoming as famous in Salt Lake City as she had been in Ogden." He says, "Richard Evans asked her to study the Hill Cumorah Pageant with an idea of improving it. This was strictly on a confidential basis." Dil and Gladys toured Mexico in January, 1959, by car: Mexico City, Veracruz, Coatzacoalcos, and the colonies again, returning in early February. An undated entry in Gladys' journal, probably from this trip, records the many changes to her child-hood home.

> Roses & lotus & umbrella trees gone. Peach & pear trees gone. Barns & vineyard gone. Fireplace changed, rooms added where porch used to be, new picture window in dining room where Andis Gonzales serenaded and where Mother stood between woodbines shrubbery and roses in her arms—this all gone, but myrtle plants still live and bloom. Window where cream was cooled still there, stairs the same.

On February 10, shortly after their return, Dil got a call in his office. "It was Gladys. She said she was on the floor and could not use her arm and leg. She had managed to pull the phone to the floor and dial with her good arm and hand." Leonore says it hit while Gladys was sweeping the porch, and that she somehow crawled inside.

Dil continues, "I dashed home and found her south of the bed on the floor." He lifted her onto the bed and called Dr. Al Clawson, who diagnosed a stroke. Dil called Harold B. Lee to administer, then took her to the hospital that night. "I slept in the hospital every night and was with her much of each day." Dr. Clawson brought another doctor in on the case.

> On about the 5th day about 2:00 p.m. I noticed Gladys was breathing irregularly. I called a nurse and told her to get the house doctor. To my surprise in came [the other doctor]. He raised an eyelid and looked at her eyes, picked up her hand and looked at her nails, and without a word walked out. After about five minutes, I called the nurse and asked if the doctor wasn't coming back. She was embarrassed and did not know. I ordered her to get the house doctor. Soon he was there, administered oxygen, and revived her.

> Twenty minutes later Al Clawson called me and said that Gladys was dying—was probably dead by now—and that I shouldn't feel bad and it was for the best. I was by now angry.

> I said, "She is not dying or dead, but she would have been if

[that doctor] had his way. What did he mean by walking out and making the decision without consulting me? She is very much alive, no thanks to him."

Al was surprised and didn't know what to say.

Betty Baker remembers waiting for Gladys to improve enough that she could receive visitors. "Leonore had been down and stayed overnight with her, and [Dilworth] was just really upset with both of them because they stayed up and talked nearly all night. But they knew from that she was getting better." Betty came to visit Gladys with a group of friends. Dil had fixed a rose to her feeding tube. She says Gladys said as they entered, "'Did you see my rose?' And we looked at her and we looked at the rose, and we said how lovely it was, and then we sang 'Only a Rose.' And Uncle Dil stood there and the tears rolled down his face, and she cried, and he reached over and wiped the tears away, and she says, 'That rose was given to me by my darling.'" Others visited. Leonore says Gladys' niece Melba Gillette came and secretly brewed coffee. Ena Barnes came, washed her hair, and put her makeup on. On later visits at the house, Ena says, "she used to call me her doctor. She'd say, 'At least you make me feel better.' She needed company, and everybody can't be there all the time."

Gladys had lost the use of her left arm and leg. She retained the use of one muscle in her hip, which allowed her to walk, wearing a metal leg brace, with support. She could sit up and read. Dilworth says, "Her mind was good, although because of the difficulty she couldn't speak very readily." After seventy days in the hospital, he took her home for the weekend. "On Monday she had improved in morale so much that I told the doctor (by now Burtis Evans) that I would like to keep her home. He reluctantly consented." Dil borrowed a hospital bed and nursed her himself. He fixed her meals, talked to her, walked her in the yard. "The brethren supplied me with a woman to stay days, and then for a reason I have never found out the help was withdrawn." Dilworth's living allowance wouldn't permit him to hire anyone himself, so he moved his office work home and struggled along. This continued until "Mark E. Peterson told the brethren my condition and persuaded them to get me some help." A Mrs. Nye was employed for daytimes. Dilworth took care of Gladys nights, with friends or relatives spelling him if he had an appointment. Leonore and Blaine helped on weekends so Dil could go to conferences, giving up their bedroom to set up a hospital bed. Gladys, without control of her body, was terrified of the ride to their home in Provo. Nor could Leonore, with six children, easily come to Salt Lake for the weekend, so Dil hired a helper. "I paid her $20.00 no matter how long: Friday to Monday or Saturday to Sunday." He arrived at conferences late and left early. Hulda, his second wife, remembers him telling how he excused himself during the final sessions, telling the audience, "'Now, when the closing prayer is being said, you'll have your eyes shut. When you open your eyes, I will be out the door.' And he did it, time and time again."

Gladys was "fearful."

> She said to me one day . . . "Are you going to send me to a hospital or a home?" And I said "No! Of course I'm not. I don't even have it in mind. I am not going to do that." I could see she was disturbed and worried for fear that she was going to have to leave home and be put in the hands of strangers. And I had to decide how I was going to have my life after that, so I told her that I was not going to ever leave her, that as far as I was concerned, the nights I was home I was going to stay home. . . . I said to her, "I'm not going to accept any social engagements." She said, "Oh, you must do that." I said, "No, I must not, and I'm not going to. I'm not going to go out socially. I'm not going to do anything except to stay with you." And then I noticed that she seemed to be calmer. She seemed satisfied, and she seemed able to adjust herself to the situation.

Gladys painted trays and canvases in the mornings. Dil set her up with materials before leaving for work. She went to bed in the afternoon, and was up and down in the evening. Dil says, "I read to her quite a bit." Gladys' papers from the time speak of experi-

menting with pigments. "Use three primary colors, the white &
the umbers, and see what you can do with them in mixing colors
and shading. . . . Don't try to paint." She wrote throughout the
day, pouring out her boredom and anxiety. Noises agitated her,
abdominal pains, bodily smells.

> Noon and dinner is over. I am sitting quietly and will stand the
> impact of [the] vacuum. . . . Dil was quiet and subdued in his
> nerves and I am happy. My heart sings because I have passed
> another hazard. I am now calm and can rest and arise refreshed.
> Dil has work and responsibilities. Whatever happens to me
> does not matter. The only thing in the world that matters is
> that I live so that I can meet my God, my son and my parents
> on the other side. . . . Only one thing I crave above all else
> except to be in Thy presence again is please, please, God, do not
> let these agitations conquer me to the point I cannot endure
> them, but allow me to have peace this afternoon and to let this
> pass. . . . May I not become overwrought today but may the
> peace of heaven come to me as I write, and . . . [may I] wait on
> thee, Lord, and thy blessings. May I not say anything except
> these words.

Again she writes,

> I must remind myself a hundred times a day that I am entirely
> dependent for my inner and outer life on Dil and his services
> . . . and that I must spend the rest of my days returning a little
> of the debt I owe him. Oh, Lord my Heavenly Father, let this
> seizure pass and let me feel the glow of peace that comes from
> thy spirit. I can only endure this noise for a short time longer.
> Give me thy love, thy protection, and thy care.

She wrote stories for her five grandchildren, and read them to
them, memories of Rosemont, new stories of Myrtle Hill, and a
collection of stories of her Mexican childhood.

> I shall do my best to keep [this] coherent. However, if it goes
> off at angles, I'll pull it back and get on the track again. I need
> something absorbing and I can't do dramatics, gardening, house
> decorating as yet but I can write with this good right hand and

a pen, so here goes. Maybe some of it will be untrue. Some of it will be only half true. But all of it will be most sincere. I've got to save my emotional life, and as I save my emotional life, I save my soul and my physical life as well.

One story describes preparations for the annual trip from Dublan to Pratt Ranch in the mountains: her brothers rubbing grease on the horses' harnesses, then greasing the wagon wheels, repairing the box, and stretching the canvas cover. She describes the wooden steps for mounting the wagon, the barrel with spigot secured to the outside, the grub box, full of salt, soda, sugar, and various supplies.

On the sides and back of the wagon box we hung our iron pots and pans and Dutch ovens to cook our food in. We used the heavy iron pots and pans and Dutch ovens because we cooked over an open fire. We had no stove on the ranch. On the other side of the wagon box the boys made and hung a chicken coop. Into this chicken coop we put hens and roosters and a few baby chicks. We could not buy eggs on the ranch so the hens were taken along to lay eggs for us and the baby chicks were taken along to feed and fatten so we could have fried chicken once in awhile. We took seeds so we could plant a vegetable garden. [We also took] . . . the wooden churn which rode up near the front seat of the wagon. It looked like a wooden barrel with a lid on it. The lid fit tight and had a round hole in the very center of it. Up through this hole came the long handle of the dasher which was pushed up and down, up and down, and dashed the cream into butter. But even more important than that was a glass jar filled with good foam yeast. We could not buy bread on the ranch, neither could we buy yeast cakes, so we had to save a little start of yeast in the bottom of the [bottle] every time we used the rest of it to mix bread. To this little start we would add sugar and potato water, and more yeast would grow in the bottle. Then we would have yeast enough for our next loaves of bread. We guarded the yeast very carefully so it wouldn't spill nor spoil. Children do not live happily without bread.

Dil continued as a popular speaker and storyteller. In general conference he addressed himself more and more to the problems of youth. Parents could only influence children if they involved themselves in their lives. Youth must follow the prescribed course to gain a testimony. He condemned pornography, alcohol, gambling, racy literature, cultural decay in general. One talk preaches against comic books and television, and speaks in favor of early reading. His April 1956 talk asks the hearer to imagine himself in the family of Joseph Smith. A similar talk in April 1961 before the Deseret Sunday School Union Conference, tells the Christmas story from the point of view of James, the Lord's brother. This was later published, as *The Testimony of Mary,* in pamphlet form. Dil continued too with poems and varied articles in Church magazines. In October 1962 he wrote in the *Improvement Era* on "destiny" and the circumstances that brought the family of Brigham Young close to that of Joseph Smith in the 1830s. A 1964 BYU devotional covers Brigham's life through the council at Nauvoo after the Prophet Joseph's martyrdom. These reflected Dil's research for his books from the period. *Young Brigham Young,* a part-fictionalized account of Brigham's childhood, illustrated with Dil's own drawings, was published in 1962. This was Dil's second novel for young readers, and shares *An Adventure in Faith's* strengths. His history is authentic, and his conjectures strike the reader as plausible. *Young Brigham Young* is smoother and more poetic than the earlier book, as Dil perfects the form. In 1964 appeared his full scale treatment, *Here Is Brigham,* again following his great-grandfather's life through his assumption of the mantle in 1844. In style, the book is marked by frequent, lyric asides on the landscape and seasons, together with speculation as to his subjects' thoughts and feelings. Dil wrote for a faithful audience, and saw no reason to address the more specialized concerns of professional historians. Nevertheless, he did his homework, and *Here Is Brigham* became a principal secondary source on the prophet's young life.

Grandson Dilworth Blaine Parkinson remembers watching his grandfather at work. "He'd sit at his desk and write. . . . I just remember, I'd say, 'What book are you working on now, Grandpa,' ever since I was a little kid, and he'd tell me. And I'd say, 'Can I see it,' and he'd show me. . . . And he'd hand me something and I'd read it and then I'd say, 'That's good, Grandpa.'" He remembers him telling Brigham Young stories, and talking about deciding what to include and what to leave out. S. Dilworth wrote longhand, in his cramped script. Dilworth Blaine remembers him calling publishers, arranging for maps and illustrations, but mainly writing. "He spent a lot of time on it. He'd say, 'I have to write now,' and he'd go write. We'd come to his house and there he would be writing. . . . I remember specifically thinking of my grandfather as a writer."

Dil's Care

The elevator car Dil installed in the stairwell, enabled Gladys to sit in the cool of the lower floor. He and the helpers changed sheets six to eight times a day. "I washed those sheets and [ironed them in the mangle iron] most of the time. In all the time she was ill Gladys never had a bedsore." He took her to parties occasionally, "one to Duff Hanks', I remember, and one to the after-conference dinner for the authorities at the Hotel Utah. I had a reclining collapsible chair which I carried and set up at each place." Charlotte Fry says at home, Dilworth always fed Gladys in the dining room. He had considered eating himself in the kitchen, but decided, "No, if I'm going to preserve any self-dignity . . . I'm going to eat like I would." Leonore remembers Dil quietly replaced Gladys' coffee with hot water. Dil writes, "I gave dinner parties and cooked the meal myself." He became famous for his bread, and his shrimp cocktail. Dil says Gladys wouldn't eat in front of the others but would be nearby, lying on a couch or sitting on a chair, "enjoying the conversation. Everybody was happy, a little more than happy. They'd be a little extra vivacious to make the thing go." Mary Wilson remembers Gladys murmuring a question, having to repeat herself several times, and Dil interpreting finally. "Dil could understand her."

All who visited said what good care Dil gave Gladys. Ena

Barnes says, "He kept her immaculate. She couldn't have been taken care of any better by anybody. I'll say that for him." Dilworth writes, "I was not always a good nurse, but most of the time I made real effort to ease her boredom." Dorothy West remembers Gladys cheerful, uncomplaining. "Once in awhile when we were there alone, we'd catch some tears in her eye, and how horrible it was to have to sit and do nothing when you wanted to be out using your talent and doing things, you know. And then, all of a sudden, she'd just break off and shut up," not let it show. Dil said many friends would come and visit once and then never return. One admitted to him when he met him in the street, "We can't stand to look at her. Remembering how she used to be, we just can't. It's too heartbreaking." Leonore and Blaine, with seven children now, moved into the basement in 1962 for Blaine's last year of graduate school. Dil writes, "At first we feared that so many children around might make Gladys nervous, but we soon found just the reverse. It made the days shorter. They ate and slept on the lower floor—crowded, true, but not as crowded as the apartment at the 'U' built to hold no more than four and into which were crowded nine." Blaine was hired at Weber State, and the family moved to Ogden the following June.

Gladys deteriorated as the years passed, wasting down to ninety-five pounds. Dil says,

> She couldn't wear her false teeth—I wouldn't let her for fear she'd swallow and choke on them, so her mouth was pulled in. . . . She'd look in the mirror and she says, "How can you look at this old hag?" "In the first place you're not a hag. In the second place, it gives me pleasure to look at you. In the third place I love you." And then she'd get thinking she was pretty good looking, that she wasn't a hag. And she wasn't of course.

Leonore describes Gladys' nerves as "unsheathed," to where it was almost unbearable to be in a room with her. The doctor prescribed a variety of tranquilizers, which left her like a "vegetable," until finally he found one that seemed to soothe her without incapacitating her. Dil says gradually "she lost her ability to do things and spent more time lying than sitting."

> There were times when I'd wake up at night, and I couldn't tell whether she was alive or not, her breathing was so quiet. I got so I would wake up if the least rhythm of her breathing changed, even the least bit. . . . I've stood many a night over her in the semi-darkness, with my ear down close to her mouth, trying to detect even the least breath. And I'd turn the light on in the other room and see if I could see that her eyes were shut. Then I'd see a finger move, and know she was all right and go back to bed.

Dil's money problems continued. Hulda says, "He just got to such a desperate condition, he didn't have anything to survive on, and he was ready to sell the home and everything." Dil writes in his history, "I have learned that, in general, folks do not want to help because they are apparently fearful they will be involved later on." He mentions many in his history who did help. Spencer Kimball delivered a check for $100 from an anonymous donor, and added $100 himself. Mark and Emma Peterson came to the door one Christmas day. "They visited for a few moments and then Mark said that his Oldsmobile was in the driveway, in good condition, gassed up, and handed me the keys. 'It's yours!'" Dilworth desperately needed a car. The Petersons were going to Europe for three years and wouldn't be needing theirs. "I couldn't think of anything to say at the moment, so all I did was ejaculate, 'I'll be damned.' He laughed and they went home." Another time Dilworth answered a knock on the back door, only to find an envelope "from some friends who love you both," containing a bank passbook with $770.00 marked inside. "Apparently the giver included the tithing he knew I would pay." Dil, as late as 1972, could still only write, "I never found out who it was."

Leonore visited Gladys in late March of 1964 to show her Samuel, Gladys' and Dil's ninth and last grandchild. She remembers Gladys apologizing for many, little things, the kinds of things Leonore herself felt she should apologize for. On Friday April 3, Dil's sister Louine Cromar and her husband Kenneth visited for conference. Dil ate lunch with them at the house at noon. Louine recorded her impressions of the day in a letter to her children. Gladys' appearance she describes as "more shocking than usual, for you know she has had a partial paralysis of the throat and her jaw has sagged" and she wore no teeth. "She was very alert and we carried on a conversation, even though she had to speak laboriously with a guttural sound in her voice." They talked about Leonore's baby, Dil explaining the new kind of anesthetic injected into the cervix as it dilates. He "compared this modern discovery to the terrible experience Gladys had in bearing Dil," who had come breach. He said "she had been indoctrinated with the idea that a woman should experience all the pain of childbirth, so she would be more appreciative of this great privilege. Gladys then spoke up and said that she would go through all of that again if she could have Dil back. . . . Dil [Sr.] kissed her on the forehead and we bade her goodbye until later." Dil's history mentions the conversation as well. "After a cheerful speech from Louine, I said, 'Gladys and I have been married 42 years. Gladys, what do you say we make it 50 years?' She said, 'I'm game, let's do it!' And so it stood." Dilworth returned to the office (Louine has him attending the Primary conference first). Grandchildren Dilworth Blaine and Charlotte came down from Ogden after school to visit and attend the general session on the weekend. Dilworth Blaine remembers, "We went to her bedside, talked with her for awhile, then we went downstairs and played." They became aware something was wrong. Dilworth Blaine remembers Gladys' heavy breathing, and being aware she was dying. He remembers feeling solemn, but also playing. "We knew we were supposed to be solemn, but we were kids. . . . We didn't have anything else to do but play. . . . So we played around."

Louine's letter records the nurse's account. Gladys ate a little, and drank a little water, after complaining of a pain in her side. "The nurse helped her raise up and then she noticed that Gladys was turning a greyish color and her mouth was twisting a little. She then hurried to the phone to call Dil, and returned immediately to the bed. Gladys gave two or three gasps and was gone. It

THEIR LONG ROAD 267

was probably a blood clot in the (coronary) valve of the heart, as the pain on the right side up under the ribs is one of the signs." S. Dilworth's history gives the cause as massive cerebral hemorrhage, and the death certificate agrees. Dil writes that after feeding Gladys, Sister Nye lifted her up to "burp" her, when it struck. "Gladys sighed and that was all." He describes the phone call, at about 4:30. Sister Nye said:

> "Something has happened; you'd better come home!" "What's the matter," I said. "Has she died?" All she would say was, "Hurry home!"

> I dashed out on the run and drove home. Gladys was on the bed. One look told me she had gone.

Dil held the funeral Monday, April 6, the last day of Conference, at 6:00 p.m. so people from Ogden could come. "We had no viewing. Gladys disliked them—so did I." There were few flowers beyond the two red rose buds in a vase on the casket. Louine explains, "During Gladys' illness whenever there was a funeral in the ward they would bring Gladys a floral piece. She got so that she could not stand the smell of the flowers they would bring. . . . Maybe it was suggestive of death, but she had an aversion to the floral pieces. So I suppose that was Dil's reasoning." Louine says all the general authorities except President McKay attended, and many friends. Alice Thornley Evans, Richard L.'s wife, was among the speakers, telling her childhood memories of Gladys as Kaysville recreation director. Ena Barnes told of the Ogden pageants, and Gladys' special "ability to bring the beauty out of life." Mildred Koew and Dorothy Nielsen spoke of New England. Dorothy Holt told of Gladys' dramatic efforts in the Ensign 4th ward, how she prized authenticity, and how "after her first success, with the road show, she was a new person." Harold B. Lee spoke of her insistence that Dil continue to take assignments during her illness, and told also of Gladys' experience in Mexico with Young Dil. Two Pratt relatives sang "La Golondrina." Dil had asked Betty Baker to sing "Estrellita," as she had so often in their home. She says she couldn't bring herself to do it, visiting the grave later instead, where she sang it to her alone. Dil wanted no cortege, so buried her the next morning in his little family plot high in City Cemetery, beside Dil Jr., with just a few friends and family there. He supposes, "I was branded further as an eccentric person for doing it that way," but says, "It was very quiet and peaceful."

Five years of constant looking out for all of Gladys' needs softened Dilworth. He told James E. Faust, then in a stake presidency, the stroke "is the worst thing in the world that could have happened to Gladys and the best thing for me. It made me decent. I learned what love really should be." Leonore says, "I don't know what lesson my mother had to learn with that ordeal. I don't know what good it did her. I just know it turned my dad into an angel." Dil would sometimes be incensed when people would sympathize with him while he cared for Gladys. "Why, I'd take care of her the rest of my life, just for the joy of having her with me. I think it's a privilege to take care of her." To Gladys' nephew Stanley Cardon he said, "What would it be to me if I were to come home and that house were empty." He spoke to his grandchildren of his years of care:

> I want to tell you young folks that it did me good to do it. I learned a few things about life, and I learned things about patience, I learned how patient she could be, we grew to love each other more. And people would say they feel sorry for me and tell me how much of a burden I was bearing, but I wasn't bearing any burden at all. I was really happy doing that. . . . We had really a very happy life together.

On another occasion he said:

> I have perfect peace in regard to her. We had our quarrels when we were young . . . of course. But I think that five years that I had this experience, there was burned out of me any feeling about those, and was burned into me that here in her emaciated condition was the most beautiful, lovely person I had ever known. And I don't have any conscience about it. I have perfect peace. I did all I could.

CHAPTER 12

Second Chance

Alone

Leonore says Dil never complained of loneliness after Gladys' death. "He buried himself in his work." Dil writes:

> I kept house and tried to keep things up. Mrs. Riley cleaned once a week—not very thoroughly; and I set a table each meal with a cloth and proper utensils and cooked a hot meal twice a day. I tried not to be lonely, read, wrote, had music, and spent many evenings visiting quorums. A few kind people invited me to eat, but that soon stopped. As the months wore on, I thought that I was making out all right.

A 1964 poem speaks of "echoes" in the empty house. The Staffordshire dishes remind him of her plates of many little pancakes—he thinks to pack them away. He looks at the mirror in the bedroom, only to see her deftly combing her hair. Should he give away the oriental statue, which she liked to decorate with necklaces? He looks over the old sideboard, and thinks to hide the bottle of wax polish. "Her / Pleasure, as she / Caressed it with the cloth to make it shine, / Is too vivid." He surveys her drawer in the bureau, her things laid out in neat array. "She could not / Endure confusion." He imagines her reunion with Young Dil and Victoria. "Such things . . . do not cross this / Gulf which / Separates." He considers putting a rose in the silver filigree vase and displaying it on the mantle. "Perhaps she'll see."

He writes in his history,

> No sooner was Gladys buried than people began to hint that I
> should begin to look about for someone to marry. In the eleva-
> tor one day one of the Twelve said that soon I should begin to
> look around . . . for a little woman to grace my home. It was all
> meant in kindness and I took no offense, but it wasn't very good
> taste.

Bruce R. McConkie, then Dil's colleague in the First Council of
Seventy, says, "He was very affirmative in saying that he was not
going to do anything or look at another woman for a year, and
that that was one of the amenities that he'd learned from Gladys."
Leonore remembers "he made the remark that it was easier to be
single and do his job without worrying about the welfare of someone at home."

He writes, "One day I was eating lunch when suddenly I had a
sharp pain in my stomach. It lasted through the meal." Each day
the pain returned at mealtime. He decided he had better be examined, and went to Ogden to "tell Leonore so she would not worry
about me when she heard I was in the hospital.

> I told her the difficulty. She laughed and said, "You don't need
> a doctor or a hospital!" Me: "Oh, what do I need, Dr.
> Parkinson?" She: "You need a wife. You are lonely and need to
> get some social life. I advise you to go looking. Don't wait a
> year—go now!"

He says the advice was good. People frequently made suggestions
as to whom he should look at, but none appealed to him,
"although some were good and pleasant people." Bruce
McConkie remembers friends would invite Dil to dinner, sometimes without telling him some eligible woman had been invited
as well. Bruce teasingly recommended Clare Middlemiss,
President McKay's longtime secretary. Leonore points out
Dilworth's difficult position, as a general authority. "He had to be
very careful about looking around for a wife, because whoever he
was seen with would be the subject of talk, and if he didn't want

to marry them, it would be an embarrassment to the woman."

Dil's assignment at the time was to oversee Spanish translation for the Church. His call stated he should not leave Salt Lake City. "Marion Romney could see the futility of this and had me called to a conference in Mexico City and thereby to see the translation facility." The Mexico City Stake had been organized in December of 1961. Stake president Harold Brown says, "This was a difficult time as far as translation was concerned, because there were no foreign-speaking stakes in the world." Few materials for stakes and wards—as opposed to missions, districts, and branches—existed. Harold was authorized to translate and publish some items, but these were a year behind. Dil struggled back in Salt Lake to establish a basis for the Mexican Stake to receive materials early. Harold says, "Everything that was discussed and everything that was initiated, he very systematically followed up on," which impressed Harold a good deal. Without materials, local leaders had trouble learning their jobs. General authorities, general board members, priesthood committee members, all would arrive "prepared to talk to us about a program that we were not carrying out." He says Dilworth, when he visited, "gave the most thorough and useful instructions on Church government and Church procedure that our people had ever heard."

Harold and Leonore Brown had befriended Gladys and her Leonore when they were in Mexico City in 1944. Gladys had introduced them to Dil—Leonore B. remembers, "It took him about six introductions before he really had us pegged. He never did brag on remembering people." Now he renewed acquaintances. He confided in her as he helped her fix a meal, "I'm not going to get married again. Do you know how many women want to marry general authorities? . . . I don't want to get married again. I was so happy with Gladys." He said it several times. Leonore says, "I thought to myself, 'Uh-huh, he's getting lonesome. He's thinking about it.'" Leonore was stake relief society president, and had gotten to know Hulda Parker, General Secretary, during a three-day trip to Acapulco. To pass the time, in fact, each traveler had told his or her life story. Leonore told Dil,

"Well, if I were thinking of getting married, do you know who I'd go see?" And he said, "Who?" And I said, "Hulda Parker." He says, "Who's Hulda Parker."

I said, "You know who Hulda Parker is. She's the General Secretary of the Relief Society."

"Oh, that Hulda!"

Dil's own account reads, "As she said it, I felt a heavy blow strike in the pit of my stomach." He adds, "for the first time I felt warm to a suggestion." Leonore B. says later he told her, "You know, when you said her name, a whole electric charge just went through my body, like there was something that I had agreed to before this life." Hulda remembers him speaking of the "blow." "And he says, 'It didn't ever leave, it was just there.' And then he says, 'For days afterwards, it was just like a big neon sign that kept going around, *Hulda Parker, Hulda Parker.*'"

Dil had had some dealings with Hulda with regards to Spanish translation and knew her from her days as secretary to different members of the Twelve. He spoke at a stake conference in San Antonio, hosted by President Birch Larsen and his wife Melba. When he learned Melba was Hulda's niece, he asked enough questions to arouse suspicion. Hulda says she heard from Melba before Dilworth ever approached her. "Has Elder Young been around? Has there ever been any contact there? I think he's interested in you." Hulda says, "I didn't pay any attention to it. There were no grounds for that." Dil's history continues, "When I came home from Mexico, it was general conference. I attended the conference of the Relief Society. Hulda was there and I watched her closely. My impressions were that she was the one." Unsure how to approach her, he called her in her office one day and told her he needed to talk to her, the assumption being to discuss a translation matter, though Hulda doesn't remember him saying so. She asked if he wanted to come over, but he said, "No, I want you to come over here." Hulda says, "That was not usually Brother Young's style. He would never inconvenience us by having us walk over to his office. He would be the one who would come to our office." She told him she couldn't come, she was supposed to be in a presidency meeting, starting right then. Dilworth told her, "I said for you to come now!" Hulda, surprised, said alright, then explained the request to the presidency, who, she remembers, were "dumbfounded." But as she says, "What can you do when a general authority puts it that way."

She headed down Main Street from her office in the Relief Society Building and turned the corner. Dilworth left his office in the old Church Office Building on South Temple and met her in front of the Hotel Utah, then accompanied her back toward the Relief Society Building. He told her his situation in allegory—he needed her advice, he knew an older man, interested in marrying a woman, and these were all his faults. "This man is strange, he forgets, he has a very difficult diet," Hulda remembers him saying. "He listed all these queer things about him. . . . And finally when we got just in front of the Relief Society Building, he said, 'Well, do you think you could be interested in marrying that man?'" She said, "'Well, I don't know. I don't know. I'd have to think about it, I'd have to pray.' At that point I was finally putting it together. And then he said, 'I want you to know, I am committed. As for me, I am committed.'"

Dil's history reads, "As I talked to her, I knew it was right." He told her to think about it, not to be pressured, to take all the time she needed, and to let him know—he would not call her, but would wait for her to call. Marion Romney happened along, on his way back to his office from the Mission Home. He walked up to Hulda, who had been on a conference trip to Alaska with him, took her arm and warmly asked when she would like to go again. She said anytime he would assign her, she would love to go. Marion teasingly ignored Dil, walking right by him. Dil said, "Well, Marion, aren't you going to speak to me?" Marion said, "Oh! are you here?" He took his arm and down the sidewalk they went. Dilworth writes, "He said as we walked, 'Dil, if I were looking for someone, Hulda would be one of those I would look for.' I thanked him, hoping he hadn't guessed that I was proposing."

Hulda went into the Relief Society Building, ducking into a conference room, in tears.

That same afternoon, Dil sent his secretary to Hulda's office with a love poem. He had said he would wait, but called that night, and sent roses the next morning. He went to a stake conference in Idaho Falls that weekend, calling twice more. Hulda says, "I couldn't help but appreciate" his considerations. "You know, he's a very gracious, proper man. . . . I was very touched by his feeling that I could tell was coming through. But then I just was ready to collapse even more, because it made me feel more and more, he wants a decision right now. . . . I cried all weekend." The next week Dil and Hulda both were to travel to Oakland for the dedication of the temple. Dil gave her a large orchid, which she didn't dare take, for fear she would have no explanation if anyone asked where it came from. For his own partner Dil brought daughter Leonore. He told Hulda he wanted her to join him for breakfast, but that the invitation would be directed to Belle Spafford, the Relief Society General President, and her son Earl, one of Dil's missionaries, so no one would suspect. Hulda remembers Belle returning to the motel and saying, "'Well, I have a breakfast appointment with S. Dilworth Young. Since the rest of you are not invited, I don't know what you're going to do. . . . And I sat there and listened to it, and I thought, 'Well, fiddle! I'm not going to sit here in this motel and let her go to breakfast with him and me sit here." She called a sister in Oakland and arranged to stay with her for the two days they were there.

Dil liked to tell about the meal:

> I offered a blessing publicly on our food and then explained that Paul Royal had lunch with Roy Rogers the cowboy actor who did just that and told Paul that he was a Christian and always did it. Paul and I decided to henceforth do it. . . . After breakfast outside, Leonore took me to task for being a show-off, and praying just to attract attention. I denied the charge. Later, on the plane home, we were served supper. When it was put before us, before Leonore could do anything, I said, "Heavenly Father, bless my food but don't bless Leonore's. She doesn't

want her food to be blessed in public." Leonore gave me a dig in the ribs with her elbow. I was sore for a week.

His purpose in bringing Leonore was to introduce her to Hulda surreptitiously, which he says happened "very naturally one afternoon." Leonore describes sitting by a window on the bus taking them from the temple to their hotel, with Dil and Hulda standing outside talking to each other. Dil introduced her through the window—Hulda was gracious, as usual. When Dil joined Leonore on the bus a minute later, Leonore said offhandedly, "Why don't you marry her, Daddy?"

Dil began to fear the difference in their ages was too great—he was sixty-seven, she forty-three. Hulda says, "Some way he slipped a note to me or something that made me feel that he was cooling off. And I didn't quite know what direction to go. . . . I [was] in such turmoil." She took two or three days vacation and visited her brother in Ukiah, to think and pray. In Salt Lake, Dil called Margaret Parker, her niece and roommate, nearly every day: "Now when is she coming?" Hulda remembers him visiting as soon as she returned, with a loaf of warm bread, and on subsequent nights. Dil writes, "I didn't want to be seen taking anyone out, for fear I would be the laughingstock of the people, should I be turned down. So I went calling on Hulda at night and wore a big hat in the car. We talked a good deal." Hulda and Margaret lived in an apartment with Hulda's mother, Matilda, who was beginning to be senile. Dilworth, breaking bread for his Thanksgiving stuffing one evening, said to himself, "Why should I break this bread alone?" He called Hulda, who was watching television as she did her mother's hair, and Hulda invited him down. Dil left the bread in the car. Hulda introduced him to her mother by saying, "This is S. Dilworth Young, our home teacher." The two of them sat and visited with Matilda, waiting for her to go to bed, but Matilda was suspicious. Dilworth had to leave the house before she would retire. He returned with the bread from the car, but no sooner did he and Hulda start to break it than they heard Matilda in the hall. Dil grabbed the bread and left on the run.

276 S. DILWORTH YOUNG

Hulda struggled with the decision and cried and prayed. "I just suffered intensely." She told him he had been considering this for some time and had had a chance to weigh out all the issues, but that she was just starting the process. "'Well,'" she remembers him saying, "'I won't hurry you.' And so here comes the telephone call and the roses and a loaf of bread. . . . He knew my every move and my schedule and everything along the way." He told her he was willing to sell the house, or change parts of it, buy a new bedroom set, whatever it took to make her comfortable. Hulda confided in Caroline Kimball Berrett, who talked it over with her. Dilworth had Hulda, Caroline, and her husband, Golden, to dinner. Hulda describes the meal: roast, baked potatoes, avocado in the half-shell with blueberries and maple syrup. Afterwards, Dil said, "Well, Honey, Golden and I will go in the front room and we'll sit down and talk men's talk, and you and Caroline go ahead and look at the house, and look at closets, cupboards, anything you want to, and decide whether you can live here." The two women went through room by room, all the while thinking how easily each of Hulda's things would fill the different spaces. Alone, later that evening, she says, Dil asked her, "'Well, what do you think of it.' And I said, 'Honey, I think I could live here. I think this is where I'm supposed to be.' And then was when I told him yes." They set the date for the first of the year.

Hulda called a meeting of her brothers and sisters, refusing to tell them the reason but insisting they break away to come. Dil arrived last—they rose as he entered the room. Hulda led him to Matilda, and said, "Mother, this is S. Dilworth Young, you're future son-in-law." Hulda's sister Mary Frandsen's jaw dropped down. Dil reached over with one finger and gently nudged it shut. Matilda said, "Young man, I want you to know, my daughter would never marry a scrud." She repeated this, and then said it once more, to which Dilworth responded, "Thank you, Sister Parker, for the testimony that I am not a scrud." Bruce McConkie says Dil announced he had an item of business for their Thursday First Council meeting in the temple. "I'm going to marry Hulda Parker," he told them, out of the blue, when his time came. He told the story of his courtship, start to finish, then explained, "I figured that some of you brethren might some day be in the same position I was, and I thought you ought to know how it should be done." Hulda and Dil attended a Beneficial Life Christmas social together in mid-December. She says, "By then he had given me a ring. . . . It did cause a stir when we came in." After that, they didn't feel the need to keep their relationship so quiet as before. She remembers how busy she was with Christmas and wedding preparations and parties in their honor. "All my work was stacking up on my desk. I wasn't getting it done. And then, 3:00 o'clock in the morning, here would come a telephone call. And he'd call me, 'Honey, I can't sleep. Do you mind if I talk to you for awhile?' So then he'd lie there and talk to me for an hour or two in the middle of the night." They considered moving the wedding back, but decided it was best to go ahead with the early date after all, in hopes their lives would settle down.

They were married in the Salt Lake Temple, Monday, January 4, 1965, at 2:00 p.m. to accommodate Dilworth's mother, now ninety-five and in the last year of her life. The night before, Viola Martin, a New England friend, asked Dil to speak at her husband Gero's funeral. He writes, "I said I would if she would hold it at 11:00 in the morning, as I had an engagement to meet at 2:00. She agreed. The next morning I left the office to go to the funeral. I got in the car and went home, took a nap, bathed, ate lunch, and went to the wedding at 2:00," completely forgetting the funeral. Friends, family, and general authorities filled the sealing room at the temple, wives on chairs, husbands behind. Dil had told Hulda to invite only her closest friends and family, but had not been so careful himself. The crowd, all standing, in white, filled the celestial room. Hulda says when she "looked out and saw all those people there, I about died. I had no idea there were going to be that many there." They held no reception, though those present came and greeted them after the ceremony. Dil says, "The funeral didn't enter my head from the moment I left the office until 7:00 p.m. when Hulda and I were having dinner in Farmington. The next morning I took Mrs. Martin a bouquet and an apology. She was gracious and blamed the forgetting on the wedding."

Hulda Parker Young

Joseph William Parker grew up in a pioneer home in Heber. A dairy farmer in the community of Joseph, near Richfield, he filled a mission to the Southern States, while married with four children, and later became bishop of the Joseph Ward. His wife Margaret bore him fourteen children—ten of whom lived to maturity—before she herself died. William then married Olena Matilda Olsen Dalton in the Manti Temple, for time. Matilda, the daughter of Norwegian immigrants, had been sealed to Edward Dalton, who died from an explosion in a Marysvale, Utah, mine four months before the birth of their first child. William and Matilda, with fifteen children between them, had four more daughters of their own. Hulda, the youngest, was born in Richfield on May 8, Mother's Day, 1921.

Hulda writes in a life sketch, "Father was most strict in his discipline, yet he was also strict in being sure that justice and right prevailed. . . . He was a hard worker, and all of the family were taught that they too must work. . . . Mother also [was] a hard worker, a most unselfish person," possessing "the rare quality of making peace and . . . resolving misunderstandings that may arise in such a family." She says her father was less strict with his four little ones, and that he doted on them.

> I think he didn't ever have time to really enjoy his first family that much, and I think when we came along, he kind of let down some. . . . I remember Mother saying that she would wake up at night, and he was lying there awake, and she'd say, "Bill, why aren't you sleeping?" And he'd say, "Til, I don't know what you're going to do for me in the eternities, but I cannot think of not having those four daughters. You've got to do something to make it up to me for taking those four daughters from me."

One of Hulda's earliest memories is sneaking under the seat of his milk wagon so she could go to the post office with him. William delayed in town, talking business, religion, politics with the town men. "I don't believe anyone enjoyed getting down town and talking with the men more than father did." She went and showed herself finally. "Where did you come from?" he exclaimed, and she told him, to the hearty laughter of all the men, including William. "In his heart I believe he was pleased to think that I wanted to go with him." Hulda also suspects he liked her spunk.

William wanted better schools for his children, and to be nearer a temple when he and Matilda retired. In 1926 he sold his successful diary farm in Joseph and put the proceeds into "a one-hundred acre greasewood and alkali farm in Draper," in the south end of the Salt Lake Valley. Local farmers thought the water table was too high, and warned him he would never get it properly drained and producing. William saw what surrounding plots produced. In his mind, sage and greasewood were the very things the pioneers found on entering the valley, and he intended, like them, to make this holdout "blossom as the rose." Hulda remembers bonfires of the brush her father cleared, in which they roasted potatoes. She remembers herding cows until her mother raised a flag, or in the evening until she could see five stars. The children sat in the grass and read church magazines through and through while they tended the animals—they had few books and no library. The family lived in a newly-built chicken coop until their house was ready. "In the chicken community of Draper this was quite a common practice especially for families that were just trying to get established."

Hulda's sister Olena died of spinal meningitis in 1930. Hulda, nine, was helping out at her sister Edna's, under quarantine for scarlet fever. "I remember when they brought her home in the casket, the folks let . . . me slip over one night and view her through the window. . . . On the day of the funeral, I remember our standing out by the fence watching the funeral procession go by." Five weeks later, her father, age sixty-five, died of a stroke in his sleep. Hulda remembers the "sweet spirit" at the funeral "though I was very young at the time." Her father had been prosperous in

Joseph, and the living children gathered to divide their inheritance. Hulda says some hadn't realized he had sunk all he had in the farm, and was still in debt. The children divided the land, each assuming a part of the debt, including the little ones like Hulda. Matilda, with her three daughters, one step son, and two sons-in-law, tried to make a go of farming with twenty-five acres and a milk route between them. She hired out on the side, mainly housework for her neighbors, as did the girls. Circumstances forced her to move, finally. Hulda lived for a time with Edna, tending and doing chores. Then Matilda and the younger girls cared for an elderly man in exchange for rent and a small wage.

Hulda writes of one winter,

> I remember it was necessary for me to come directly home from school as soon as it was out. I would hurry and have a bite to eat and then dash over to the home of Brother and Sister Less Nelson and put in about four hours' work washing and ironing, or cleaning house, preparing meals and doing dishes. For this work I would receive fifteen cents a night. It was usually after eight before I would get home and I would then start on my home studies and the personal chores I would have to do at home. Then on Saturdays I would work the full day receiving fifty cents for my day's labors.

The girls worked to support each other through college. Hulda, after five quarters at BYU, was offered a high school teaching position in Duchesne. She accepted, partly "because of our strained financial condition," though she had had no education classes. She taught six different subjects without a break, and had to study hard to keep ahead of her students, some of whom were only a year younger than her. "Fools rush in," she writes, noting too, "I was the third teacher those children had had that year in that capacity and they had prided themselves in the fact that they had driven out the two previous ones." Hulda admits to some discipline problems, but notes, "all concerned said that I had done much better than the two teachers before me." She was hired back for a second year, teaching five subjects instead of six. "That summer [I] went back to summer school at BYU, where I took a very heavy course." She writes, "I thoroughly enjoyed . . . the second year, was much more relaxed, had more self-confidence and, I am sure, did a much better job." She taught a third year also, during which she directed a play, The Calamity Kids, that drew a large audience from Duchesne and surrounding towns.

She quit in 1944 to prepare for a mission. She had helped support her sister Olive in the field, and now it was her turn. During wartime, she remembers, "missionary activity in the Church had been restricted, barring all young men of physical ability." Young women might serve in secretarial capacities. "In order to qualify in this category, the girls had to have six months of actual office experience." Hulda found the position she needed at Fort Douglas, and on February 4, 1945, entered the Mission Home. She remembers arriving in Toronto shortly after one of the worst snowstorms on record. Snow was piled so high she could not see the houses from the street. Only nineteen missionaries made up the Canadian mission, including two married couples and "two or three single elders whose health would not permit them to serve in the military." Hulda spent ten of her nineteen months in the mission office, partly because of a bad back. She performed secretarial duties and served as Sunday school supervisor. She helped orient new missionaries, particularly when they started to arrive en masse after the war. She remembers taking pairs of green elders out tracting. "Technically I was the senior missionary." She filled a special assignment with Sister Glenna Foote, when President Ursenbach was considering closing down the city of Toronto. For twelve days the two "spot tracted" the city. "We would get on a streetcar and ride until we felt impressed to get off and as we went down the streets we would call on just a sprinkling of the homes as we felt impressed." Few homes did not receive them. They left many pamphlets, loaned many copies of the Book of Mormon, and had many discussion. They recommended the city remain open, and the President followed their advice.

After her mission, Hulda worked to get on her feet, then returned in January 1947, to BYU. That October she received a

telephone call from Elder Ezra Taft Benson, of the Twelve. He
needed a secretary, and President Ursenbach had recommended
her. Hulda interviewed, did well on the trial dictation, and left
with a peaceful feeling. When she began to realize he was serious
about hiring her, she started to worry, and like Dilworth, avoided
the call from Salt Lake. She went to Olive's and stayed several
hours. When she returned, her roommates said, "Salt Lake operator Such and Such is calling." She slipped into her bedroom and
prayed: "I was afraid, I felt inadequate; . . . I was happy where I
was and . . . I didn't want to go to work in the Church Offices and
be an old maid. I told Him, however, that I did want to do His
will." She writes, "In the midst of my tears a strong witness came
to me that I was supposed to work for Elder Benson and also that
in time I would marry." As she states elsewhere, "It doesn't matter
how many boyfriends you have. The only thing that matters is
that you find the right one." She accepted the job, reporting for
duty November 1, 1947.

> Before coming to the Council of Twelve, Brother Benson had
> been used to the best secretaries money could buy in
> Washington, D. C., and I really was not that qualified. Before
> starting work I was given a blessing . . . that if I would trust in
> the Lord, he would increase my abilities. When taking my dic-
> tation, if I would lose myself in the Lord and carefully listen to
> every word, that even though I may not get it written down or
> I may write the wrong form, if I would truly trust, when I came
> to transcribe my notes, the accurate wording would come to my
> mind. This I soon found to be true. When I feared, I made
> blundering errors, but when I trusted, I was indeed blessed.
> Brother Benson was patient, but expected much both by way of
> quality and quantity of work, so my work was indeed a chal-
> lenge to me.
>
> As time passed, my abilities increased.

For ten years she worked for various Apostles, including one
and a half years with Elder Benson when he served as Secretary of
Agriculture in Washington, D. C. Here she helped with telephone

calls and appointments, took Elder Benson's personal and Church dictation, took down his journal, and kept scrapbooks of press clippings.

> There [were] on the desks of us two secretaries a telephone with four direct lines to The Secretary, one separate white telephone which was a direct line to the White House, and intercommunication connections to fourteen top policy offices in the Department of Agriculture. It was most interesting to sit in on a press conference, to attend an agricultural hearing on the Hill . . . to monitor telephone conversations with legislators, White House staff and even the President. Working that closely at the hub of the national government indeed increases one's insight into the functioning of government, to the influences of pressure groups, the cunningness of politics and also the great need for integrity in government offices.

She writes of her admiration for Elder Benson and how he met the demands of the job and "failed to be discouraged in spite of all the opposition and criticism." She feels he was "magnified through the power of the priesthood," and says of him, "Even men who disagreed with him in politics or agricultural policy, personally respected him and tempered their manner because of his calm presence and dignity."

From 1953 to 1957, except while in Washington, Hulda served on the Beehive committee of the YWMIA General Board. On January 2 of that year she was called to be the Relief Society General Secretary-Treasurer.

> My responsibilities . . . included the handling of much correspondence, and telephone and personal contact with stake and mission Relief Society leaders throughout the Church. I took minutes for all of the General Board meetings some of them all-day meetings, which minutes were meticulously prepared, edited, indexed and bound for permanent storage in the large walk-in records vault adjoining my office. This vault contained all of the minutes of the General Officers of Relief Society since its founding in 1842 by the Prophet Joseph Smith.

I also spent a great deal of time in the Executive Officers meetings with the General Presidency, three days a week, carrying on the business of all of the areas assigned to the General Presidency. At that time it included in addition to the regular R. S. program of the Church world-wide, special programs such as garment distribution, the making of temple-burial clothing and baptismal clothing, operating the Mormon Handicraft Shop, the Relief Society Magazine, the Social Services Department and matters relating to the Indian Student Placement Program.

I devoted long hours to my work at the office and almost every evening brought work home that needed to be done. I am confident that I could not have managed my work nearly as well as I did had I not had the experience I gained in working for various of the Brethren and also my work with Brother Benson both in Salt Lake and in Washington, D. C. . . . I had the services of as many as three or four secretaries at a time to assist me.

My responsibilities also included a great deal of travel . . . attending conferences, conventions and institutes instructing Relief Society leaders. . . . I was particularly responsible at the Relief Society General Conferences for the instruction to Relief Society secretary-treasurers throughout the Church and for the preparation of all of their record keeping tools and instructions regarding them.

Hulda continued as General Secretary until November 1967, three years after her marriage to Dil.

Dil and Hulda traveled to stake conferences and toured missions, not just in North America, but in the entire world now. Her life sketch lists "most of the United States, Canada, Alaska, Mexico, Guatemala, most of South America, all of the Islands of the Pacific, Australia, New Zealand, Hong Kong, Tokyo, England, Ireland, Scotland, Norway, Sweden, Denmark, Finland, [West] Germany, far into East Germany, Holland, Belgium, France, Switzerland, and Austria." When Hulda accompanied

Dil, she remembers, "the Brethren would say, 'Sister Young, you go with him, and you do everything you can for the Relief Society.'" Sister Spafford, the Relief Society General President, wasn't always comfortable with the situation, and would say, "You can't have it that easy," and assign her to go elsewhere. But often, when the assignments were sent to the First Presidency, President Joseph Fielding Smith would change Dil's assignment to correspond to hers. Hulda remembers herself and Dil so busy that their adjustment after the marriage seemed simple, their relationship almost like that of missionary companions. "It's as though we were thinking together on everything regarding both of us twenty-four hours a day." The Church News published the general authorities' weekly travel assignments, until several of their homes were broken into. Dil and Hulda were robbed twice, once shortly after their marriage. The second time, Dil installed a burglar alarm.

Dil grew famous for his eccentricities, continuing to pack along his sleeping bag lining to keep warm. Rosemary Fletcher remembers him getting her to remove his contact lenses with a little suction tool when he visited alone. Dil took to carrying a rope he could secure to his bed for a fire escape. (In about 1970, he writes, their reservations at a hotel in Denmark were canceled without notice. "That night the . . . hotel had a fire in which a dozen or two people were killed, many of them American tourists. Had the reservations stood, we would likely have been burned.") In late 1967, while Hulda attended a series of regional Relief Society conferences in the British Isles, Dil spent a month touring Rarotonga in an orange freighter. Hulda had been assigned to go with him, but as General Secretary couldn't miss the conferences in Britain either. "I had handled all of the details here for all of those meetings over there, so it was almost imperative that I go." It occurred to her that if you stuck a pin through the globe, you couldn't have separated them further. Dil was stranded at one point, without the food for his diet, and when she met him at the airport, she found him pale and gaunt, having lost fifteen pounds. "That trip," Hulda says, "made me realize that I had finished my work with Relief Society. It was now time for me to be a full-time wife." She resigned as General Secretary, but continued to travel with her husband. She looked after Dil, monitored his medicine, kept him on his diet, and all agreed he seemed to grow younger instead of older. He loved her company. "Honey," he told her, "I can't tell you how much I appreciate your being available to go with me. The way it is now I can just call you, you will go with me, to a funeral, to a wedding, to anything. I've gone alone so much of the time."

Hulda is five-foot-six and trim, with a warm smile, blue eyes, slight chin, a pink, even complexion, and a nose not large but on the prominent side. Hulda's blond hair was already turning white when she married Dil. She wears it styled in a short, full dome. Her voice is clear and loud, slow in cadence, with a melody suggesting her Norwegian heritage. Hulda is ambitious, busy, opinionated, spiritual, loyal to the gospel, confrontive, unusually forgiving. Intensely energetic, Hulda always has two or three more projects going at a time than she can handle. A strength to those around her, Hulda spends hours a day talking on the phone. Her natural bent is to take command, yet she is utterly loyal and defers in all things to the Brethren. Hulda is a health food enthusiast. She got Dil to wear a copper bracelet for his arthritis, which stained his skin green. He was quite open about it, and told James Nielsen, a nephew, in her presence, "I wear this because it makes Hulda feel better." Dil writes, "She is of a deeply spiritual nature. People who meet her and, or, work with her soon find out she lives very, very close to the Lord." He speaks of her "faith that gets her answers to questions asked of the Lord," and once told James he liked a particular statuette of a woman in prayer "because it reminded him of Hulda, that she was always on her knees."

Hulda devoted herself to Dil, and Dil would have done anything for Hulda. He tried to give her a child. Hulda told him, "I've always wanted to have a son." He even took her to fertility specialists, but she says, "it just did not materialize." He confessed his relief some time later, as he so enjoyed traveling with her, and a child would have kept her home. Hulda says Dil was a "sweet lover," gallant, a gentleman, wrote her poems, gave her flowers, often a single rose. Once she answered the doorbell to find roses on the porch with no one in sight—Dil was hiding behind a tree. Dil told the family, "She tells me every morning she loves me, and I got so I believe her." Hulda said, "And he didn't at first. When I'd tell him, he'd say, 'What are you trying to do, talk yourself into something?'" Hulda treasures the long walks they took in the early mornings, where he would tell her everything. Dil writes, "Many of my friends have said to me and to others that Hulda is the best thing that has ever happened to me. I would agree she is the best thing which could possibly have happened to me in this day of my greatest need."

The Written and Spoken Word

Hulda remembers their hosts at stake conference being "delighted" to see them together. "Every one of them referred to it as our honeymoon, coming to their stake conference . . . We had a honeymoon, in their words, for a number of years." She says the tour that seemed a honeymoon to them was to Toronto, a month after their marriage. "That was my old mission field. And so that was a thrill." Dil told her prior to their departure, "I feel like I want to do something on the Prophet Joseph Smith . . . You know, I so admire [him]," he said. "I've been wondering about doing something in poetry." "Well, why don't you try it?" she urged, and he answered, "I don't know whether I could handle it or not." He made up his mind, and brought along materials. The story he knew, if nothing else from his research on Brigham Young. She says, "He'd get into that, and he'd write and write." This long poem, entitled *The Long Road . . . from Vermont to Carthage,* published in 1967, had been through nine printings by 1977, and was produced as a drama in the Promised Valley Playhouse, with Ralph Rogers directing. Charlotte Fry remembers Dilworth reading sections of the uncompleted work at firesides. "Some were just small groups in homes, and some were in church-es." Dil's voice was plain, deep, humorous, unstudied, homespun, the roughness accentuating the lines' melody. According to

Charlotte, "His voice had real emotional impact . . . and his spirit . . . just sort of [came] through . . . It was just so impressive to me." Dil got Cynthia M. Gardner to edit the poem. Cynthia says, "I tried not to change the meaning or anything, but I just tried to make him say it in good English . . . He said he had a real problem because people would read it, and they'd say, 'It's just great, it's just grand.' . . . I think the thing he liked about me was, I didn't mind telling him if something needed changing."

The Long Road is written in Dilworth's mature style. His free verse is predominately iambic, and often reads like blank verse, but made light by frequent short lines and unexpected rhymes. More regular, rhymed stanzas mark changes of mood or scene. This surely is the book Dilworth was meant to write. If the book is not quite epic in scope, it is true to Dilworth's insight that the lives of these great men were heroic. And if, in the view of some, Dil's pausing in *Here Is Brigham* to set the tone or speculate as to people's thought and feelings, weighs down the narrative, here it liberates it. The lines shine brightest when probing the hearts of his subjects—Joseph contemplating sending Hyrum back from Carthage, or earlier, Emma losing her children:

> *Walk with quiet step into the room,*
> *The darkened room.*
> *Emma Smith lies grieving on the bed,*
> *Her swelling breasts*
> *Find no relief, no tiny head*
> *To nestle or to nuzzle.*
> *In the next room her first born son*
> *Lies dead.*
> *His life but*
> *Hours old, the warming*
> *Spirit gone,*
> *The body cold.*
>
> *Once more with solemn tread*
> *Carry to the cemetery,*
> *Not one new born child,*
> *But two. Lay them in the*

Quiet earth,
The new turned quiet earth.
And Emma Smith lies grieving on the bed,
Finds no relief, no tiny head
While Joseph holds a funeral for the
Dead.

Dil continued to publish articles and poems regularly in the Church magazines. He wrote poetry in letters, on Christmas cards, and more than once, while traveling, on his hosts' unfinished walls. He wrote tributes to the living prophet: Joseph Fielding Smith, Harold B. Lee, and Spencer W. Kimball. Several more selections on the life of Joseph Smith appeared in the Instructor from 1968 to 1970, matched to paintings by William H. Whitaker. One of these poems, on Joseph's boyhood operation, was included in the dramatic version of *The Long Road.* He matched his book on Joseph to one on Brigham Young, covering the years 1844 to 1847. Dilworth Parkinson remembers him worrying over it, wondering whether he would have time to finish it, pondering how to get it all in. "There were times when he felt his genius was running dry, and it just wasn't flowing anymore. I don't think he felt that he finished it." He self-published the work, together with other meditations, eulogies, light verse and love poems, in 1976, under the title *Thoughts of Heart and Hand,* and distributed it to family and friends.

Dil's talks in general conference during these years center as often as not on the role of seventies as missionaries. Stake mission leaders should be selected from among the seventies presidents. Seventies should be trained, some to teach the discussions, the remainder to fellowship families. The seventies undertook to support missionaries called from foreign lands. Many quorums, and other members of the church and even nonmembers, contributed to the fund. Dil talked about Christ, the Book of Mormon, and on one occasion the mystery of infinite space. He talked on preparing boys for missions, reflecting on his own power as a storyteller.

> Firelight . . . reproducing itself endlessly in the lapping waters of a quiet lake, the moon making a delicate filigree through the canopy of leaves, the mysterious stars winking their eternal signals of distant worlds—all have put a boy in a receptive mood to hear my message.

He regrets not telling of the adventures of Wilford Woodruff or Samuel H. Smith, rather than "The Wendigo."

> That story never sent a single boy on a mission . . . Rather it tended to pull the covers over his head.

He spoke of a visit to Tonga, and the Saints' memory of the visit of David O. McKay. He honored President Harold B. Lee in a blend of prose and poetry, as eloquently musical as any word Dilworth ever spoke. He encouraged those without callings to redouble their efforts at compassionate service. He urged youth to be obedient to parents, and, again and again, to seek after the Holy Grail, the highest adventure. He spoke to them of Samuel, David, Joseph of Old and Joseph Smith, and told them not to wait to be great men, but to be great boys.

Dil spoke well in general conference, but liked to get out in the provinces, where he could bring all his powers to bear. Hulda remembers him teaching stake organization, picking people out of the audience to represent the bishop (never a real one, so that he wouldn't be embarrassed if he gave the wrong answers) and other ward leaders, and presenting them with the problem of an inactive girl. At his prodding, they would talk it out, and if they got going the wrong direction (for example leaving out the home teacher), his gentle teasing would bring them back. Hulda says it was effective, but never as effective as in new stakes, particularly in foreign lands, where the leaders had no experience. These watched wide-eyed. Charlotte Fry tells of a stake conference session in Grand Island, Nebraska, where he taught how to fellowship new members. He suggested someone pin a corsage on them as they entered the chapel, so that everyone would know to greet them. "And then he'd have someone come in with this corsage on. And at first no one would do anything. And then he'd explain to them and make them go back, so that everyone in the audience as that person came in would shake their hands, and come over to the aisle, and stand up." She describes them all standing, reaching down the aisle, saying, "Hello, hello." "It was just so visual," she remembers. "The emotional impact was so terrific."

Her husband Robert Alan (Bob) Fry remembers Dil talked to the missionaries in Grand Island, demonstrating his story about walking down the tracks in Louisiana, too impatient to wait for his limping companion. "He was using that whole big room—it was a Relief Society room—and the missionaries were sitting in a big circle, and he had them move their chairs back, and he walked his big strides, and he . . . had that whole group just laughing." Charlotte and Bob helped Dil give a talk on the plan of salvation in Bountiful and also Richfield. Dil had the two of them hold a string, to represent eternity, with two knots representing earth life. Bob recalls, "It was the entire length of the chapel . . . You couldn't even distinguish earth life." Dil called others out of the audience. Charlotte says he put a veil over the first person, "representing the spirit, and then he'd get the littlest baby in the audience, and usually there was a week old baby. And he'd say, 'Now this big spirit's going to telescope down into this little baby.'" He called up an eight-year-old child, then boys representing the different ages of the Aaronic priesthood, then a missionary, a young engaged couple, an old person, and talked about each stage of life. Bob remembers Dil taking the part of the old person himself. "And he says, 'See these crooked fingers? These are earthy.' And that was the word he used . . . He said something to the effect that, 'They're not really like this. They want to be young. They think they're young.' And he says, 'They're so earthy they hurt'" A manikin represented the body after death, which together with the string and all the volunteers lined up made for a strikingly visual demonstration. Bob says, "He was really a master teacher."

Dil spoke frequently at stake youth firesides, at institutes of religion and at BYU. Several talks dealt with Brigham Young. Also, *The Long Road* had one of its early readings at the Church school. Dil spoke of honesty and the staying power of false rumors. He quoted secular historians arguing for the Church's complicity in the matter of the Danites and the Mountain Meadows massacre, then gave contradictory evidence from his own research. He said he had not come to prove or disprove anything, but to point out how strong the seeds of doubt could be, like a persistent rumor long ago shown to be untrue. He spoke of genealogy, honor for priesthood and womanhood, the concept of covenants. He spoke of the deep things of the Spirit and the scriptures, often with the goal of showing how a testimony could be got and understood. He spoke of passages that had struck him only in middle age, though he had read them any number of times before: Doctrine and Covenants 18:36 on testifying of the Lord's voice, even though the voice the apostles heard was Oliver Cowdery's reading an earlier revelation; 1 Nephi 17:45, where the Lord speaks in a still small voice, but Nephi's brethren cannot feel his words. Once Dil spoke of the feelings of the Spirit, which he said were not unlike the feelings accompanying beautiful words and music, and he demonstrated with scriptures and musical selections. Olga Gardner sang "In My Father's House are Many Mansions," interrupted in the middle by a "glitch" in the sound system that brought the blaring words of a rock song crashing through the Marriott Center: "I love you baby, I need you baby, I want you baby, let's live together. . . ." That set the students up in their seats. Dil had arranged with the sound booth in advance. Olga remembers Vice President Robert K. Thomas picking up a phone and talking—even he didn't know. Dil explained afterwards,

> May I say that that was done purposely so that the boy won't be fired. And I apologize, Sister Gardner. She knew it was going to happen, but to spoil your beautiful song that way. I wanted to make a point, folks. You see, when you get the Spirit to study the scriptures, and you get the Spirit of the Lord in your hearts, it also carries forward over into your studies, doesn't it. You come to the 'Y' to study by the Spirit. You get into your rooms, and you start to study, and you turn on that thing and interrupt it.

The audience laughed, but there is no doubt they got the message.

In several speeches Dil developed the theme of "the priesthood quorum of the home." Fathers should counsel with their children. Temple marriage was the highest covenant. Husband and wife shared the priesthood. Dil often told personal stories—Hill 13 from his army days, losing the two hundred dollars, Bybee the highway patrolman, all on the theme of integrity. "Just one lie told and you have committed yourself to remember every facet of the situation to protect that lie. Furthermore, once you lie and are discovered, just once, all the rest of your life that person will not trust you . . . On the other hand, if you tell the truth always, no matter what, it will someday save your reputation and perhaps your honor." Other stories—Long's Peak, his two courtships, the grand jury, his callings—deal with help from the Spirit.

> I discovered too that one is guided sometimes even if he does not ask for it. Nearly all of the occasions in my life when I've had great events foretold me by the Spirit, I have never invited myself to ask about it. They've just come. And I can see why that is, because every person who joins the Church and is a member of it in good standing has a right to receive the constant guidance of the Holy Ghost. He is given the right at baptism and he keeps that right as long as he is righteous. And I have come to the conclusion that this Spirit and whatever influence he uses to reach us is more anxious to help us than we are anxious to be helped. I found that out quite early. So you may be sure that if you are doing your normal things in righteousness, there will come to you intuitions, feelings, revelations which will guide you if you can understand that Spirit and know you're having it.

He adds, "It takes a little bit to get that, but you can learn that also."

CHAPTER 13

The Seventy

Home and Office

In Dilworth's time, the seven Presidents of the Seventy oversaw local seventies, including ordaining them and setting apart quorum presidencies, (duties later given to stake presidents), and exchanging correspondence with the quorums. In the early days, local seventies were assessed fifty cents dues annually, which was all the travel budget the seven Presidents had. Local seventies staffed and sometimes led stake missions, and raised money for an international missionary fund, administered by the First Council. The seven Presidents helped out on other Church committees, and at one point ran the missionary department under the direction of the Missionary Committee. The First Council met on Thursdays in their room in the temple, and also once a month with the Twelve. Members sometimes had special assignments, like Richard L. Evans with the Tabernacle Choir. Along this line, Dilworth wrote and illustrated the brochure for the restored Beehive House. With the other general authorities, they set apart missionaries, and in the early days interviewed prospective ones. Phyllis Peterson Warnick, Dilworth's and later Marion D. Hank's secretary, says Dil delighted in grilling them. "I really gave him one today!" she remembers he would say. Bruce McConkie says he sent his own missionary sons to him. "I figured that they'd get the toughest interview in the building out of Dilworth, and it would be good for them." The Presidents also counseled individual members. Phyllis Warnick says people would call or come in off the street, and say, "I need an answer to this," or "I have to see somebody." That could seem like an imposition, happening day after day, but she says, "He was always willing to take the phone call or listen to the person . . . [That] impressed me, his willingness to help."

Phyllis describes the atmosphere at the Church Office Building as businesslike, but with "a spiritual overtone." "They were always talking about serving the people and doing what the Lord wants . . . Always there were scriptures talked about and read." She says Dilworth was hard working, like the Brethren in general. She remembers disagreements within the First Council, but "not ever an argument." "They are really strong men, all of them. And they obviously don't agree on everything." During the discussions, "I don't recall ever anyone saying, 'You're wrong.' They would just say, 'Well, I think that this is the way it should be said,' or 'I think this is the way it should be done' . . . If Elder Young was the Senior President, then he had the final [say]. And I saw then only absolutely cooperation." Phyllis speaks of a "unique closeness among those seven Brethren, just a brotherhood that I've really never known anywhere else."

She remembers when Marion Hanks was called to the First Council, Elder Evans was using the extra office, and no one bothered to find Elder Hanks a temporary one. "They let him wander in and out, and nobody took care of him or anything." If he had interviews or setting aparts to perform, he was obliged to look around for one that was empty. Finally Dil pulled an extra desk into his and said, "Now listen, Duff, you and I are going to work this out, and here's the schedule." So they shared. Once in a meeting with all the Brethren, President Joseph Fielding Smith urged all to go immediately afterwards to the third floor to set apart missionaries. Some had been skipping out—he reiterated twice, go to the third floor immediately. Dilworth, called on to pray at the end, said, "Heavenly Father, take us to the third floor in peace and safety, Amen." Some of the brethren could hardly control their laughter. Dil's attitude toward policy comes through in advice he gave John Hale Gardner when he became a branch president in a BYU student branch. Hale says, "I was to follow the program of the Church—very emphatic. However," Dil added, "'You must work through the Spirit. If that leads you into conflict with the program of the Church, you follow the voice of the Spirit.'" Phyllis remembers Dil as helpful, solicitous, gruff but playful, blunt but never intentionally unkind. Once he wore a face mask at work for several days. "I have this terrible cold and I don't want to contaminate people." He liked to tease the stenographers by seeing if he could get ahead of them. He delighted in gifts to colleagues and office workers of biscuits, poetry, and paintings.

Eb Davis, a young mission president in Figi, saw Dil in the field. He remembers him working hard to get everything done. He didn't concern himself with sight seeing, or with duty free shopping, like some visitors, but buckled down. He remembers Hulda helping him, looking after him, trying to get him to bed on time. "She was always very quiet," he says, ". . . She obviously knew just what he was going to do, and went along to try to help and aide and keep the thing going." He found Dil's advice unusually practical, and yet squarely in line with a vision of where the Church was moving. Dil said the Church gave unusual freedom to mission presidents, more than to stake presidents, because they were on the front lines. He said they had to change them every so often, because each had his own "hobby horse," his own talents and specialties—genealogy, tithing, home teaching—so that little by little the whole program got implemented. Also, of mission presidents, he said, "For the first year, no matter what you ask, we say no. No matter what you say, we say, that's wrong. That's part of the process in humbling a mission president to the point that he's 'Church broke,'" willing to bend himself to the Church's policy and seek the Lord's will. Dilworth said the Church was trying to avoid a lengthy "colonial" period, with long-term mission presidents who, if they tended to dominate in other missions, in the Islands sometimes took on some of the trappings of "great white fathers." In Figi the Church could skip that whole step if it worked from the beginning for stakes and wards and strong local leaders. Eb, like Harold Brown, speaks of Dilworth's follow-through: "Usually, when the people come through, be they lower level bureaucrats, or the highest level of the Brethren, you talk about things, and something slips. And everything [Dilworth] said, 'I'll check on it for you,' or, 'I'll look into it,' or 'I'll let you know about this'—it all happened."

Dil spoke frequently at funerals. Bruce McConkie remembers Dil's axiom that "a funeral was never properly attended unless you also went to the cemetery." Weddings multiplied. Hale and Olga Gardner tell how he waited in a line that extended around the block at their daughter's reception. He visited with the people for the hour it took, refusing to go ahead of the others even when the Gardners sent someone to bring him in. "Never mind, never mind," he told them later. "I have long since learned that you do not use your position to get favors." He loved to perform temple marriages. At Charlotte and Bob Fry's, he said, "Today is the beginning of a new universe." At Marie Parkinson Johns', (another granddaughter), he taught that all the ordinances in the Church were covenants, from baptism and sacrament through the endowment, and that all of them led to this, the highest covenant and the key to exaltation. Rosemary Fletcher tells how her son's future parents-in-law, not members of the Church, were unhappy at not being able to see their daughter married in the temple. "He went and talked to them and they felt very good about it. He just had a way of explaining to them what the marriage ceremony was about, and how nice it was for their daughter to be married in the temple. He was beautiful, and they were very pleased."

Hulda's nephew James Nielsen says of Dil and Hulda, "Whenever he was performing his calling, she would always defer to him, and know exactly what her role was." This trait stands out the more for Hulda's inclination to take charge, as James observes, in non-Church contexts. "She tried to direct, wherever they were." He continues, "I . . . remember him saying that he was the boss, but she was the boss in the house, and he would always defer to her when they were in the home." He did what she said, at parties, arranging furniture, though not always without grumbling.

"But the minute they were to go someplace or to do something out in the yard . . . the roles reversed and he would direct." James' wife Giana, when she first married into the family, was surprised to see a general authority and his wife argue. Once they disagreed over whether to take a certain plant during an extended stay in California. He objected; Hulda had James put it in the car; Dil put his foot down when he noticed; Hulda reasoned with him: "Well, Honey-Dear," (which was her pet name for him). Eventually Dil gave in.

Dil continued to paint with watercolors, and delighted in giving his efforts to friends and associates. He studied perspective, experimented with colors, turned a critical eye to his work, and improved. Dil's son-in-law and former mission secretary Blaine Parkinson remembers how eager the old New England missionaries were to have one, if nothing else as a memento of Dil. Dil made bread ahead and froze it, snacking on it with Roquefort cheese. He made bread fresh for friends and neighbors, and recommended it for fellowshipping non-members. His recipe appears in the January, 1965 *Improvement Era*. One must remember Dil's childhood, his camps, his care for Gladys, and his courting Hulda, to glimpse what gifts of bread meant for him. Dil continued playing practical jokes, often exchanging them with Bruce McConkie. He once wrapped a mud pie in the foil from a fine cheese and presented it to Bruce. Bruce gathered his family around for a taste before discovering what it was. Another time Bruce said some outrageous thing about Dil in the *Church News* to get his goat. Dil refused to acknowledge he had done so, but a few days later Bruce got a letter, ostensibly from Willis Ritter, Utah's controversial federal judge, calling him in for slander. The most elaborate joke involved Gurcharan Gill, an East Indian mathematician and BYU professor, married to Gladys' niece. Bruce had published Mormon Doctrine, so Dil typed up a list of questions under the name of Balwant Singh, and used Gil's contacts in India to provide the postmark. Letters went back and forth. Finally Singh said he would be visiting the United States with wife and friends Ghlema Rhoodh (Glen Rudd), Vulmh

Arveh (Velma Harvey, Bruce's secretary), and Seehkmoor Dhl Jung. Singh states, "I hope that you have a large faimly [sic], because if you do, we would like to meet them in their natural behavior and function." Bruce agreed to host them for dinner. Dil and friends intended to disguise themselves as Indians, and even learned some Indian phrases to use, but decided not to go through with it at the last minute, for fear of what members of the Church would think if word got out.

Dil believed in caring for his own. His father died in 1941, leaving a large bank debt, which Dil and his siblings paid, though they had no legal obligation to do so. Seme's health had kept him poor, and he preferred to go on state welfare rather than be a burden to his children. Once he was gone, the children prevailed upon Lou to drop the welfare and let them help instead, which they did until her death in 1965. Leonore says that one of Rey L. Pratt's dying wishes to Dilworth was to look after his children, which he tried to do. One divorced daughter supported herself for a time with fortune-telling, to the consternation of some in the family. Dil helped out with loans, some of which he forgave when she couldn't pay. Gladys' sister Amy, and Dil's sister Emily, found themselves widowed. Hiram married his sweetheart Rhea late, and had no children. All four were fixtures at Dil's home at holidays. Dil visited and looked out for his maiden aunts. Hulda's mother lived in their home for some time after Hulda resigned the relief society. Matilda, vigorous enough to raise her daughters alone, was now reduced by senility. Always a gentle, loving soul, now she spent her days tearing rags for rugs and babbling nursery rhymes.

The grandchildren, living in Ogden or attending BYU, visited often. They loved to discuss the gospel with him—he had thought much and read much, and he had an answer for every question, though he never pretended his was the final word. When there was nothing to talk about, Dilworth's easy, playful way with small children stood in contrast to his sometimes awkwardness around adolescents and young adults. Family members learned to sit with him in comfortable silence. At times he might enter a room where a grandchild was sitting, blurt out some word of advice, then walk out again. Dil was a conscientious if infrequent letter-writer. If a grandchild wrote with a doctrinal question, he went the whole route in researching the answer, including lengthy explanations and Xeroxed excerpts from printed sources. Grandson Benson, age about ten, got caught up watching a football game at his house when the family had to leave. "Let me know who wins," he said in his frustration, though he forgot the incident in the days that followed. Dilworth surprised him with a letter describing the fourth-quarter action, the big plays, the final score. As good as his sermons were, that lesson in integrity to a ten-year-old boy said more.

Dil reflects on his life in a 1978 journal entry, "I had no buddies. I don't know why . . . I have never had in my life a man in whom I confided. So I guess I'm a loner. I don't think I was secretive. I seemed more to live in a sort of world apart. I had my place and my dreams—other people's places seemed no real part of me."

Dil and Hulda tried to give useful gifts, often things their children and grandchildren could not so easily afford. They bought Leonore a sewing machine. As the grandchildren left home or on missions, they bought them luggage and leather-bound scriptures. Newlyweds they presented with queen-sized, longboy beds, to lighten their burden during their years of poverty, but also, Hulda later admitted, to weigh them down. Dil doted on his grandchildren's accomplishments, the languages they learned, the poems they wrote, the degrees they earned. The grandchildren tried each year to out-do themselves in their after-Thanksgiving-dinner presentations. What started out as talent shows grew into costumed dramas with uproarious dialog and complex choreography. Dilworth's bellowing, joyful laughter was the one accolade that mattered. Dinners at the grandparents were ever a pleasure. Hulda, who had the large, black, armless chair nearest the kitchen, was forever scurrying between stove and table, trying to manage each detail. Dilworth, opposite her in the matching, black captain's chair, dominated with his wit, put all at ease with his good humor, held the floor with his stories, his jokes, his clowning with Hi. A single conversation flowed across the noisy, crowded table, washing up under itself like surf as neighbors repeated this and that for the benefit of the young and the hard of hearing before the next wave came. This seemed the natural order of things in the family, though it ceased when Dil was gone.

Dilworth Young wanted nothing more for his family than that they live up to their highest ideals. He told them the same things he told the youth of the Church—be honest, honor priesthood and womanhood, obey your parents. After bearing his testimony on the end of a tape after his eightieth birthday celebration, he added:

> What does this mean then to you my descendants. It simply means this, that if it's true, then you have a promise of eternal life if you keep the commandments. Eternal life is the only life you'll want. You might be happy in the telestial kingdom if you did not know there was a celestial kingdom. And you might be happy in the terrestrial kingdom if you didn't know there was a celestial kingdom. You even might be happy in the celestial kingdom if you didn't know there was eternal life in the celestial kingdom. Eternal life in the celestial kingdom means that you live in such a way that you keep all the commandments, all of them.

He dwelt specifically on temple marriage and living faithful to that covenant to the end.

> [That] done, we'll all meet together in eternal life, which is the only one we want. That is where the Lord lives. That is where the extreme joy is. That is where we're all working for.

First Quorum

Dilworth, who in writings and speeches often recited the history of the Seventy, returned many times to one particular scene. On Sunday, February 8, 1835, soon after the brethren's return from Zion's Camp, Joseph Smith approached Brigham and Joseph Young after services and asked them to come sing for him in his home. "Brigham and Joseph were possessed of excellent and pleasing voices, which blended together well in duet." After they sang, the Prophet told them of the blessed state of those who had died on the Camp. He asked Brigham to call a conference. "'I shall then and there appoint twelve special witnesses to open the door of the Gospel to foreign nations, and you, Brother Brigham, will be one of them.'" He spoke further on the Twelve's duties, then turned to Joseph Young and said, "'Brother Joseph, the Lord has made you president of the Seventies.'" The quorum of Twelve was organized on February 14, and the Seventies on February 28, both predominately from the faithful men of Zion's Camp.

This must have had special resonance to Dilworth. Brigham Young, whose life he had devoted years to chronicling, was his maternal great-grandfather. Joseph Young was his paternal great-grandfather, the source for him of the Young name. Joseph served as a Seventy until 1881, most of that time as senior President. Others in the family held the office, as did Dilworth in his turn.

This was the first mention of the office of Seventy in the new dispensation. There were many questions to be answered. Was this to be a local or a general quorum? The Doctrine and Covenants speaks of the Seventy as equal in authority to the Twelve, when they operate in unanimity. (D&C 107:26-27) What was the quorum's role? The same section states the Seventy are "to preach the gospel, and to be especial witnesses unto the Gentiles and in all the world." The Twelve are to call on the Seventy for assistance, "instead of any others." (D&C 107:25,38) Are the seventies higher or lower in authority than high priests. In a history of the Seventies, Dilworth tells how members of the original First Quorum "got to quarreling over who had most authority, seventies or high priests. It is likely there were some of each in the quorum as well as in the presidency." Joseph Smith finally removed all the high priests from the presidency and returned them to their former quorums. (It was at this time that Joseph Young became Senior President.) "Brigham Young said that Joseph Smith took the action to satisfy caviling men who did not understand what the priesthood was."

Joseph Smith filled three and a half quorums of seventy, all presided over by the presidents of the first quorum. Dil says in a BYU fireside that the seventies did missionary work, "some for one month, some for two months, some for a year, or whatever the time was; they were on call perpetually to do missionary work." The seventies organized and led a migration of saints from Kirtland to Far West in 1838. A group with Joseph Young arrived at Haun's Mill just in time for the massacre. Brigham Young reorganized the seventies in 1844 into ten quorums, with the sixty-three members of the First Quorum presiding in groups of seven over the other nine quorums. Seventies continued to serve missions, and sent books from the field to Nauvoo to furnish the large library in the Seventies Hall. Dil wrote in an Ensign article that, during the exodus, the seventies were "left in charge of and supervised temple ceremonies." When the saints arrived in Utah, the seventies retained membership in their old quorums. The practical effect was that few quorum could muster a majority. John Taylor in 1883 reorganized the seventy such that quorum boundaries corresponded to stake ones. The Seven Presidents, who came to be known as the "First Council of Seventy," presided. If a meeting of the First Quorum were needed, this quorum would be made up of the Seven plus the senior presidents of the first sixty-three quorums, though no such meeting was ever called. The quorums had no responsibility, and the members had only their individual responsibility to preach the gospel. The local quorums functioned under the direction of the First Council, and some so thoroughly ignored the local leaders that, Dil reports, "they were often asked when they were going to join the Church." Finally B. H. Roberts, Senior President of the Seventy, and Rudger Clawson, President of the Twelve, instructed stake presidents to supervise local quorums and to recommend presidents and members. The First Council approved or vetoed the nominations, and set apart and ordained those chosen.

In 1935, the First Council received responsibility for stake missions, and local seventies frequently served as stake mission presidents and stake missionaries. In this they sought to fill their responsibility to preach the gospel, and if the were limited to their stake boundaries, at least they were making the effort to be "especial witnesses" in their own corners of the world. One of

Dilworth's ongoing concerns in speeches was to get the bishops to leave the seventies alone, release them from their other jobs, so they could concentrate on fellowshipping their neighbors. It was easy, during these years, to think of the office of seventy as being above that of elder and below that of high priest. Quorums typically consisted of men in their thirties, older than the elders and younger than the high priests. Seventies were not made bishops or stake presidents without being ordained high priests first. Dil states that for a time most missionaries were ordained seventies, with the result that the average attendance at elders quorum dropped markedly.

> When I came back from presiding over the New England mission it was eighteen or nineteen percent. We were taking all the possible presidents of elders quorums out and making them seventies, and what was left was not presiding material. So the Brethren ruled that a boy must go on a mission first, give a little time to the quorum when he came back, and do you know what happened: The attendance rose up to thirty-six percent immediately after.

The seventies later found themselves on the other side of this situation. In 1952, Dilworth states, the First Council was released from responsibility for stake missions. "Almost overnight stake mission presidents were called from the high priest quorums and the seventies were released in many stakes. This presidency over the stake missions was later given back to the First Council."

Always on the backs of the minds of the First Council was the organization of the First Quorum. Dilworth remembers Antoine R. Ivins, age eighty-four, expressing a wish that the Quorum be organized before his death. "Well, Antoine," Dilworth told him, "if we had one, what would we do with them?" As Dil pointed out later, until recently two general authorities had been sent to each quarterly stake conference. Members of the Twelve and even the First Presidency were assigned to run auxiliaries. There wasn't enough for them to do. But the work increased as the Church grew outside Utah. Dilworth writes of discussions in about 1941

on forming a "committee to watch over elders quorums as did the
First Council of the Seventy over the seventies quorums."
President Heber J. Grant called five high priests and named them
"Assistants to the Twelve," general authorities not mentioned in
the scriptures, ranking between the Twelve and the First Council.

> Immediately the First Council reacted, pointing out the
> "instead of any other" phrase in the 107th Section. They were
> ignored. As time went on, the number of Assistants was
> increased. They performed the exact service as the revelations
> said belonged to the First Quorum of Seventy.

Dilworth related how once President Lee was delineating the
duties of the various quorums and "the duty of the First
Presidency and the Twelve to call upon the Seventies," but left out
the phrase "instead of any other." "He wouldn't say it." But, as
Dilworth often taught, a living prophet is not bound by a dead one.

Bruce R. McConkie states, "Now what we did, over the years,
time and time again, was study and evaluate and figure out how
we thought the First Quorum of Seventy might well be organized
and used. Dilworth was a moving spirit in that." In the last years
of President McKay's administration, the First Council went so far
as to draft a proposal, expressing all their feelings but penned by
Bruce McConkie. Ideas such as making mission presidents First
Quorum members, together with auxiliary heads and the president of BYU, were discussed. Specifically, the paper suggested
placing the Assistants in the First Quorum. The Seven Presidents
stated their willingness to step aside and be members of the quorum if the Brethren preferred the Assistants in the presidency.
They showed the draft to Harold B. Lee, who, Dil's history states,
"suggested improvements in our presentation if it was to survive
the meeting of the Twelve." Bruce McConkie says Elder Lee called
Dilworth in and told him if the Brethren decided to go with that
approach, "there was going to be no stepping aside"—the seven
current presidents would remain in their posts. The paper was
never presented, but, Dil writes, "that proposal had an effect for
many of the leaders read it privately."

President McKay had made the members of the First Council high priests and given them the same keys as the Assistants. Dil told his family it was "because President McKay said . . . we couldn't go to a stake conference and ordain bishops or set apart stake presidents or do anything because we weren't high priests. That was the big bone of contention. We thought we could do it anyhow. A seventy can do what anybody can do, but President McKay ruled it had to be a high priest to ordain a bishop." Dil was ordained June 11, 1961, by Henry D. Moyle. When Rex D. Pinegar was called to the First Council in 1972, Harold B. Lee set him apart without making him a high priest but gave him all the keys. Dil continues, "When the meeting was over with, I walked up to Brother Lee and I said, 'Brother Lee, you didn't ordain Brother Pinegar a high priest. Did you intend not to?' And he said, 'I intended not to.'" Harold B. Lee was a deliberate man, firm in his decisions, and Dilworth didn't press him further. Spencer W. Kimball became President of the Church at the end of 1973. Rex Pinegar was assigned to a stake where he needed to ordain a bishop, and he asked Dilworth if he had the authority. Dil told him, "You have full authority to ordain that bishop, and I'd go and do it if I were you. Only, I happen to know that President Kimball is touchy on bishops. You better go ask him if it's alright." President Kimball had no objection, and Rex attended that conference and others, ordaining bishops and high priests as needed. Once, when a stake president questioned the practice, President Benson assigned someone else to visit that stake in his place. Some time later, in a meeting with Presidents Kimball and Benson, President Kimball said it might be best "for the convenience of the Church" to make Rex a high priest, which he did the next morning.

In 1975, President Kimball informed the First Council of his intention to organize the First Quorum, and asked for the names of eligible seventies. "We submitted about ten or twelve names." The quorum was sustained in that October conference, to consist of the seven presidents (including Gene R. Cook, a new member), plus Charles A. Didier, William R. Bradford, and George P. Lee.

President Kimball and his counselors set these men apart in the temple after the Sunday session, October 5, without ordaining them high priests. Dilworth, describing Gene R. Cook's setting apart, tells how President Kimball "gave him all the keys that the Assistants to the Twelve had, and told him his calling was apostolic. He could do anything an Assistant to the Twelve could do. It was an apostolic calling. He had every key an apostle has, except two, and he named the two he couldn't use. And he did the same thing to those three seventies." Their keys included the sealing power, but excluded the power to restore blessings and the power to appoint and instruct patriarchs. "All four thus held the keys as Seventies." The First Council continued to press the idea of calling the Assistants to the Twelve to the First Quorum. "We talked to [President Kimball] like that and wrote letters and went privately to . . . other members of the First Presidency and talked to them." A problem the quorum had faced was finding seventies with the experience to organize stakes, counsel bishops, and run the Church in general. In April, 1975, without saying anything to the First Quorum in advance, President Kimball called four new members to the Seventy, one of them an elder and the other three high priests. Again he gave them all the keys, but ordained each a seventy. "They were high priests—he ordained them seventies. Had they been seventies, he reordained them seventies. But he impressed us all that they were all high priests and seventies. 'I ordain you a seventy and a high priest.' 'I ordain you a high priest and a seventy.'"

Three weeks prior to general conference in October, 1976, President Kimball called the Seventy in, told them he intended to put the Assistants in the quorum, and asked how they would feel if he reorganized the Presidency. "Well, we'd laid the groundwork for that, because three months before that, I went to one of the Twelve and one of the First Presidency, and so did some of my colleagues privately, and told them that as far as the First Council was concerned, all of us would be very happy if they wanted to release us." And so at conference the Presidency was reorganized, with Franklin D. Richards as Senior President in Dil's place, retaining only A. Theodore Tuttle and Paul H. Dunn from the old Presidency. The quorum now numbered thirty-nine, which gave them the majority necessary to conduct business. Various quorum members, under the direction of the Twelve, took charge of the various auxiliaries and committees, some of which were run previously by the Assistants. Dilworth could write, "There has not been a ripple in the Church organization by the creation of the Quorum." Further, President Kimball appointed the local seventies quorums to be the stake mission organizations, with the seven local presidents as stake mission presidents. Local seventies could be appointed "teachers" or "finders" as circumstances warranted without being set apart.

Dilworth said to his family of the change, "When I heard President Grant say there'd be five Assistants to the Twelve, and they'd be senior to the Seventies, everybody rebelled, and I rebelled in my own mind too. But it was right. You couldn't organize the first quorum then if you wanted to." There weren't enough seventies in the Church who knew what to do. He spoke of the experience of the Assistants as a training period, "and when he got them trained, he moved them into the First Quorum, a trained quorum. We've got thirty-[nine] trained men who can do the job. Only a few of us haven't been stake presidents or bishops. And so I think the Lord's hand is in it to not have it organized until now." If the First Quorum filled up and there was need, other quorums could be added. "As much as the world expands, we can expand." He continued, "Modern revelation is not what Joseph Smith said. Modern revelation is the revelations of the Lord to us as interpreted in the application by the living President of the Church, the Prophet . . . So we see an example of modern revelation practiced four times, once by Brigham Young, once by John Taylor, once by President Grant, and once by Spencer Kimball. That's modern revelation." He wrote in the Church News that if it were not so, the Church would become as bound as the ancient Israelites "who believed they could not deviate from rules set up by Moses. As a result they lived in a social condition unfitted to their times 1,000 years later . . . Simply stated, modern revelation is revelation today to the living prophet."

Dil had long hoped and agitated for this change. His humility and willingness to step aside may have been a factor in its coming when it did. Some of his friends expressed their sympathy—the Seventy may have gone up in status, but Dilworth and the others had come down. Dil spoke in the Sunday afternoon session of that general conference.

> A week or so ago I wrote an address which I thought I might give at this conference, but the events of the past two days have made that a little inconvenient. So I thought perhaps I ought to begin by apologizing to the translators who have to change these things into foreign tongues for not giving them more time to do what they have to do now.
>
> Since last Friday the number of people who stop and offer their arms as I walk or climb stairs has increased fourfold. I assure you that I am not retired: I am retreaded.
>
> There have been several times when I have looked about as my name is mentioned with affectionate tones, as did Golden Kimball, wondering who had died. (This last part I put in after Hulda read the speech.)
>
> A friend said to me last Friday, "How can you bear what you have lost." I replied, "I have lost nothing. Rather I have gained."
>
> I have gained a new group of close friends and associates in a quorum which I hope will have such unity of purpose that it will be as a banner of righteousness before the world.
>
> I have gained seven leaders far beyond me in ability, strength, and wisdom, which, had there not been this enlargement, I could not have had.
>
> I have gained the opportunity to serve rather than to direct. In that service my arms will extend in the wide world, as far as I

can find the strength to extend them, and my upward reach will be as high as I can see.

Now the only limit to my personal service, which I myself originate, is my strength of body, facility of mind, and compassion of heart.

I have gained a personal knowledge and understanding of the meaning of the words of President J. Reuben Clark: Not where I serve, but how.

He paused to remember Seventies he had known: his grandfather and uncle, B. H. Roberts in Europe, J. Golden Kimball at home, Samuel O. Bennion, Rey L. Pratt, John H. Taylor, Oscar Kirkham, Richard L. Evans, Antoine R. Ivins. He quoted David Copperfield: "'Barkis is willin'." He mentioned he and the others had been consulted "for our feelings and input." He spoke of the Church's "increased power" in having not two presiding quorums but the third as well, filled with well-trained, loyal men. "It thrilled me to see something come to pass for which we had so long hoped." He mentioned Antoine Ivins' wish to see the quorum, and said he himself had feared he would only see it from the spirit world. "When I get there, I'll report to President Ivins that he should have stayed here a few years longer." He testified of the Church, rededicated himself, and closed.

Some days after, he told the family of a letter from the mother of a little girl who had taken notes during all the speeches, and for his wrote that he hadn't been retired, he'd been "'reshredded.' That may be nearer the truth than the first one!" he joked. "I'm not sure!" He mentioned a call from President Kimball thanking him. "Brother Kimball was kind of on a spot, too, because . . . you see, it looked like he was just dumping an old man . . . Brother Kimball didn't want to be [remembered] for that, and he hesitated a long time, I'm sure before he ever decided to do it." People wrote Dil from all over the Church to say how moved they were by the talk. As he pointed out to the family, the church was full of people who had been released from something they didn't want to be released from. A former mission president had waited for him by the door in the tabernacle, in tears. "He said, 'For five years I've been frustrated and left out, let out, dropped.' They hadn't picked him up in the stake, and they hadn't picked him up in the ward . . . And he says, 'I hoped I'd find some peace in this conference, and I went down there, and when you spoke . . . I want you to know I found it.'"

Last Mission

One chapter remained to be written in Dil's history with the Seventy. He filled assignments in Salt Lake and the Midwest, and continued to speak and write (notably a long poem on Adam and Eve), but increasingly he felt his age. He wore hearing aids now. Cataracts left him needing contacts in addition to his glasses, and able to read only large type. His teeth, as he joked to a BYU crowd, were "extractable." (The upper left ones had died, though he retained the others.) He developed arthritis. His gout had not improved. And after all the years since his Annapolis examination, his heart had gone bad. Hulda remembers, "The doctor would not let him take a conference assignment that would take him through Chicago. He said, 'You cannot stand the stress that is involved in making airplane transfers'" in that particular airport. Once when he did fly, and Hulda went to pick him up at Salt Lake International, she found Daniel H. Ludlow pushing him in a wheelchair. He explained he had seen Dil sitting in the terminal, and said, "Brother Young, are you in trouble?" Dil said, "Yes, I am." In general conference, September 30, 1978, N. Eldon Tanner announced the creation of a special "emeritus" status to be granted some of the general authorities. "Some of our associates have served for many years with complete and unselfish dedication, and they deserve every honor and recognition for such devoted service. It is felt advisable at this time to reduce somewhat the load of responsibility they carry." To this point, general authorities had been released by death only. Emeritus brethren, while not released, would receive no travel or committee assignments, and were free, as a later *Church News* article puts it, "to spend [time] with their families, to write, to work in the temple, to home teach, attend ward meetings, or accept such other assignments that might come as ordinary Church members, as their health and circumstances allow." Dilworth, eighty-one, was one of seven made emeritus that day.

Dil once again was the epitome of grace. "I am certain and bear witness," he stated the next day in what would be his last general conference speech, ". . . that the calling which has come to me and my colleagues in the last two days is as much the inspiration of the Lord as was my call thirty-three years ago." Dil had been aware he would eventually have to slow down. He had said to the family that prior to the reorganization of the First Council, when the seven Presidents offered to step aside, "I told President Kimball personally that he ought to release me anyhow because I was too old to be the Senior President of a big organization like that." But likely he was not thinking of retirement per se. Always busy, right through his scouting and Church careers, now he faced the prospect of having nothing to do. His assignments continued through the end of that year, including the writing of a book-length, internal history of the Seventy. Nevertheless, Olga Gardner, who saw him at funerals, thought him discouraged, and remembers him saying, "They've put me out to pasture." Hulda says, "It's an adjustment. It's a feeling of being let down . . . He knew it was alright, and he agreed with the decision, and he wanted it. It's just the personal, emotional adjustment that does come." On October 13, as she and Dil toured the Denver Mission, they received a phone call in Pueblo from President Benson, assigning them to head the Los Angeles Temple Visitors Center, effective February 20, 1979. Leonore speaks of this as a blessing. "He told me once he wanted to die with his boots on."

Dil's final stake conference trip, in November, was in the Los Angeles area, which gave them a chance to scope out the assignment. He finished the large history of the Seventy and referred it to the brethren January 8. The Church created a three-room suite for them in the temple-worker apartments behind the Los Angeles temple by cutting a door between two smaller apartments. That

314 S. DILWORTH YOUNG

meant just a short walk across the parking lot to work each morning. Dil writes the call was for an "indeterminate" period. "I suppose that meant that when I ceased to be able to function well I'd
be released." He says, "The center is a real opportunity geared to
Emeritus brethren." Hulda points out, "He was able to control
[his work load]. He was busy every day, and if he wanted to stay
at the center part of the time, he would. If he wanted to come
home and rest, he could." As his health declined, he sometimes
got one of the missionaries to drive him the little distance to the
apartment, where he spent his afternoon.

Dil had charge of ten full-time missionary couples, who led
tours around the displays, ran films, and manned the front desk
on rotating schedules, in addition to other duties, such as keeping
the books. Each missionary couple attended wards in a different
stake in the region, where their job was to promote the center. For
the tours, the couples worked from a twelve-page script, which
Dil insisted they not follow too closely. Reed Brown quotes him
as saying, "'You cover those points, but do it in your own words.'"
Dil wanted them to aim for a friendly, less formal quality. He
would say, "Now you sound too preachy. This is no place to
preach." Dil listened, critiqued, encouraged. Once Reed para-
phrased a scripture during a tour. Dil told him later, "'Never
quote a scripture, unless you quote it verbatim.'" With the rest he
wanted their own words, "'but on the scripture itself, quote it verbatim.'" Thelma Brown, Reed's wife and missionary companion,
remembers Dil smoothing over glitches and irritations. "He
would sit there when we were greeting people and things, and he
could seem to feel if there was any tension or friction within the
group of missionaries." Dil concerned himself with their health.
Reed walked with a cane, and was in some pain. Thelma says,
"[Elder Young] was just so concerned . . . He'd say, 'Oh, are you
sure you're not getting too tired?'" She found this all the more
striking in view of Dil's own poor health.

Mary Pratt Parrish, Gladys' niece, and her husband Boyd, were
called to the visitors center in late June of 1979, and told to report
to the MTC July 18. Mary recalls, "The very next day we got a

call from Dil that said, 'You come down here next Friday.'" So they rented the house, packed, made arrangements hastily, sold a duplex because they couldn't rent it in time. When they arrived, Mary says, Dil explained, "'The reason why we needed you here is, we're just up against it for Spanish people.' And I said, 'Dil, I don't speak Spanish.' He said, 'Okay, I'll give you three weeks.'" She adds, "And I did it." Mary had sufficient background to memorize the script and pronounce it properly, and managed, over time, to carry on conversations with visitors afterwards. "I wasn't real good at it, but I did it." Dil accepted numerous speaking engagements all through the area, averaging three a week his first year. James Nielsen, who visited, remembers Hulda driving while Dil navigated. "He knew that city backwards and forwards, and he could tell her everywhere to go . . . She'd just go wherever he said, and they'd always get there." Or Dil got one of the missionaries to chauffeur, often Boyd. "He was awfully good company," Boyd says, but jokes, "he claimed he couldn't see, but if you got up over sixty miles an hour, or cut in too close in front of another car, he could see that." Boyd's license lapsed, and Dil called the mission home for an elder to give him a ride. "He wouldn't even let me drive my car down" to get it renewed.

One of the first changes Dilworth made at the visitors center was to move the piano from its alcove to a raised platform in the concert room. The center had been hosting Saturday night "cultural programs," which Dil says "attracted about 40 people mostly [temple apartment] inhabitants. We could see some possibility for enlargement there." Hulda says she and Dil had attended the dedication of the women's monument in Nauvoo the previous summer, and that Dil became convinced something like it was needed in Los Angeles. He said, "We have got to devise some way of telling the true story of womanhood here without invoking criticism or contention." They decided to fill the empty alcove with bronze miniatures of the Nauvoo statues, paid for, at Elaine Cannon's suggestion, by the area's young women. An outdoor dedicatory program in August featured girls' choruses, a banner parade, a slide show on a huge screen erected on the front of the building, and poems for each of the statues by Dilworth, with readers including Laraine Day. Ezra Taft Benson, his wife, and other dignitaries attended the event, which Hulda describes as almost a miniature "June Conference." Over two thousand people attended on each of three nights. Dil came to realize Los Angeles likely was home to more Latter-day Saint actors, musicians, dancers, artists, and sound, stage, and lighting people of every description than any city on earth. He started to push the Saturday evening shows as ideal places to bring nonmember friends and neighbors. He used the talent in the local wards and stakes, but of course that was where the world-class talent lived. By the end of the first year attendance at the concerts averaged a hundred and twenty. At Christmas Dil and Hulda revived the tradition of lighting the temple grounds, and held cultural shows nightly, including string quartets, hand bell ringers, a two-hundred-and-fifty-voice children's choir, a production of Amahl and the Night Visitors, Polynesian choirs, traditional carols, the musical Scrooge, and a range of other offerings.

The following year Dil moved the women's statues to a sculpture garden in front of the building. That June he repeated the previous August's pageant, this time with living tableaux on a rotating stage. Hulda remembers print and radio reporters, and camera crews from all the network affiliates. A Cambodian women's choir that sang "I am a Child of God" brought an invitation to tape a twenty minute segment for a Sunday morning program on NBC-TV. The pageant drew large numbers. Hulda says, "They estimated then that we had at least eight thousand people out in front of the visitors center seeing that—every standing spot available right back against the [temple] wall." Dil had his poems from the pageant published as a brochure, set against photographs of the sculptures, entitled *Woman—a Precious Jewel.* These poems resonate with two of Dil's old dictums: honor womanhood, and the man is not without the woman, nor the woman without the man, in the Lord. Reed Brown remembers, "They were the hottest selling thing we had down there . . . We'd get two or three letters a week from somebody far off." Dil privately donated the proceeds to the visitors center. Dil generated a level of excitement about the center such as there had rarely been—and one that proved difficult to maintain after. For all that, towards the end he spent a good part of an average day resting in a recliner in his apartment. Hulda, zealous and impatient, filled in the details, typed and got on the phone for him, nursed and looked after him. As she says, "[Dil] made the decisions, but Hulda did the legwork. You're not kidding."

Hulda remembers several blessings Dil received from the local priesthood. "Every one of those blessings told him, 'You will be able to complete your mission and return home in safety.' But that's all they ever said." Dil went into heart failure the night of March 24, 1981. Hulda had a difficult time finding a security guard to let them off the grounds. To her further consternation, the cardiologist would take no responsibility, even to admit them. Dil improved enough to attend conference, and, on April 13th, the funeral of Cannon Young. Hulda says, "I don't know how [Dil] ever got through the funeral. I expected him to collapse right there. But he hung onto that pulpit, and he spoke." Dil made up his mind to ask to come home, though he wanted to stay on for one more June women's pageant. The written release, dated the 1st of June, sets the date for the 1st of July. Hulda and Ross Tucker, one of their missionaries, struggled to find a new cardiologist, finally convincing Dr. MacAlpin at UCLA to see him. The previous doctor had apparently overprescribed diuretics, leaving Dil starved for salt and potassium. Dr. MacAlpin gave him the potassium, but put him on a regimen of eight ounces of water a day to bring up his salt. He asked Hulda what she had been doing for him—she listed both the doctor recommended treatments and the "multiplicity of vitamins" and special care she herself provided. Hulda remembers him saying, "Mrs. Young, I don't know what it is you have been giving him, but whatever it is, keep on doing it. You have kept him alive for at least ten years beyond what he should have been."

Hulda writes that during their off hours, Dil had been preparing her "in every way—to make sure I was fully informed on our financial and legal matters and everything I would need to take care of when he was gone. He would talk very openly to me about it[,] . . . more freely about it than I could." She writes of Dilworth's nightly prayers, on his back in a hospital bed in their apartment. "It seemed that his greatest concern was whether he was worthy to go—to meet the Savior . . . Because of his unique and choice sense of humor, not everyone knew of the depth of his spirituality." Grandson Benson, who visited during the June pageant, remembers how tired, pale, and sunken-cheeked he looked, draped out in his recliner, the afternoon of the day before it went on. Benson had asked that morning, "What do you plan to do when you get home." Dil, without hesitating, and with more than a trace of gloom in his voice, said, "Die." Hulda remembers he said as much to many people, sometimes with a chuckle. "He knew he was going to go."

Dil and Hulda returned to Salt Lake on Tuesday, June 30. Colleagues from the First Quorum and their wives came to the airport to greet them. James and Giana Nielsen had been taking care of the house. James speaks of Dil's easy way with his little girls. "The kids loved him, and they seemed to trust him." He describes them going into the master bedroom, where Dil lay exhausted on a hospital bed, and saying, "'Hi, Uncle Dil,' and he'd grin at them, and they'd say, 'Take out your teeth!' And I'm sure he'd just as soon that they would leave the room and not bother him, but he'd take out his teeth and make faces for them and make them laugh." Sunday, after he coughed up a blood clot, Hulda checked him into LDS Hospital. Dil, with congestive heart failure, was slowly drowning from the fluid in his lungs. Lying down, he was as starved for air as if running. Friends and family visited, though he couldn't always talk to them for lack of breath. Boyd Parrish remembers, "I was holding his hand, and standing there close to him, and Hulda says, 'Well, I think you better go now, I think Dil's tired.' And he hung onto my hand, and he said, 'Don't go.'" He counseled grandson Dil to finish his dissertation. Granddaughter Charlotte he told he wished he would live to see her children grown. Leonore, in an effort to distract him, told him of various adventures trying to handle her teenage boys, and in spite of herself began to sound discouraged. She finished by saying, "Daddy, what I've learned from having nine children is that I don't know how to raise children." Dil answered, "Neither did I." Then he added, "Neither did my father."

Hulda wrote in a planner, "I love him and it is hard for me to think of letting him go. I felt that after I had worked so hard in LA with everything at the Center that now . . . the Lord would let us have some time together." She pressed the attendants, brought in specialists, until the house doctors took her aside and told her there was little they could do for a heart so worn out. So she sat with him, twenty-four hours a day. "They put up a little cot there by him, and I was there all the time." She remembers, "I had ahold of his hand." She would touch him gently to sooth him. "The minute I'd stop, [he would say], 'Oh, don't stop, don't stop." Once she went home to shower and freshen up. On her return, she remembers Leonore saying, "Hulda, please do not leave his side again. He gets so anxious when you are gone." Leonore too sat with him day after day, and some nights. Once he asked, "When is this going to end?" Leonore answered, "I think Heavenly Father wants you to come home now." Dil said, "How soon?" Leonore said, "Maybe a week." Another time, out of the blue, Dil told Leonore, "I don't care." Leonore said, "About what?" He said, "I don't care about anything." Arza Hinckley, a friend and longtime neighbor, visited and blessed him to recover. Bruce McConkie blessed him too, on the 8th, but did not tell him he would live.

> I've never had such an experience in all my life. When I placed my hands upon his head, it was as though I were in a dark room. There was no light at all. The room was dark and I was against a black wall. And there was no promise and no assurance and no hope of recovery or improvement or betterment, simply a prayer to the Lord that he might have rest of body and be free from unnecessary pain. And that night he had a measurably good night, I am told.

Leonore, Hulda, and a friend from California were present the next day when Dil's heart and breathing stopped. Hulda remembers Leonore had just been talking about the process. "We were both just intently watching him. I guess our heart and souls were with him, as to when he took his last breath, because we knew it would not be long." As Leonore remembers it, her back was turned—she thought Hulda's too—when Dilworth's heavy breathing stopped. She says Hulda walked over and removed his oxygen mask, hurrying to replace it when Dil gasped one last breath—Hulda has no such memory.

S. Dilworth Young died at 2:10 p.m. in room 701 West of LDS Hospital in Salt Lake City, Thursday, July 9, 1981, at the age of eighty-three. The funeral was held Monday, July 13, in the Ensign Stake Center, with Ezra Taft Benson, President of the Twelve, conducting. Music was provided by members of the Tabernacle Choir. Dilworth B. Parkinson spoke on behalf of the family, painting his grandfather as a master teacher and a wise, funny, eccentric, humble man. Oscar W. McConkie Jr. spoke of travel without purse or scrip in New England. A. Theodore Tuttle called Dil unique, creative, colorful, a teacher, poet, painter, scouter, writer, humorist, missionary, special witness, and a link to the general authorities of the past. He spoke of his eloquence at the pulpit, his stories, his rubber face, his humor, abruptness, earnestness, common-sense judgment, square-jawed tenacity, modesty, integrity, and love for God. He said, "There have been three occasions when a man of true faith, true obedience, was needed:" the organization of the First Quorum, the reorganization of its Presidency, and the creation of emeritus status. "In this he has been a crucial link." Of Hulda he said, "She gave us S. Dilworth Young at his best, sixteen years of his best." Bruce R. McConkie spoke next, giving a doctrinal sermon on probation.

> If we die in the faith, that's the same thing as saying that our calling and election has been made sure, and that we will go on to eternal reward afterwards. As far as faithful members of the Church are concerned, they chart a course leading to eternal

life. And because this life is the time that is appointed a probationary estate for men to prepare to meet God, as far as faithful people are concerned, if they are in line of their duty, and doing what they ought, although they may not have been perfect in this sphere, when the day comes that they pass into the next sphere, their probation is ended. Now there'll be some probation for some other people hereafter, but for the faithful saints of God, now is the time and the day, and their probation is ended, and they will not thereafter depart from the path.

He concluded, "[I] am pleased to bear witness that our good friend and associate, Brother S. Dilworth Young, was the sort of individual that we've been speaking of." Grandsons and nephews bore the casket, preceded by the entire First Quorum of Seventy, honorary pall bearers. The train followed the hearse to his little family plot in City Cemetery, a few blocks from his home on "J" Street. There, Blaine P. Parkinson dedicated the grave.

Dil had always gone out of his way for funerals. Charlotte Fry remembers he maintained, "Births and marriages and deaths, [those are] the important social things." Bruce McConkie says that of the general authorities, Dil "attended more funeral services than any one of us or any group of us combined." Yet it seems likely Dil did not linger over his own funeral. There was the matter of reunion with wife and son and other family members, but one imagines too that, as in Gladys' vision, S. Dilworth would soon be busy. The one thread running all through his varied life is scouting, which in its simplest definition means getting in front and looking around.

- END -

Dilworth's father
Seymour Bicknell Young, Jr.
11 January 1908

Dilworth's mother
Carlie Louine Clawson Young
ca. 1909

Dilworth
7 September 1899
at age 2

Dilworth at age 11, Emily, and Hiram on the coaster wagon, made by Otto
Oblad, blacksmith, for the Youngs

At Mountain Dell, summer 1914; from left, Melvin Wells, Hiram,
Richmond, Dil's mother, Louine, Dil (with guitar)

Missionary picture,
April 1921

Gladys near
the same time

Debonair Dancing Club, organizing committee, *from left, rear,* Dil, Herbert Woods; *second row from left,* Maggie Gamwell, Reed Gamwell, Gladys, Mrs. Herbert Woods, Delora Hurst, Guy Hurst, Mrs. Ira Davis, Ira Davis; *front row from left,* Lucille Petty, Russell Petty, (middle couple not named on photograph by Loveland, 1932) Irene Croft, and Russell Croft

"Uncle Dil" performing surgery on scout's blistered foot during one of the Carson Hikes, ca. 1933

Stories around campfire in Yellowstone Park, 1933, first Carson Hike; Dil, *center,* silhouetted in glow of fire; one of many classic scenes captured by Paul S. Bieler, professional photographer and neighbor

Probably en route to national Jamboree, ca.1933, Dil in uniform

A Bieler photograph, of the family before the fireplace with Brownie, ca. 1940,
Dilworth, and Gladys on couch, with Leonore, at 14, and young Dil, at 16.

First Council of the Seventy, 1946, when Elder McConkie was added. *Front row from left,* Levi Edgar Young, Antoine R. Ivins, Richard L. Evans; *standing, from left,* Oscar A. Kirkham, S. Dilworth Young, Milton R. Hunter, Bruce R. McConkie

Elder Young photographed for General Conference October 1955.

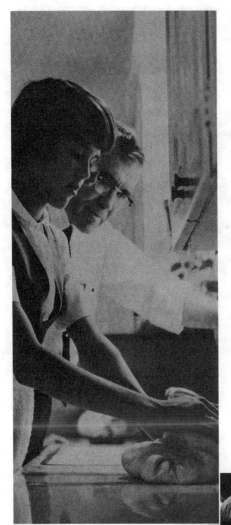

Bread was a recurring theme in Dilworth Young's life. He learned to bake during his elementary school years, while caring for his ill mother; made "hike bread" on all campouts; baked while caring for Gladys after her stroke; courted Hulda with it. Nearly all who knew him had at some time or other received a loaf of Dil's bread. He would rise at 5 a.m. to begin the dough, which he would then deliver himself to a friend or relative. This photograph of Dil and his granddaughter, Charlotte Parkinson, making bread together appeared in the *Improvement Era*, in January 1965.

Pensive yet attentive during a Conference session, ca. 1970

Speaking from the pulpit of the Tabernacle, at General Conference,
7 October 1974

Hulda Parker,
at age 33, when she
went to Washington, D.C.,
as secretary to
Ezra Taft Benson

Dilworth
and Hulda were
married in the
Salt Lake Temple
in January 1965

Elder and Sister Young, in 1980, directing the Visitors Center at the Los Angeles Temple

The last photograph taken of Dil and Hulda together, taken the week he died

Writings of S. Dilworth Young
(In Chronological Order)

In addition to the following works, Dilworth had poems, articles, and speeches published in various Church periodicals throughout his years as a general authority. Most of these periodicals have been indexed. A number of speeches are available from Brigham Young University in written form and/or audiocassette.

1. *When a Boy Goes Camping,* c. 1936.
2. "An Experience on Longs Peak," *Pioneer Stories,* ed. Preston Nibley, Deseret Book, 1940.
3. *An Adventure in Faith,* Bookcraft, 1956.
4. *Family Night Reader,* Bookcraft, 1958.
5. *More Precious Than Rubies,* Bookcraft, 1959.
6. *The Testimony of Mary,* Deseret Book, 1961 (also published as *Mary's Testimony,* Keepsake Paperbacks, 1990).
7. *Young Brigham Young,* Bookcraft, 1962.
8. *Here Stand I—Looking!* Deseret Book, 1963.
9. *"Here Is Brigham . . .": Brigham Young . . . the years to 1844,* Bookcraft, 1964.
10. *The Long Road: From Vermont to Carthage,* Bookcraft, 1967.
11. *Thoughts of Heart and Hand,* 1976.
12. *Woman, A Precious Jewel,* 1979.
13. *S. Dilworth Young,* recorded live on cassettes, Covenant Communications, 1979.
14. "The Priesthood Quorum of the Home," in *Collector's Classics,* Covenant Communications, 1981.

Index